W9-CDG-958

WINNING THE
WEALTH
GAME

WINNING THE
WEALTH
GAME

How to Keep Your Money in Your Family

Andrew D. Westhem & Donald Jay Korn

Dearborn
Financial Publishing, Inc.

While a great deal of care has been taken to provide accurate and current information, the ideas, suggestions, general principles and conclusions presented in this book are subject to local, state and federal laws and regulations, court cases and any revisions of same. The reader is thus urged to consult legal counsel regarding any points of law—this publication should not be used as a substitute for competent legal advice.

Publisher	Kathleen A. Welton
Associate Editor	Karen A. Christensen
Cover Design	Mary Kushmir

© 1992 by Andrew D. Westhem and Donald Jay Korn

Published by Dearborn Financial Publishing, Inc.

All rights reserved. The text of this publication, or any part thereof, may not be reproduced in any manner whatsoever without written permission from the publisher.

Printed in the United States of America
92 93 94 10 9 8 7 6 5 4 3 2 1

Hardcover ISBN 0-79310-376-2
Paperback ISBN 0-79310-309-6

Library of Congress Cataloging-in-Publication Data
Westhem, Andrew D., 1933–
    Winning the wealth game: how to keep your money in your family / Andrew
D. Westhem, Donald Jay Korn.
        p.   cm.
    Includes index.
    ISBN (hardcover) 0-7931-0376-2   (paper) 0-7931-0309-6
    1. Inheritance and transfer tax—Law and legislation—United States.
2. Trusts and trustees—United States. 3. Estate planning—United
States.   I. Korn, Donald Jay.   II. Title.
KF6572.W43   1992
343.7305′3—dc20   91-39318
[347.30353]   CIP

"*Winning the Wealth Game: How To Keep Your Money in Your Family* lets you KISS an aloof subject. You'll love the experience because you'll get paid for your time—you'll *make* as well as *save* money by reading this book!"

—Peter A. Dickinson
Editor, *The Retirement Letter*

"There are just a handful of leading estate and tax planning experts whom I follow carefully. Andrew Westhem is one of them, and *Winning the Wealth Game* is sure to be a winner. Andrew has saved hundreds of thousands of dollars for our seminar attendees over the last decade!"

—Kim K. Githler
President, Investment Seminars, Inc.

"Andrew Westhem is my kind of estate planner. He shows you how to live like a king, die like a king, and leave absolutely nothing to the IRS. The only way to go!"

—Mark Skousen
Editor, *Forecasts & Strategies*

"What a revelation! Finally, a book on estate planning that is not only easy (sometimes even *fun*) to read but also chock full of ways to save on attorneys' fees, insurance premiums and—most of all—taxes. Your heirs will bless you for following the sound advice in this book."

—Richard E. Band, CFA
Editor, *Profitable Investing*

Dedication

To the memory of Jordan Olivar (1915–90), All-American football player; coach at Villanova, Loyola of Los Angeles and Yale; Andrew's friend, partner and mentor. Once, after explaining pension benefits to employees of a state mental hospital in California, Jordan was stopped on his way out by a guard, who said, "You can't leave here."

Jordan assured the guard that he was just visiting for the day. "That's what they all say," replied the guard. So Jordan asked, "Don't you recognize me? I'm Jordan Olivar, Yale's football coach." The guard stuck out his hand and said, "Pleased to meet you. I'm Knute Rockne."

Jordan convinced the guard of his identity. He was a real winner, not a pretender, on the football field and in the game of life. You can be a winner, too, in the wealth-transfer game, if you take our message to heart. As a winner, you'll ensure your family's well-being, while your own prize will be peace of mind.

Contents

Acknowledgments   xi
Preface   xiii
Introduction: Why You Need a Wealth-Transfer Plan   xv

Section I: Basic Training   1

1. The Cruelest Bite, and How To Avoid It   3
2. The Seven-Figure Hitch   11
3. Where There's a Will . . .   17
4. Deflate Probate   25
5. Title Games   30
6. 'Tis Better To Give   34

Section II: Trust-Worthy   41

7. Trusts Without Fear   43
8. Cleaning Up with Q-TIPs   53
9. A Trusted Way To Double Your Money   61
10. Making Sure an Inheritance Trust Is Truly Tax-Free   68
11. Give and Take   76
12. Bridging the Generation Gap   90

Section III: Beyond Trusts   111

13. Keeping Good Company   113
14. All in the Family   125
15. Henry Ford, John D. Rockefeller—And You   136

16. The 15 Percent Solution   144
17. Gambling with Death   150

Section IV: Policy Matters   **155**

18. The Short-Term View   157
19. The "Death" of Whole Life   173
20. When Second Is Best   184
21. . . . And Congress Created MECs   193
22. Don't Believe Everything You Read   202

Afterword: The Winning Team Wins   213
Appendix A: The Wealth-Transfer Numbers Game   223
Appendix B: A Tax-Free Inheritance Trust—
             Plus How a Charitable Remainder Trust Works   231
Glossary of Wealth-Transfer Terms   269
Index   273

Acknowledgments

I would like to acknowledge and publicly thank the following persons for the valuable knowledge that they contributed to help me make this book a reality.

First, I would like to thank my partners in Wealth Transfer Planning, Inc., for their time and assistance: Mark Fielder, Paul Colflesh, Jacques Hunter and Donald Lievsay.

Next, I would like to thank Steven Sciarretta, Esq., of Boca Raton, Florida, and Stanfield Hill, Esq., of New York City for all the time they spent devising and reviewing many of the legal strategies presented in this book.

Marty Greenberg of Los Angeles and Marvin Meyer of New York City deserve much credit for assisting us with the insurance funding chapters.

Special thanks to Charles Parisi for his fine contributions on variable annuities and variable modified endowments.

Thank you to Mark Skousen, a long-time friend who originally gave me the idea for this book.

A very special thank you to Donald Jay Korn, my co-author, without whose financial writing experience, great patience and hard work this book would not have been possible.

Last, but far from least, a super thanks to my lovely wife of 36 years, Emily. And to my son David and my daughter Lisa for their wonderful encouragement.

ANDREW D. WESTHEM

Preface

This isn't a book for the selfish. If you're truly self-centered, you won't care what happens to your children after you and your spouse have died. In that case, the information in this book will be moot: you'll spend all your money, so there will be no wealth to transfer.

For most people, that's not the case. You probably want to leave as much as you can to your children or grandchildren. Or, you want to make sure the IRS collects as little as possible from your family after you die.

That's what we call wealth transfer, the process of keeping everything you've worked for in the hands of your kids and their kids. Our strategy consists of two parts.

First, there's estate-tax reduction or elimination. We'll show you how to cut your estate-tax bill, legally and ethically. If you're interested in a tax protest or tax fraud, you'll have to buy another book. Our message is tax avoidance, not evasion.

Often, estate taxes can be reduced but not eliminated. That's where the second half of our strategy comes in. We recommend that you set up a separate pool of funds, outside of your estate, to pay the unavoidable estate taxes. If you plan well and far enough in advance, you can put aside a few dollars today to cover the future tax bill, and all your wealth can pass to your family.

To understand what this can mean, consider Peter and Catherine, a New York couple who would never consider themselves "wealthy." They got married right out of college and had two children in fairly short order. Peter now is a mid-level executive for an international office products company; Catherine is an office manager for a medium-sized bank. They have a decent combined income, but for the past 20 years nearly all of it has gone to put their two children through private schools and college. There's not much money in the bank; they own little except a small condo apartment. Instead of saving or investing, they are relying on retirement plans sponsored by their employers.

But there's wealth in Peter and Catherine's future. Their older child, Sam, is about to graduate from college while Mary is getting ready to finish high school. Within a few years, if all goes well, both kids will be out in the world, earning their own living.

At that point, Peter and Catherine will be in their late 40s, with substantial incomes but few responsibilities. They'll enjoy a surplus. Already they're starting to talk about buying a vacation home. Unless a tragedy strikes, they can expect 15 or 20 years of capital accumulation before retirement.

What's more, both Peter and Catherine have living parents, hard-working people who own homes, bank accounts and small investment portfolios. At some point, possibly in that same 20-year period, those parents will die, further enriching Peter and Catherine.

It may well be 30 or 40 years before Peter and Catherine both die, leaving their estates (and estate taxes) to Sam and Mary. By then, Peter and Catherine may well own real estate, savings, investments and whatever they've inherited and accumulate substantial amounts in their retirement plans to boot.

What will this all be worth in 2025? $1 million? Probably, barring catastrophe. $2 million? Not impossible. What will the estate taxes be? Several hundred thousand dollars, in all likelihood.

Let's say the final accounting comes to $1.5 million. With no planning at all, Sam and Mary could owe $400,000, or even more, in federal taxes, state taxes and various expenses. That $400,000 would have to be paid in cash within a few months after their parents' deaths.

If Peter and Catherine read our book, and take it to heart, they could save their kids $400,000 by spending less than $15,000 today. First, some basic estate planning can reduce that $400,000 tax bill to $100,000 or so. Second, an investment of around $10,000 can provide the $100,000 their kids will need, 30 or 40 years from now. Everything else can be passed on to Sam and Mary.

That's what you'll find in this book. We'll tell you how to relieve your children of a huge financial burden. Death and taxes may be inevitable, but you can make your own death less taxing for your loved ones.

Introduction: Why You Need a Wealth-Transfer Plan

Life, John F. Kennedy once said, isn't always fair. Even the venal can get rich. One such individual, whom we'll call Vic, was implicated in a nasty Wall Street scandal in the 1970s. After a forced retirement from New York, Vic ran a successful small business in northern California. By the time he was in his mid-60s, he had a net worth of around $6 million.

At that point, Vic's three children were grown and doing well, so he decided he wanted to leave $4 million to his grandchildren after his death and his wife's. He consulted his attorney, a San Francisco lawyer who moved in the best social circles.

"No problem," the attorney said. "We'll set up another trust." The lawyer's fee for this penetrating advice was $2,500. "By the way," the attorney said, as Vic was walking out the door, "your bequest to your grandchildren may be subject to a 55 percent estate tax and a 55 percent generation-skipping tax on the remainder." By the time all the taxes come out, as little as $800,000 of the $4 million might go to the grandchildren: as much as $3.2 million might go to the IRS.

There might be some poetic justice to such an outcome, but Vic didn't appreciate it. So he went elsewhere for advice. How can I provide for my grandchildren, he asked, rather than the IRS?

There was, indeed, a better way. Vic set up an irrevocable life insurance trust to hold a $4 million second-to-die life insurance policy. Over the next ten years, he'll likely pay $700,000 in premiums, but the trust will receive $4 million, tax-free, when Vic and his wife die. Then that trust will sunburst into three trusts, one for each of his children. His children, as trustees, can parcel out the money as need be. If the money's not used, the total may grow to $20 million by the time Vic's grandchildren, the trust beneficiaries, are adults.

If some of the expressions in the paragraph above are unfamiliar to you, don't worry. By the time you're finished with this book, you'll know all you need to know about second-to-die life insurance, irrevocable life insurance trusts, sunburst trusts and more. They're easy to understand, once you have the background.

But why bother to understand them? Because these and other tools are vital if you want to keep what you have in your own family, out of the reach of the IRS. Do you really want to work all your life, just to leave a fortune to the taxman?

The Wealth-Transfer Problem

The word *wealth* may conjure up visions of Rockefellers and Fords and Mellons or, in today's world, of Michael Jackson and Michael Jordan. Unfortunately, the reach of the IRS doesn't stop there.

To the IRS, anyone with over $600,000 is wealthy. When you die, the IRS will take a cut of that wealth. As we'll see later, the tax rates you face at death are now higher than anything you're likely to encounter while you're still alive.

Still, $600,000 sounds like a lot. Not many of us have $600,000 sitting in the bank. Surely we don't have to worry about a "wealth" tax.

Don't count on it. Maybe if you've spent your entire life on a factory assembly line or a retail sales floor, you're not wealthy enough to catch the taxman's eye. But if you're reading this book, chances are that you own a house and a car or two. You probably have a retirement account that's been building up. Maybe there's a collection of art or antique furniture, some other real estate, an investment portfolio, life insurance policies. When you die, all those assets will be added up to get your final score. That tally may be well over the $600,000 mark and your heirs will face a hefty tax bill.

If you own part or all of a small business, one that's even moderately successful, you certainly fall into the definition of *wealthy.*

That's today. Suppose you add up all your assets and find yourself a millionaire, at least on paper. Let's say you'll live for another 15 years: you're 60, for example, and you'll live until age 75. Assuming a growth rate of 8 percent—what you can earn now on Treasury notes—your $1 million will grow to $3 million. As a three-millionaire, you could owe over a million dollars to the IRS when you die.

That's right. One million dollars. After you've worked hard and saved, paid taxes on current income and reinvested what was left, you manage to accumulate $3 million in assets during your lifetime. Then, when you want to leave those assets to your children or grandchildren—transfer your wealth to your family—the IRS steps in and takes another million, in addition to all the income taxes you've already paid year by year. Too often, the IRS turns out to be the greatest beneficiary of your life's work.

Imagine yourself dining at a fine restaurant, a meal you've been looking forward to for some time. With great fanfare, the waiter comes to your table with a covered dish, lifts the dome and—there's nothing underneath. That's how your family will feel, after taxes bite into your estate.

Life may not always be fair, but some aspects are patently outrageous.

The Better Way

Fortunately, you don't have to accept your fate passively. You can minimize estate taxes, even avoid them altogether. Looking at the glass from a different perspective, you can keep much more of your wealth in your family.

You can do it by taking control. That doesn't mean you have to become a tax lawyer. Indeed, one key step in successful wealth transfer is to find and use an experienced estate-planning attorney. But you can't just rely on your attorney—as Vic found out, in our example above, not all lawyers are estate-planning wizards. (All the examples in this book are real, by the way, although names have been changed.)

You're the one who has to make the decisions, even if you're aided by lawyers and accountants and financial planners and insurance agents and actuaries and astrologers. Therefore, you need to know what you're deciding about. If you know the basics, you can implement the strategies we describe.

These strategies aren't too complicated to grasp. You don't need to be a tax attorney or a CPA to understand the ground rules; the technicians can grapple with the fine points. If you've been able to accumulate hundreds of thousands or millions of dollars' worth of assets, you can follow the fundamental strategies we'll reveal.

Implementing these strategies will take some work. You'll need to put together a team of experts and supervise them. You shouldn't sign anything you don't fully understand, so you'll have to do some homework. But isn't it worth putting into successful wealth transfer just a fraction of the time that you now spend on acquiring wealth or spending it?

Perhaps most important, you need to start now. After you die, there's precious little tax planning your family can do.

If you begin now, the payoff can be substantial. You may be able to pay as little as 10 cents on the dollar, compared to your family's cost without a wealth transfer plan.

More than Money

Don't think wealth begins and ends with money. Your real wealth also includes the reputation you've built up over your lifetime, your friendships and, most of all, your family relationships. When you plan your wealth-transfer program, you want to keep that kind of wealth intact. It's not worth sacrificing just to squeeze out the last drop of tax saving.

For example, you have two children. Your daughter is a successful venture capitalist married to a shopping-mall developer, while your son teaches disabled youngsters in a big-city high school. Naturally, you want both of them to remember you with love after you're gone, but you want to steer more of your assets toward your son, where the need is greater.

Or you're remarried to a younger spouse, who has children from a previous marriage. If you die first, as you anticipate, you want to provide for your spouse, yet you want your assets to ultimately wind up with your own children.

Or you have a charity or religious organization to which you've devoted considerable energies. You want to leave something to this charity and you want to be recognized, yet you don't want to unduly penalize your own children by doing so.

The list could go on. Every family has its own unique situation: circumstances where the human factor has to be considered along with the financial in a wealth-transfer plan.

We certainly don't expect to be able to cover every conceivable circumstance, but we will describe the most common situations, based on real-life examples. We'll show you how to deal with them, and we'll provide you with guidelines for handling those nontextbook scenarios you'll have to confront on your own.

Keep It Simple

The rule of thumb for financial writers is to K-I-S-S (Keep It Simple, Stupid), so that readers can understand what you're trying to get across. That's especially true of complicated subjects such as estate and gift taxation.

We'll keep it simple, but we'll stop at K-I-S. We don't think you're stupid. Not if you've managed to build up a sizable estate, and certainly not if you've bought our book.

In the following chapters, we'll start with the basics: how the estate-tax laws work, why you need a will, and what should be in it. Then we'll cover some traditional estate-planning techniques—living trusts to avoid probate, lifetime gifts to reduce your taxable estate, using life insurance proceeds to pay the estate tax.

From there we'll go on to more sophisticated strategies: Q-TIP trusts, irrevocable life insurance trusts, charitable trusts and family limited partnerships. Before throwing you into deep water like that, though, we'll let you tiptoe into the area of trusts. We'll explain how a trust is set up, who the players are (trustee, grantor, beneficiary) and how much you can reasonably expect to pay for set-up and maintenance.

Many of our strategies may involve the use of life insurance. Therefore, we devote an entire section of this book to a discussion of when life insurance should be used and what type is most suitable. The more you know about life insurance, the more likely you are to get the right coverage, rather than a policy that's overpriced or unneeded.

In particular, we'll introduce you to the new wave of life insurance, sometimes called *survivorship* or *second-to-die* or *joint-and-survivor* insurance. This is different from traditional life insurance, which usually is bought to make up for lost income in the case of a breadwinner's untimely death. Instead, second-to-die life insurance is specifically intended to pay estate taxes after both spouses die. We'll show you how to make the best use of this competitive, efficient new type of life insurance.

Well-Covered

Often, having the right wealth-transfer plan in place means that you can live more comfortably while you're alive, in addition to providing for your heirs. Take the case of Dr. L, a 62-year-old physician with a 58-year-old wife. Dr. L would like to retire in eight years. About half his estate is in his pension plan, which now adds up to around $700,000. His original plan was to draw out as little as possible from the pension fund to let it grow, so that his children will have a substantial inheritance.

When he discussed this plan with a wealth-transfer pro, he found that income tax, estate tax and a 15 percent excise tax on large pension funds (see Chapter 16), would eat up most of his legacy. If he leaves a $1 million pension fund when he and his wife die, their children might receive as little as $300,000.

So Dr. L was advised to start taking sizable distributions from his pension fund right now. In the next eight years, paying $15,000 per year will likely buy a $1 million life insurance policy for the children. And even after paying income tax and premiums on the insurance policy, he's likely to have enough excess cash from pension-fund withdrawals to build up a $300,000 portfolio of securities in addition.

At the end of his eight-year plan, he can retire and live comfortably off the income from the securities, supplemented by continued large withdrawals from his pension fund. He'll be able to do the things he wants: play tennis and ride horses. Yet he'll know that his lifestyle won't hurt his kids' future, because they'll have $1 million worth of life insurance proceeds coming to them; because the insurance policy is held in an irrevocable trust, the proceeds will be tax-free.

Taking care of our children as well as ourselves: that's a truly successful wealth-transfer plan. This book will show you how to do the same in your circumstances. Surely, you spend your life working for your family and your own well-being rather than the enrichment of the IRS.

I

BASIC
TRAINING

1 The Cruelest Bite, and How To Avoid It

If you've ever received a paycheck, you know what a maddening experience it can be. By the time federal income taxes are withheld, plus state and local income taxes, plus Social Security taxes, you may see 30 percent, 35 percent, even 40 percent of your income snatched away before you ever receive it.

You may shudder at the thought, but estate taxes are even worse. They currently start at 37 percent and go as high as 60 percent. Those are federal taxes—your state may impose its own taxes. And, as we'll see later, there may be supplementary taxes that jack up the tax bill even more.

How does the estate tax work? When you die, all your assets are counted up. It's like a Monopoly game that ends when the popcorn runs out: you value all the cash, deeds, hotels, etc., to see who has the most and thus wins the game.

In real life, you have to include everything. Your house, of course. If it's owned jointly, half the value goes into your estate. Other real estate counts too, whether it's a vacation home or a piece of property held for investment. Then you add in assets such as gold coins or artwork or jewelry. If you're a collector—anything from rare stamps to baseball cards—the value of your collection will be included in your estate. Add all your financial assets—bank accounts and CDs and stocks and bonds and mutual funds and limited partnership interests and insurance policies and annuity contracts. Don't forget what's in your retirement plan or plans. The grand total, minus any debt, is your estate. (See Appendix A for our Asset Inventory Worksheet, to help you project the size of your estate and thus determine your wealth-transfer needs.)

In Chapter 13, we'll discuss wealth transfer for business owners in detail. For now, let's just say that any business interests must be valued by

3

accepted techniques. If you own a company that earns, say, $100,000 per year, that company may be valued at $1 million, which is included in your estate on top of all your other assets. (That's just an example—business valuation is a complex subject deserving of a book by itself.)

Once you have an estimate of your estate—your net assets—you can see what your family will need to satisfy the IRS.

A Numbers Game You're Bound To Lose

Under present tax law, everyone gets the equivalent of a $600,000 estate tax exemption. The federal government gives you a tax credit that completely offsets the estate tax on the first $600,000 worth of assets in your estate. Therefore, if your total estate is $300,000, $400,000, even $600,000, you owe no federal estate tax. (Throughout this book, we refer to a "$600,000 estate tax exemption." Technically, it's an *exemption equivalent*.)

Once your estate goes over $600,000, the estate tax kicks in at a 37 percent rate on the excess. From there, as your estate grows from one tax bracket to the next, the rates escalate like this:

Size of Estate	Marginal Estate-Tax Rate (Percent)
$600,001–$750,000	37
$750,001–$1,000,000	39
$1,000,001–$1,250,000	41
$1,250,001–$1,500,000	43
$1,500,001–$2,000,000	45
$2,000,001–$2,500,000	49
$2,500,001–$3,000,000	53
$3,000,001+	55
Special rate on estates between $10,000,001 and $21,040,000	60

As you can see, you can roll up a huge estate tax bill fairly rapidly.

Examples:

Value of Estate	Tax Owed
$1 million	$153,000
$2 million	$588,000
$3 million	$1,098,000

That's the federal estate tax. You'll probably owe state estate taxes, too; in some states, your heirs will pay an inheritance tax as well. Your state tax may effectively be deducted from your estate subject to federal tax, so your total tax bill won't go up. In more than half of the states— including New York, Pennsylvania, Michigan, Ohio, Oregon and Wisconsin—state taxes will add to your total estate-tax bill. (See Appendix A for our state-by-state listing.)

The estate tax can be a daunting sum. Your heirs have to pay within nine months, in most cases. Not until the IRS is paid in full, in cash, will your family get their share. (If you own a small business, a 15-year installment plan may be possible.) Your heirs may be forced into distressed sales of prized family assets in order to raise the necessary cash.

Riding a Gift Horse

You may react to these numbers by saying, Why die with your money? Why not just give it away? Suppose you're in your 80s and you have $3 million. Why not just give $2.4 million to your kids, keeping a tax-exempt $600,000 for yourself?

Don't worry, Congress hasn't overlooked this one. There's a federal gift tax that's "unified" with the federal estate tax. Gifts you make during your lifetime use up your $600,000 exemption. Excess gifts are subject to tax at the same rates as the estate tax. And those gifts are counted when it comes time to value your estate.

For example, suppose you give away $1 million during your lifetime and die with a $2 million estate. The first $600,000 you give away is tax-free, but the next $400,000 is taxed at estate-tax rates. And your $2 million estate will be taxed at rates of 41 percent to 53 percent, the rates you'd have to face with a $3 million estate.

Original net worth	$3,000,000	
Lifetime gift	$1,000,000	
Tax-free portion	($600,000)	
Taxable portion	$400,000	
Gift tax (37% and 39% rates)		$153,000
Estate at death	$2,000,000	
Estate tax (41–53% rates)		$945,000
Total gift and estate tax		$1,098,000

This example is rough, not precise. On the one hand, paying a gift tax of around $150,000 will reduce your remaining estate to about $1.85 million. On the other hand, in the interim between making the gift and dying, your estate may grow back to around $2 million.

Once you finish with this balancing act, the total gift and estate tax you'd pay is about the same as the tax on a $3 million estate. So giving away your money won't solve your estate-tax problems.

Nevertheless, there are times when it makes sense to give away your wealth while you're alive. We'll describe those situations in Chapter 6.

Convenience of Marriage

There is one certain, Congress-approved way to avoid estate taxes: leave everything to your spouse. The estate-tax laws provide for an *unlimited marital deduction*. Whatever you leave to your spouse can be deducted from your estate. If you have a $1 million estate and leave $1 million to your spouse, you'll wind up with $0 in your estate and no tax bill.

This surely is easy and definitely will win you points at home. The problem with this strategy is that you're wasting a prime tax deduction: the $600,000 tax exemption.

Let's say that Charlie O has assets worth $500,000 while wife Charlene has $300,000. When he dies, he leaves everything to her. No taxes are due.

Five years later, Charlene dies. By that time, the $800,000 in total assets has become $1 million. She leaves that to the couple's two children. They'll owe around $150,000 in tax on the $1 million they inherit.

		Estate tax owed
Charlie leaves to Charlene	$500,000	$0
Charlene already has	$300,000	
Now Charlene has	$800,000	
By Charlene's death, her estate is	$1,000,000	
Their children owe estate tax of		$153,000

A better way would be for Charlie to leave his $500,000 to the kids. Thanks to the $600,000 exemption, that would be tax-free. Then, when Charlene dies, her $300,000 also would be tax-free. Total estate taxes paid: $0. Estate taxes saved: $153,000.

		Estate tax owed
Charlie leaves to children	$500,000	$0
Charlene leaves to children	$300,000	$0
Estate tax savings		$153,000

This works out well financially, but you can see the human weakness. Charlene, with $800,000 in assets, might live comfortably. With only $300,000 in assets, she might not be so comfortable. Charlie doesn't want to see Charlene suffer in her widowhood just to beat the IRS out of some money.

Can you have it both ways? One solution is for their children, who'll inherit $500,000, to support their widowed mom financially through regular gifts.

Not all families, though, are ideal. Suppose their daughter Cherie is married to Chester, a wastrel. He takes Cherie's share of the $500,000 and blows it on a lizard ranch. Where does that leave Charlene? In reduced circumstances.

Charlie can prevent this by using a trust. We'll tell you more about trusts in Chapter 7, but assume for now that this is about as simple as trusts go. When Charlie dies, his $500,000 goes into a trust set up for the benefit of his children. Again, the bequest is tax-exempt because it falls below the $600,000 limit.

During Charlene's lifetime, all the trust income can go to her, so she won't be dependent on the children's largess. When she dies, the assets pass to the children. Charlene's own $300,000 will also pass to the children tax-free because it's under the $600,000 limit.

Of course, life (and death) doesn't always work out that easily. Suppose Charlene dies before Charlie. To cover this possibility, each spouse should provide for a trust to be set up at the first spouse's death. Then if Charlene dies first, her $300,000 can go into a trust, with the income going to Charlie during his lifetime. Again, all their assets can pass to their children with no estate tax.

You may hear estate planning jargon talk about *A-B* trusts or *credit shelter trusts* or *marital and nonmarital trusts*. They're all the same thing. A married couple, in their wills, set up a trust apiece to go into effect when the first spouse dies. The trust will be funded with up to $600,000 worth of assets; the couple's children usually will be the ultimate beneficiaries. The surviving spouse can get the trust income as long as he or she lives. When the surviving spouse dies, the trust assets go to the children.

Now you can see how a married couple can pass up to $1.2 million to their children free of estate tax. At the first death, $600,000 can go to the children outright (if the surviving spouse will have ample income) or via a trust, as described above. That $600,000 is outside the surviving spouse's estate. When the surviving spouse dies, another $600,000, for a total of $1.2 million, goes to their children.

		Estate tax owed
Charlie has	$600,000	
Charlene has	$600,000	
Charlie dies and leaves to the children, in trust	$600,000	$0
Charlene has the income, during her lifetime, from	$1,200,000	
Charlene dies and leaves to the children her	$600,000	$0
Total left to the children	$1,200,000	
Total estate taxes	$0	$0

Suppose now that the couple has $800,000 in assets, as in the first example, but that Charlene has $700,000 while Charlie has only $100,000. If Charlene dies first, and her $700,000 goes into a trust on behalf of the children, there will be a tax on $100,000 worth (the excess over $600,000). That means writing a $37,000 check to the IRS.

This can be avoided if Charlene gives away $100,000 to Charlie. The unlimited marital deduction applies to lifetime gifts as well as bequests: couples can give away as much as they want to each other without incurring a gift tax. A $100,000 gift reduces Charlene's assets to $600,000, which she can pass on free of estate taxes.

As long as you and your spouse get along, you should use tax-free gifts to equalize estates, at least up to $1.2 million. Then whoever dies first leaves half the total assets to your children in a trust that can pay income to your surviving spouse. The other half remains with the survivor. After the death of the survivor, everything is in the hands of the next generation.

If both spouses fully use their $600,000 exemption, $1.2 million can be passed on to children and grandchildren tax-free. It takes a little foresight, a little knowledge of the estate-tax law and a little planning. That's really all you need for successful wealth transfer.

- When you die, federal estate tax is levied on all of your net assets, which may add up to much more than you realize.
- Everyone gets to transfer up to $600,000 worth of assets, free of federal estate tax.
- On estates over $600,000, the tax bite is considerable, ranging steeply upward from $153,000 on a $1 million estate.
- State taxes may drive the bill still higher.
- Generally, the IRS must be paid in cash, within nine months, before your family gets anything.
- You can avoid estate tax by leaving everything to your spouse. However, the tax bill will be even steeper when he or she dies.
- Always try to take advantage of a key tax break: don't waste your $600,000 exemption.
- A married couple can leave up to $1.2 million, tax-free, with this simple strategy:
  - ☐ The spouses equalize their estates through tax-free gifts from one to the other.
  - ☐ Each spouse sets up a trust that contains up to $600,000 at his or her death. The children are beneficiaries, but the surviving spouse gets lifetime income.
  - ☐ At the first death, up to $600,000 of that parent's assets goes into a trust tax-free. The trust assets are out of both parents' estates.
  - ☐ At the second death, another $600,000 tax exemption can be used. Thus, up to $1.2 million can be transferred to the next generation tax-free.

2
The Seven-Figure Hitch

As we just demonstrated, a married couple can pass on up to $1.2 million to the next generation free of estate tax. But there's more to successful wealth transfer. Even with this "A-B" strategy, you have to be sure you're working with competent professionals and that the paper is all pushed properly. Besides, you may be in a special situation, such as

- The couple with "only" $1 million who would like to enjoy retirement and yet still leave some wealth to their children
- The couple with $1 million that's virtually all tied up in one retirement plan, where the A-B strategy may not work
- The couple who has $1 million, virtually all belonging to one spouse, who has children from a first marriage but is remarried to a spouse who has his or her own children

Therefore, even families below the $1.2 million figure may need some sophisticated wealth-transfer planning, as we'll describe later. On the other hand, if your assets are greater than $1.2 million, or if they're likely to be that great in the future, you definitely need savvy wealth-transfer planning. Without such planning, the IRS will be a great deal richer at the expense of your children.

In subsequent chapters, we'll show you how to keep all your wealth in the family, even if your estate winds up at $2 million, $5 million, $10 million or more. In case you can't sit down and read our book cover to cover, here's an overview of our strategy:

1. Inventory Your Assets

Find out what you're worth now and what you're likely to be worth by the time you and your spouse die. Thus you'll have an idea of your eventual estate-tax liability.

To simplify matters, subtract $600,000 from your total estate and divide by half to get the approximate expense.

Projected estate	$1,000,000	
Exemption	($600,000)	
Difference	$400,000	
Approximate obligation (@ 50%)		$200,000
Projected estate	$2,000,000	
Exemption	($600,000)	
Difference	$1,400,000	
Approximate obligation (@ 50%)		$700,000

And so on. You may notice that these estimated obligations are higher than the federal estate-tax obligations listed in our last chapter. That's because the federal estate tax starts at 37 percent, not 50 percent. If you include state taxes, funeral costs, estate administration fees, etc., you'll probably wind up with a figure close to these approximations. In any case, this method allows you to plan without memorizing the federal estate tax tables.

2.   Establish a Will and a Revocable Living Trust

Most of your assets should be held in your living trust, to avoid the time, expense and public exposure of probate. A *pour-over will* can cover miscellaneous assets. In either your living trust or your will, provide for trusts to be established at your death. These trusts, as described in our previous chapter, will enable you to make full use of your $600,000 estate-tax exemption and pass on up to $1.2 million to your children tax-free.

3.   Make Lifetime Gifts

You can give away $10,000 per person per year, free of the gift tax. So can your spouse. When you reach that stage in your life where your need for income and wealth buildup is secondary to your concerns about estate tax, it's time to start giving away your wealth.

Let's say you're a 75-year-old widow or widower with two children and four grandchildren. You can give each child and grandchild $10,000 each year, reducing your estate by $60,000 per year. If you live another ten years, you'll have reduced your estate by $600,000. At the same time, you'll have removed those assets' appreciation and income from your estate. An estate of $1.5 million, with an approximate estate-tax obligation of $450,000, can be reduced to $900,000 with an approximate obligation of $150,000. You can save your heirs $300,000 just by giving them some money early.

For another example, suppose a married couple in their 70s has three children, three sons- or daughters-in-law that they fully trust, and six grandchildren. They can give away $20,000 per year to each of these twelve, or $240,000 each year while they're both alive. After the first spouse dies, another $120,000 per year may be given away. In this way, even a large estate can be reduced substantially.

4. Set Up an Irrevocable Trust To Pay the Projected Estate Taxes

We call these trusts *tax-free inheritance trusts* because they enable heirs to receive their inheritance tax-free. They're *irrevocable* because they can't be canceled or substantially altered after they're created.

Therefore, assets you transfer to such a trust can't be taken back. By the same token, assets transferred to an irrevocable trust are outside your estate. With few exceptions, you can't be the trustee, because you're not allowed to control the assets once they're in an irrevocable trust and outside your estate. Your spouse may be the trustee, in some cases, but you need to act cautiously.

Often your heirs can be the trustees as well as the beneficiaries. Typically, one or more of your grown children will act as trustee(s) of your tax-free inheritance trust. As trustees, they control the trust assets.

Their object is simple: get enough money into the tax-free inheritance trust to provide liquidity for estate tax and other obligations.

In a "plain vanilla" situation, where a married couple will want to pass assets to their children, the trust won't be needed at the first death.

That is, the first spouse who dies will leave $600,000 to the children and the rest to the surviving spouse. No estate tax will be owed because of the $600,000 exemption and the unlimited marital deduction. At the death of the second spouse, taxes will be due on any assets over $600,000, so that's when the tax-free inheritance trust will be desirable.

In other situations, in which you're widowed or divorced or remarried, you might want the tax-free inheritance trust to provide funds after one death (yours), if that's when you plan to leave a taxable estate to your children.

When the time comes, and your heirs face an estate-tax obligation, the tax-free inheritance trust can provide the money to pay the estate-tax bills. This will allow your heirs to receive the full amount in your estate.

Here's an example:

Donna and Phil's estate	$2,000,000	
Phil dies, leaving his kids	$600,000	
Donna with	$1,400,000	
Donna and Phil estimate Donna's estate at	$1,400,000	(assuming no net increase or decrease)
If she leaves $1.4 million, their kids will owe about		$350,000
Thus, they establish a tax-free inheritance trust to provide		($350,000)
At Donna's death, the trust will provide the funds to pay taxes and expenses of		$350,000
Leaving their kids with	$1,400,000	
Total assets passed to their kids	$2,000,000	

How will Donna and Phil get $350,000 into the tax-free inheritance trust in order to cover estate taxes? They can make cash gifts to the trust. Then the trustee can invest the money.

Commonly, the trustee will choose to hold a life-insurance policy in the trust. Why? Because, with life insurance, two things are certain: the amount the trustee will receive and when the money will be collected. Here, Phil and Donna can buy a $350,000 policy that will pay off after they both die. The total premiums might be anywhere from $35,000 to $100,000, depending upon their ages. But they'll know that the trust will receive $350,000 when the second spouse dies, in time to pay the estate taxes.

That doesn't mean that insurance is the best investment. Donna and Phil's trustee might take their $35,000 and invest in stocks or municipal bonds or modified endowments or just about anything. If Donna or Phil lives for 30 or 40 years, that $35,000 might grow to $400,000, $500,000 or more—better than the life-insurance policy—before estate taxes need to be paid. If on the other hand they both die the next year, there's no way that a $35,000 investment will pay off $350,000.

So life insurance is typically used for tax-free inheritance trusts in wealth-transfer planning. If you're not insurable, or if you just don't like life insurance, you can invest your money elsewhere and hope that you have enough time for the buildup to cover the estate-tax bill.

5. Advance Planning

That's the simplified version. We'll explain this strategy in greater detail later. We'll explain special strategies for special situations:

- *Q-TIP trusts.* If you're remarried, or if you have another reason for not giving your surviving spouse complete control over your assets, you can use a Q-TIP. This type of trust allows you to give your surviving spouse a comfortable lifetime income but makes certain that your assets wind up with the beneficiaries you choose.
- *Charitable remainder trusts.* If you have appreciated assets, donating them to this type of trust avoids the capital-gains tax. You also can get current tax deductions and a lifetime income.
- *Generation-skipping trusts.* Assets you give to your grandchildren, within limits, won't be taxed in your children's estate. This is a long-term wealth-building device.
- *Family limited partnerships.* Instead of giving assets to a trust, give them to family members who are limited partners in your wealth. You'll still be general partner, with control over the assets.

- *Private foundations.* This is another form of charitable giving, but your descendants retain the responsibility for choosing the charities; they can receive compensation for managing your foundation.

Many of these strategies serve another role in wealth transfer: asset protection. You won't have much wealth to transfer if you're on the losing end of a major lawsuit, and the courts these days can be unpredictable when it comes to distributing wealth from "the rich." If you transfer assets to a family member, to a trust or to a limited partnership, you have extra layers of protection against creditors. It's more likely that your wealth will be transferred to your children, rather than to a disgruntled customer or employee.

- Shrewd wealth-transfer planning allows a couple to pass on $1.2 million to their children free of estate tax.
- Larger estates will owe tax, so a plan is necessary to keep wealth intact.
- Vital to any plan are a living trust, to avoid probate, and a will, to distribute assets not otherwise covered.
- A will or living trust can call for the establishment of trusts to make sure $1.2 million is passed to your family tax-free.
- Large estates can be trimmed with a long-term strategy of giving away assets, $10,000 or $20,000 per year per recipient.
- To cover estate tax on larger estates, an irrevocable trust can be established. The trust can be funded with gifts from you. Your grown children can act as trustees and control the trust assets. When the estate taxes are due, they can be paid from trust funds, leaving your estate intact as it passes to the next generation.
- For predictability, life insurance usually is used to fund tax-free inheritance trusts. Other investments may be used, if desired.
- While the tax-free inheritance trust is the key to wealth transfer, other strategies can help in special situations.
- Wealth-transfer strategies not only ease the bite of estate taxes, they also move assets out of the reach of creditors and render those assets less vulnerable to costly awards from lawsuits.

3 Where There's a Will . . .

As we go through this book, we'll introduce you to some fairly sophisticated wealth-transfer strategies. But you have to crawl before you can walk, walk before you can run. So it is with wealth transfer. You have to begin at the very beginning: with a will. No matter how advanced your wealth-transfer planning, no matter how high-powered your advisers, you must start out by drafting a will.

Why? A will is a formal document in which you spell out how you want your wealth transferred. If you don't write a will, your state government will write one for you. And you probably won't like the results.

You may have heard horror stories about people who died without a will or a viable substitute. Well, they're true. Without a will, you die *intestate* and your estate will be distributed under the laws of your home state.

Is that so terrible? If you're confident about the generous intentions of your state government, you can do without a will. In some states half your assets may go to your children, not your surviving spouse. Minor children may become wards of the state.

In that situation, your surviving spouse will have to account to a court for every penny spent on the children's behalf. If large amounts of money are involved, the court usually will appoint an attorney to represent the children. The lawyer gets paid off the top, reducing your estate. Plus, many layers of reporting are involved.

If your children are minors, when they come of age they may demand a complete accounting from your spouse. If they're dissatisfied, they can sue. When they come of age, your children may receive all the assets they inherited from your estate with no further safeguards.

Moreover, if your spouse remarries, the new husband or wife may be entitled to those funds your spouse inherited from you, with no obligation to use them on behalf of your children. Other relatives of yours, including your parents, may have no claim on your assets.

And, of course, the court handling your estate will make no effort to reduce estate taxes.

Will Power

A will can avoid these potential problems. You, rather than a state government, will make the decisions.

As we'll explain in Chapter 7, sophisticated wealth-transfer plans often include living trusts, which cover most of your assets. Nevertheless, a living trust can't cover everything—a will is necessary even if it covers only the loose ends.

Must a will be written? Some oral wills have held up, but don't count on it. Not only should your will be written, it should be drafted by an attorney. Wills that you write yourself, or fill-in-the-blanks preprinted wills, aren't likely to suit your particular circumstances. In fact, you and your spouse probably should have individual wills, rather than a joint will, for more flexibility. If you're locked into a joint will, you may miss out on potential tax savings.

After you've made your will, have copies made but sign only the original. In some states, signing duplicates can cause technical problems. Store the original in a safe place, such as a fireproof safe or a filing cabinet in your home or office. If you leave your will with your attorney, it may be misplaced.

Should you store the original in a bank safe-deposit box? Probably not. Many states seal those boxes immediately after death to prevent tax cheating. There may be delays in getting the will.

In any case, be sure your family knows where to find the original copy of your will.

Good-Will Games

Naturally, your attorney should know what belongs in a will. Just to make sure, check it over to see that it contains an introductory clause with your complete name and address. This clause should state that this is your official will, replacing any previous ones.

Your will should explain how you want your funeral expenses, debts and estate taxes to be paid. If part of your estate is tax-exempt and part is taxable, you'll likely want these expenses paid out of the taxable portion, which will reduce your taxable estate.

Part of your will, of course, should direct how your assets will be handed down. Leaving assets to a surviving spouse is fairly simple. Things get a little more complicated when you have to decide how to leave assets to your children and their children.

Lawyers use two expressions for the main techniques, *per capita* and *per stirpes*. Per capita means that each beneficiary receives the same amount. Suppose you plan on leaving your money to three children. One of your children dies before you do, leaving three of his own children. Now you have five beneficiaries. Under a per capita arrangement, each would receive 20 percent of the assets to be distributed.

Under a per stirpes arrangement, the assets are divided evenly among your children. If your children predecease you, their children split that share. In our example, the two surviving children would each get 33 percent of the assets while the three children of the child who died would get 11 percent apiece.

Per Capita			Per Stirpes	
Dorothy	(your living child)	20%	Dorothy	33%
Tina	(your living child)	20%	Tina	33%
Ray	(children of your child Harriet, who has predeceased you)	20%	Ray	11%
Peter		20%	Peter	11%
Edgar		20%	Edgar	11%

Your will also may include specific bequests. Don't assume that your son Curtis "knows" that he's to receive your duck decoy collection and sister Edith "knows" she's to receive your dad's diamond stickpin. Spell out those bequests with enough detail so there's no confusion. Don't make bequests such as "the contents of the desk in my office go to Uncle Ben," because you don't know what will be there at some future time.

When you're making bequests, don't forget debts that are owed to you. Are they to be forgiven? If not, specify who's entitled to inherit the proceeds.

Finally, after all the bequests are made, include a *residuary* clause. This clause states that anything not specifically mentioned in your will goes to your spouse, or to a specific child, or to someone else. Again, that will help reduce confusion.

Beyond bequests, your will should name the people you choose to carry out your wishes. If you have minor children, you'll need guardians—someone to raise your kids until they come of age. Family members or close friends are the usual choices. Often you'll pick guardians who are close to your own age, with children who are contemporaries of your kids. If necessary, you may want to name a financially oriented *guardian of the property* in addition to a *guardian of the person,* who'll provide nurturing.

Your will should name an *executor* (or *personal representative*) to handle all the details of transferring your wealth. Your spouse or a responsible grown child often is the best choice. If you're establishing trusts in your will, trustees should be named. Naturally, you'll want the consent of all guardians, executors and trustees before officially naming them in your will. Be sure to provide your executor with a reasonably complete list of your assets, with backup documentation.

At the end of the will, restate for the record that this is your last will, consisting of a certain number of pages. Make sure that the pages are numbered and that you initial each one. Get at least three people who aren't beneficiaries to act as witnesses, making sure to include their addresses as well.

Eternal Vigilance

Your "last will" probably won't be your last. At certain points in your life, your will should be amended. Births (of new children) and deaths (of anyone named in your will) are occasions for new wills. So are moves to new states, where the laws may be different. And you might want to change your will if your economic circumstances change (you inherit your parents' estate) or if the federal estate-tax laws change, which seems to happen as often as Washington discovers a new need for revenues. Just to keep up with tax law, you should have your will reviewed every two years.

When it's time for a change, do you have to rewrite your will completely or can it be amended by a slight modification, called a *codicil?* You'll need to consult with an attorney. But you're the one with the responsibility for forcing the issue every time you go through a major change in your circumstances. What's more, you're responsible for choosing the right attorney to update your will.

Take the case of Betty and Ed, who had an estate of just over $1 million. Back in the early 1980s, after the landmark 1981 tax act, they consulted the attorney who had drawn up their wills. Don't worry, said the attorney, who was not an estate-planning expert. If Ed dies, everything goes to Betty; if Betty dies, everything goes to Ed. After that, your kids will inherit. Because the lawyer had represented them for 35 years, Betty and Ed did not question his judgment.

In the late 1980s, driving in the California fog, Betty and Ed were in an auto accident. Ed died immediately; Betty died two months later. Under their wills, all Ed's assets went to Betty. Then all the couple's assets went from Betty to their children. Because Betty's resulting estate was over $1 million, the estate tax was around $200,000.

The estate taxes could have been avoided by a simple update of their wills. Ed's will could have called for $600,000 to be left to their children, in trust, with a lifetime income for Betty. That would have reduced Betty's estate to around $500,000. All the assets could have passed to their children free of estate tax.

So Betty and Ed's children are $200,000 poorer because Betty and Ed didn't have their will revised by a knowledgeable attorney.

Do wills have shortcomings? Certainly. They have to go through probate, which is expensive and time-consuming. A will must be filed with a local court, exposing your affairs for all to see.

Therefore, you can use a living trust or jointly owned property to reduce your reliance upon a will. However, a trust is not likely to cover all your personal property, and it can't name a guardian for your minor children. To fill in any gaps, your wealth-transfer plan should include a will.

- If you die without a will, a court will transfer your wealth for you. Your family will undergo unnecessary expense and inconvenience.
- You should have a written will, drafted by a knowledgeable attorney.
- Bequests to your children may be per capita or per stirpes.
- You may make specific bequests of certain assets, but make sure they're spelled out in detail.
- If you have minor children, you need to name guardians. Family members or close family friends are often chosen.
- You need to name an executor to handle the administration of your estate. A responsible grown child may be an appropriate selection.
- Your will should be updated whenever there's a major change in your circumstances, or whenever the tax law changes. Failure to keep a will up to date may result in needless estate taxes.

Living Will Power

You're probably reading this book after completing a triathlon or a white-water canoe trip. The last thing you can imagine is lying in a hospital bed, hooked up to a respirator, sustained by a feeding tube. For all too many of us, that's what we may look forward to. Medical science has progressed to the point where we can be kept alive long after we're getting anything out of it.

You can easily imagine the emotional strain this would put on your loved ones—and, not to be crass about it, the financial strain as well. Someone has to pay for all the doctors and nurses and high-tech apparatus. Maybe you'll be fully covered by Medicare or private health insurance; more likely, part of the wealth you'd like to transfer to your family will be diverted to the health-care industry, one of America's healthiest, for allowing you to vegetate.

To prevent such catastrophes, everyone should have a living will. This is a different document from the standard will we described earlier in this chapter. A living will is a very specific document, used solely for medical purposes, to describe when the machines should be turned off and when the force feeding should cease.

Treat a living will like your regular will. It's a formal document that should be signed by at least two witnesses, witnesses who don't stand to benefit from your death. Once it's signed, have many copies made. Sign them and give them to your doctor, your spouse, your children and so on. Don't lock your one copy in a safe-deposit box. Make sure everyone knows your wishes on this matter. You need to draft your living will while you're still competent; after you go into a coma, it's too late.

Suppose you have drafted a living will and now you're scheduled for elective surgery that might prove fatal. Don't go into a hospital until you've queried the administrator about its policy on living wills. Some hospitals refuse to "pull the plug" on patients, possibly because of their religious beliefs. This has led to ludicrous situations in which relatives of a comatose patient fight to get that patient moved from one hospital to another where a living will will be recognized. You're better off making sure before you go in.

Even with a living will, you may not get the results you want. Some doctors just aren't ready to make life-or-death decisions on the basis of a piece of paper; in some cases, the living will doesn't apply to a particular situation. That's why you should supplement your living will with a *health-care proxy,* also known as a *medical power of attorney.*

Don't confuse a medical power of attorney with the traditional durable power of attorney. The latter gives someone that you name the right to handle your affairs in case you become incompetent. A durable power of attorney generally is limited to financial affairs.

A medical power of attorney or health-care proxy gives someone besides yourself the right to make medical decisions in case you're not able to. Your proxy might be your spouse or a grown child. (Don't name two, because that can lead to a tug-of-war over your prone body.) Although a health-care proxy doesn't expire, it can be revoked.

A person, of course, is more flexible than a piece of paper, so he or she can respond to whatever situation arises. Chances are greater, too, that your proxy's wishes will be followed, if only because doctors and hospitals have less to fear from liability suits.

State laws vary in their treatment of living wills and health-care proxies. In any case, the clearer and more convincing you are in making your wishes known, the greater the chances they'll be upheld.

Be as specific as possible in drawing up your living will. You might say, for example, that if you have an incurable disease or an irreversible physical or mental condition, with no expectation of recovery, that you do not want medical treatment. You might say that if you're permanently unconscious, you want pain-killing drugs but no cardiac resuscitation, no mechanical respiration, no force feeding and no antibiotics.

For $1 and a stamped, self-addressed envelope, the Harvard Medical School Health Letter, 164 Longwood Avenue, Boston, MA 02115, will send you a form to accompany your living will or health-care proxy. This form, compiled by two doctors, lists four scenarios (vegetative state, coma, dementia and dementia with terminal illness) along with specific treatment alternatives. You can specify the treatment you'd like on this form to positively indicate how you want to exercise your right to die with dignity.

- High-tech medicine now can keep patients alive for long periods, even if there's no hope of recovering and enjoying life.
- Such a protracted condition can drain your wealth as well as your family's emotions.
- To prevent such catastrophes, you should draw up a living will.
- A living will should be a formal document, widely disseminated.
- To supplement a living will, create a health-care proxy or medical power of attorney, naming someone else to make medical decisions if you're not able to.
- Your living will should be as specific as possible, stating the conditions in which you don't wish to be kept alive by artificial means.

4 Deflate Probate

For most people, if drawing up a will is Step 1 in a wealth-transfer plan, then creating a living trust is Step 1a. A *living trust* is simply a trust that you set up while you're alive. If you have enough concern about wealth transfer to buy this book, you should have a living trust, no matter if you expect your estate will be $1 million or $100 million.

Why is a living trust so important? Because assets placed in a living trust avoid probate—the process of proving your will and transferring assets to your heirs. Depending on which state you're in and the size of your estate, the costs of probate might be anywhere from 3 percent to 7 percent of your assets. On a $1 million estate, that's $30,000 to $70,000 lost just because some papers need to be shuffled. Not only do your executor and your estate lawyer get paid, they get paid first, before your family gets a share. Their fees may be a lot for a little work, especially if your affairs are well ordered.

Probate is not only costly, it's time-consuming. Valuing all the assets and filling out all the forms will take at least six months in most states, up to two years in others. In the meantime, important assets may be tied up. If markets change, your heirs might not be able to buy or sell when they want to.

What's more, probate proceedings are part of the public record. Do you want everyone to have access to a list of your family's holdings and the debts you've incurred? If you're leaving a family business to your heirs, probate is costly and inflexible and it exposes business records to competitors and creditors as well.

If you don't leave a will, your assets will go through probate anyway. And, as we explained in Chapter 3, your affairs will be out of your family's hands, under court direction.

Do you own assets in different states? A vacation home, perhaps? Then you'll have to go through probate in that state too.

Faster and Cheaper

Are there ways to avoid probate? Definitely. Property that is held jointly goes directly to the co-owner without going through probate.

Life-insurance proceeds won't go through probate either. Just make sure you don't name your own estate as the beneficiary and don't name minors as beneficiaries. (If you must name minors as beneficiaries, set up a trust or a custodianship while you're still alive, rather than in your will, and name that trust or custodianship to receive the life-insurance proceeds.) Similarly, your pension plan can avoid probate if you name a beneficiary, following the same rules that apply to life insurance.

Some states (New York, Florida, Michigan, Minnesota and Texas, for example) have a *payable on death,* or POD, system for transferring bank accounts, including CDs. You name your beneficiary by giving a name to your bank when setting up the account. Again, if you name a minor you'll get the probate court involved.

Probably the best way to avoid probate, though, is to set up a living trust. More than that, use a *revocable living trust.* That means the terms can be changed at any time. In fact, if you're not pleased, you can simply cancel your trust while you're alive and it will cease to exist. (At your death, though, a revocable trust becomes an irrevocable trust so that its terms can't be altered against your wishes.) You can use a living trust just as you'd use a will, to set up trusts to take effect at your death.

In any sort of trust, the power resides with the trustee. When you set up your revocable living trust, you'll probably want to be the trustee. Thus, you'll remain in control.

Control of what? All your assets. Your bank accounts, your stocks and bonds, your family business—everything can be owned by your revocable living trust. You'll have to change the title so that all these assets are owned by the trust and not by you. This is a tedious process, but a necessary one. If you work with an experienced attorney, he or she can help with the paperwork.

Even though the property is held in trust, you still can receive the benefits (i.e., the income), sell assets from the trust or add new assets. If you are the trustee, you make the decisions and you won't have to pay anyone a trust management fee.

After you have created a revocable living trust, it's relatively easy to maintain. Every state recognizes these trusts, so you don't need to rewrite yours completely if you change your residence. Some updating may be necessary when you move or if there's a change in your personal situation, but revocable living trusts are not hard to modify. Trust amendments need only your signature; no witnesses are necessary.

What if you can't get all your assets into a living trust or some other form of ownership that avoids probate? You can't realistically expect to retitle every item you own so that ownership passes to your living trust. The solution is to have your attorney create a *pour-over will* to supplement your living trust. In essence, the pour-over will states that assets not already in the trust shall be placed in the trust at your death. (As we said before, if you have minor children, you'll also need a will to name guardians.)

Even though you likely will be the original trustee, you can—you should—name successor trustees. If you become incapacitated, your chosen successor will take over. In these days, with people living longer and Alzheimer's disease just one of the afflictions that can strike the elderly, it's comforting to know your affairs will be in competent hands. With a living trust in place, you won't have to worry about a court appointing a conservator to handle your affairs. In some states, a durable power of attorney can be used with a living trust, authorizing another person to sign your name to legal documents in the event of your disability or incompetence.

What's more, the transfer of power from you to your successor trustee will be done smoothly in absolute privacy. You won't have to suffer the same public humiliation that Groucho Marx, among others, had to go through, while a court hears all the intimate details of your life and decides whether you need a guardian or a conservator.

The same applies to your affairs after your death. Your successor trustee takes over and your assets are transferred according to your instructions, in private. There's immediate continuity of management.

Interest payments, for example, go to your heirs right away, without the delays of probate.

This speed of transfer makes it very difficult for a disgruntled heir (or would-be heir) to challenge your disposition of assets. So living trusts make sense if you think a will might be contested.

Take the example of William, a widower who set up a living trust while in his 70s. He retitled his home, his bank accounts, his brokerage account and his mutual funds to a living trust, naming Cal, his nephew, as successor trustee. The setup cost was $500. William died at age 80 and Cal distributed all the assets in the trust according to William's instructions in a few hours. In California, where they lived, it would have taken close to two years to move William's will through probate court.

No Tax Shelter

Is there a downside to living trusts? They're relatively expensive to set up compared with wills. Although a simple living trust might cost as little as $500, if your affairs are complicated, startup fees might be anywhere from $1,000 to $3,000. More than that, though, you'll have to identify which assets can go into a trust and retitle them.

While establishing a living trust saves probate costs, it won't reduce estate or income taxes. Assets held in a living trust are still in your taxable estate. Other techniques, which we'll cover in this book, are needed to reduce estate taxes.

In fact, setting up a living trust may complicate wealth transfer in some cases. As you'll see, gift-giving often is a key to wealth transfer. However, certain gifts made from living trusts may be tossed back into your estate if you die within three years. So you may want to take assets out of the trust first, then make the gifts personally, rather than make gifts directly from the trust. Check with your tax pro.

Naturally, you'll want a knowledgeable attorney to set up your revocable living trust. Don't bother with those do-it-yourself living trust kits you see advertised for $29.95: they'll wind up costing you more than the real thing.

- When you die, with or without a will, your assets will go through probate—the process of checking over your assets and distributing them.
- Probate is extremely expensive and time-consuming in many states.
- When an estate goes through probate, everything is open to the public record.
- Some assets can be transferred without going through probate. Jointly held property goes directly to the co-owner. Life-insurance proceeds and pension benefits go to the named beneficiary.
- For other assets, probate can be avoided by creating a revocable living trust. Virtually all assets can be transferred into this trust.
- You can name yourself as trustee and retain control of your assets, just as before, while you're still alive.
- You can name a successor trustee to take over, quickly and privately, in the event of your disability or incapacity.
- Similarly, your successor trustee will control the trust at your death, to distribute your assets according to your wishes. Assets in the trust won't go through probate.
- A living trust can't cover all your possessions. You'll need a pour-over will to include anything left out.
- Revocable trusts don't reduce estate taxes.

5 Title Games

Many years ago, sisters Lucy and Ethel were vacationing. They bought raw land to be held as an investment, each putting up half the money. When it came to filling out the paperwork, they declared themselves to be co-owners: technically, they became joint tenants with the right of survivorship.

As the years passed, both sisters married and had children. Lucy was divorced. Eventually, she and Ethel decided to sell their property, which was near a popular resort and thus much in demand. They were working out the details on a sale for around $500,000 when Lucy died.

In her will, Lucy bequeathed this property to her children. Because the title was held as *joint tenants with the right of survivorship,* her wishes were disregarded. Instead, her share of the property went directly to Ethel.

What's more, Lucy's share of the property was included in her taxable estate. It was valued at $250,000, so Lucy's children had to pay $125,000 in extra taxes (because of the laws in the state where the property was located)—even though they didn't inherit the property!

Three for the Money

As you can see by this example, your wealth-transfer strategy can be dramatically affected by how you hold title to your assets. State laws vary but, in general, there are three ways to hold title:

1. *Fee simple.* You own the property outright, by yourself. You can dispose of it as you wish.
2. *Tenancy in common.* You own property with one or more co-owners. You may dispose of your share as you wish.

3. *Joint tenancy with right of survivorship.* You own property with one or more co-owners. When you die, your share automatically passes to your co-owners.

Joint tenancy is simple and convenient. As another benefit, jointly owned property bypasses probate. If you own your home with your spouse, for example, and you want him or her to inherit your half, joint tenancy may make sense. The same with joint bank accounts.

But joint tenancy has some disadvantages, as we've just seen. Certainly, you lose a lot of your flexibility when it comes to wealth transfer.

Suppose, for example, that Cliff and Claire are married with $1.2 million in total assets. As we have described, they can pass on all $1.2 million to their children tax-free if they leave $600,000 to the kids at the first death and $600,000 at the second death.

However, suppose $400,000 of their assets (real estate, securities, bank accounts) is held jointly while Cliff and Claire each has $400,000 outright. No matter who dies first, the kids can inherit only $400,000. The surviving spouse will wind up with $800,000 ($400,000 held outright plus $400,000 held jointly). If the surviving spouse dies with that $800,000 estate, the kids will owe around $75,000 in estate taxes.

So joint tenancy allows this couple to avoid probate on a $400,000 asset, which might cost $12,000 to $40,000. Instead, their kids will pay an extra $75,000 in estate taxes. (Even without joint tenancy, probate could be avoided by use of a revocable living trust.)

Out of Step

There are other tax consequences as well. Suppose that $400,000 in joint property was a house purchased for $50,000 many years ago. If Cliff dies first and Claire inherits, in most states she'll get a *step up* in basis on the half she inherits from Cliff, to $200,000. But her half of the house still has its $25,000 basis. So, if she decides she wants a smaller house and sells this one for $400,000, she'll have a $175,000 taxable gain:

Original cost of the house (including improvements)	$50,000
Cliff's basis	$25,000
Claire's basis	$25,000
Value of house at Cliff's death	$400,000
Therefore, Cliff's basis is stepped up to	$200,000
Claire sells house for	$400,000
Claire's total basis ($25,000 plus $200,000 on half she inherited)	($225,000)
Taxable gain	$175,000

On the other hand, suppose Cliff owns the entire house and gives $200,000 to Claire to equalize their estates. If he dies first, he can leave his $600,000, including the house, to a trust. The trust will get a step up in basis to $400,000 and can sell the house for that much and not owe capital gains taxes. (Some states restrict one spouse's right to leave the family home to a nonspouse, so check with a local attorney.)

While the trust beneficiaries will be their children, Claire can be entitled to life income from the trust. Thus, she'll have access to $1.2 million worth of assets, from which she can buy a new house and still have an ample income. And all $1.2 million can wind up in the hands of their children tax-free.

So, other types of ownership may be preferable to joint tenancy, even between married couples. Certainly, joint tenancy can be unfortunate in the case of a second marriage if each spouse has children from the previous marriage. When the first spouse dies, the survivor will inherit the jointly held property, not the children of the spouse who died.

Even greater problems may arise if the co-owners are not married couples. For example, a widower and grown daughter hold property jointly, so that the daughter will have access to his funds in case of emergency. There may be gift-tax consequences when the joint ownership is first established; all the assets must pass to the daughter at his death, possibly at the expense of his other children.

Therefore, you need to be careful in how you hold title to property. You might prefer fee simple or tenancy in common, either of which gives you more flexibility. You can transfer your wealth as you'd like to. As long as you hold those properties in a living trust, rather than in your own name, you can avoid the time and expense of probate.

Again, state laws on property ownership will vary, so you need to consult with a local attorney. That's especially true in the eight *community property* states, including California and Texas, where each spouse owns 50 percent of all property acquired during a marriage. In particular, check your state's *homestead* laws to see what married couples are allowed to do when transferring a primary residence.

- There are three ways to hold title to property.
- With two of those ways (fee simple, tenancy in common), you can direct how you want your wealth to be transferred.
- With the third way, joint tenancy with right of survivorship, you have no flexibility. When one co-owner dies, the property passes to the surviving co-owner(s).
- Joint tenancy property is not subject to probate.
- The adverse tax consequences of joint tenancy may exceed the costs of probate.
- Even with fee simple or tenancy in common, you can avoid probate by using a living trust.
- Because state laws vary, consult with a local attorney when deciding how to hold title to property.

6 'Tis Better To Give

Because the gift tax and the estate tax are *unified,* you can't give away hundreds of thousands of dollars on your deathbed and thus escape estate tax. Such gifts will be included in your taxable estate.

You can give away your taxable estate, or a portion of it, if you do it right. You're allowed to give up to $10,000 each to any number of recipients (*donees*) each year. The money will not be counted as taxable income for the donees; you won't have to pay a gift tax; and your $600,000 estate-tax exemption won't be reduced. You don't even have to file a tax return.

If you're married, you and your spouse can give up to $20,000 per donee, per year, free of gift tax. Such joint gifts require the consent of both spouses, shown by the filing of a gift tax return.

Suppose you and your spouse give $35,000 to a child this year. The first $20,000 is exempt from gift tax, but the excess $15,000 is a taxable gift. Generally, you won't have to pay a gift tax; instead, that $15,000 will come out of your estate-tax exemption. Now, only $585,000 of your estate will be tax-free, rather than $600,000.

Lifetime gift/estate-tax exemption	$600,000	
Joint gift to a child		$35,000
Joint annual gift-tax exemption		($20,000)
Excess subject to gift tax	($15,000)	
Remaining gift/estate-tax exemption	$585,000	

In this example, you might want to defer $15,000 of the gift until the following year. Or give $15,000 to your child's spouse. Or give $15,000 to your child's child. All these alternatives will preserve your full $600,000 estate-tax exemption.

Riding Your Gift Horse

Your $10,000 annual gift-tax exemption ($20,000 if you're married) can be a powerful estate-planning tool. Say you're retired, with no worries about current income, and you expect to have a sizable estate. You have two children, both happily married, and four grandchildren. If you and your spouse want to, you can give up to $20,000 per year each to your children, their spouses, and your grandchildren. That's as much as $160,000 per year that you can divert from your estate.

(Actually, you can give even more. If you pay someone else's medical bills or school tuition directly, those payments won't count toward the $10,000/$20,000 limit.)

There may be situations in which you'll intentionally disregard the $10,000/$20,000 limits. As of this writing, everyone is entitled to a $600,000 exemption from estate and gift tax. That's been the case since the 1981 tax act took effect fully in 1987. Because, as we know all too well, the federal government has been running huge budget deficits for years, tax increases are likely to close that deficit and the estate and gift tax is a possible target in the next round of tax "reform."

No, we don't think the estate-tax exemption will be abolished altogether. But it's likely that the exemption will be scaled back, perhaps to $200,000 or $300,000 per person.

If you share that concern, you may want to act now. That is, give away $600,000 worth of assets to remove them from your estate. The future growth of those assets, as well as current income, will be out of your estate too. The way the tax law usually works, if you take this action while the $600,000 limit still is in effect, you won't be penalized if the laws subsequently change.

Now, you don't want to impoverish yourself just to save estate taxes. Don't give away assets you'll need to live on. But if you have assets of

$2 million or more, certainly with $3 million or more, consider making a large lifetime gift to take advantage of the $600,000 exemption while it's still available.

The Thought Counts

If you're going to make lifetime gifts, anywhere from $10,000 to $600,000, what should you give? Cash gifts are the simplest, but you may want to give away assets that are likely to appreciate to remove that future appreciation from your estate.

For example, Harry and Lee are New Yorkers in their 70s who have owned a beach house on Long Island for decades. In recent years, they've used the house less and less; their children and grandchildren are the ones who spend most of the time there now.

At the peak of the market, comparable beach houses sold for $500,000. Now prices have come down. Harry and Lee were able to find a reputable appraiser who put a current value on the house of $350,000, based on recent selling prices. So Harry and Lee gave the house to their children, using up $350,000 of their gift tax exemption. If the market rebounds, as it's likely to over the years, and the house increases in value to $500,000 again, all that appreciation will be out of Harry and Lee's estates.

Similarly, you might want to give away portfolios of stocks or mutual funds where appreciation is expected.

In rarer circumstances, where you have *too much* income, you'll want to give away income-producing assets. Take the case of Jonathan, now in his 70s, who built up a large pension plan while he worked on Wall Street. Under federal tax law, he must withdraw a certain amount from the pension fund each year, so he has an annual income over $100,000 from the pension fund alone. He likes to travel and go out to restaurants, but he still finds that his income is more than ample.

Jonathan also has a portfolio of utility and corporate bonds, paying him an extra $15,000 per year. Of that $15,000, $5,000 goes straight to the IRS in taxes. The remaining $10,000 stays in Jonathan's estate, where about $5,000 will be taxed at his death. Therefore, Jonathan has decided to give away his bonds in $10,000 chunks per year, to reduce his income tax and his estate tax. His children, to whom he is giving the bonds, can use the extra interest income, even after paying the income tax.

Present Value

Whenever you give away anything except cash, you need to establish the value of the assets. In the case of publicly traded securities, there will be no problem. The market value at the time of the transfer will determine the value of the gift.

The situation is different if you're giving away a life-insurance policy to remove the proceeds from your taxable estate. The value may be the *interpolated terminal reserve* or the *replacement cost*. You'll need to check with your agent to get a value. If necessary, you might want to reduce the value by taking out policy loans before making a gift.

If you're giving away real estate, as Harry and Lee did, or shares in a closely held business or a valuable painting, valuation is trickier. With such assets, there is no daily market with published trading prices to set the price. The best way to establish a valuation on these assets is to hire a reputable expert, not related to you by blood or marriage or business connections, and get a written appraisal of the assets, as of the transfer date.

For example, say you own all 100,000 shares of a tractor dealership, and a third party appraises the business at $5 million. Thus, each share is worth $50 and you can use that value when you give away shares. If you want to make another gift of shares next year, you'll need a new appraisal.

Giving Away a Tax Obligation

As you might expect, there are subtle as well as obvious tax ramifications to gift-giving. Suppose, for example, you own shares of Merck common stock you bought for $10,000; now they're worth $40,000. You and your spouse give them to your two children, $20,000 worth of stock apiece. This removes $40,000 worth of assets from your estate, removes any future appreciation from your estate and gives the donees (your children) any dividend income, too. The donees also acquire your unpaid income-tax obligation. If they ever sell those shares, income tax will be due on all the built-up gain.

You paid	$10,000
Shares are worth	$40,000
After you give the shares away, your children's tax basis is	$10,000
If they sell the shares for	$50,000
Their taxable gain will be	$40,000
Their income-tax liability will be (@ 35% income-tax rate)	$14,000

Let's look at a slightly different case. Suppose you had given away $40,000 worth of AT&T stock for which you had paid $35,000. Your children would have a $35,000 tax basis in the AT&T shares. If the AT&T stock appreciates to $50,000 and they sell the shares, they'd have only a $15,000 taxable gain, versus a $40,000 gain in the Merck example.

Does that mean you're better off simply retaining the Merck shares, with the large built-in gain? Not really. Suppose your Merck shares increase in value to $50,000 while you and your spouse live and then you leave them to your children in your will. The children immediately sell the shares:

You paid	$10,000
Shares are worth at death	$50,000
Their estate-tax liability will be (@ 50% estate-tax bracket)	$25,000
After inheriting the shares, your children's tax basis is	$50,000
If they sell the shares for	$50,000
Their taxable gain will be	$0

Their income tax liability will be	$0
Total taxes	$25,000

As you can see, the children are better off paying income tax at 35 percent than estate tax at 50 percent, and so it makes sense to give away the shares.

If you have other stocks without the large built-in income-tax liability, you should give them away first. In general, the assets to be given away first are those with little built-in capital gain. If you have a choice, hold onto appreciated assets until your death, when your heirs can inherit them with a stepped-up tax basis.

On the other hand, if you intend to sell appreciated assets, it's a smart move to give them to someone in a lower tax bracket, perhaps a teenaged grandchild.

Give Your Gift a Chance To Grow

Besides what to give, you need to decide to whom your gifts should be made. Your natural inclination probably is to give assets to your grown children who will inherit your assets when you die. But that merely puts assets into the estate of a middle-aged person who may have his or her own estate taxes to worry about in a few years.

If there's no pressing need for the assets, we recommend they be given to grandchildren, eliminating the estate tax for two generations instead of one. As we will explain in Chapter 12, everybody can give up to $1 million to each grandchild exempt from the so-called generation-skipping tax.

Gifts to grandchildren can be held in trust. Their parents (your children) can serve as trustees so they'll have access to the money in case of an emergency.

In general, unless there's a specific need for cash right away, we prefer making gifts to be held in trust, rather than commingled with the recipient's other funds. (Gifts to minors *must* be held in trust or custodial accounts.) Money held in trust, and managed wisely, will compound over the years, building real wealth for your family.

If you're not familiar with it already, you should learn the *Rule of 72*. Just divide a rate of return into 72 to see how fast money will double. If assets held in trust grow by 8 percent per year, for example, they'll double in nine years. If assets earn 12 percent, they'll double in six years. At a 12 percent rate, $1,000 becomes $8,000 by the time your newborn grand-children are ready for college.

That doesn't mean you have to put everything into a trust fund. Giving your children or grandchildren a few thousand dollars a year outside of a trust, allowing them to make the inevitable mistakes, may teach lessons that will come in handy when they have to deal with a six- or seven-figure inheritance.

- Gifts you make will reduce your $600,000 estate-tax exemp-tion.
- You're entitled to give away $10,000 per year to each of any number of people without reducing your estate-tax exemp-tion. Married couples can give away up to $20,000 per year per recipient.
- Larger gifts may be desirable to take advantage of current law, if you fear the estate-tax exemption may be cut back.
- Care must be taken to put a value on all gifts.
- The best assets to give away are those likely to appreciate or those that provide you with unneeded income.
- It's best to give away assets with little or no built-in capital gain.
- Gifts made to grandchildren, up to $1 million per grandchild, will remove assets from your children's estates as well as your own.
- If there is no pressing need for cash, gifts can be made to trusts. Money held in trust, if managed wisely, can compound over the long term.

II

TRUST-
WORTHY

7 Trusts Without Fear

In the old days—the real old days—all the land in England was owned by the king. Nobles held their land at the king's pleasure, and they had to leave that land to their oldest male heirs (a system known as primogeniture). In other words, they lacked control over their wealth transfer.

To solve this problem, trusts were created. In essence, land was sold while a noble was still alive, but the buyer held it on behalf of others, usually the seller's heirs. When the noble died, he didn't hold the land, so it wasn't subject to primogeniture. With this technique, land could be handed down from generation to generation, and not always to the firstborn male.

Today, trusts still exist as a legal fiction created to hold property. They may, for example, hold property for minors or for incompetent adults. They may be used to hold property so it won't be included in a person's taxable estate. They may be used to protect against litigation, divorce actions, creditors, etc. Or, as we have seen in the case of living trusts, they may be used mainly to keep your assets private, out of the reach of the probate court.

Cast of Characters

Trusts are established by a *maker*, a *trustor*, a *creator*, a *settlor* or a *grantor*, who usually provides the funds or other property to be held by the trust. At some point, the assets will go to a beneficiary or beneficiaries. While the trust exists, its assets will be managed by a trustee or co-trustees. In some situations the same person can fill two or even all three roles.

In living trusts, used to avoid probate, individuals commonly act as maker, trustee and beneficiary. New York State, though, forbids you from filling three positions by yourself, so living trusts aren't popular in New York.

Living trusts, as the name suggests, are established while the maker is alive. Lawyers may refer to these trusts as *inter vivos*. Alternatively, trusts may be *testamentary,* set up at your death, through the provisions of your will or of a living trust.

Another way to designate trusts is as either *revocable* or *irrevocable.* A revocable trust can be changed or canceled during the maker's lifetime. At the maker's death, revocable trusts become irrevocable, at which point the terms can't be changed. Testamentary trusts are always irrevocable.

What are the main differences? A revocable living trust doesn't take assets out of your estate. In the eyes of the tax code, you still control the assets because you can revoke the trust at any time. Therefore, you'll reap no estate-tax savings with a revocable trust. There are no income-tax savings either: trust income is passed through to the maker.

On the positive side, you don't have to worry about gift taxes with a revocable trust. You can transfer assets from your own account to the trust without incurring a gift tax. In the eyes of the IRS, you're merely shifting assets from one pocket to another.

Why bother with a revocable trust? Because the assets are legally controlled by the trustee. As long as you're alive and capable, you have full control over your assets. At your death, or in the event you become incapacitated, your successor trustee takes over. Your assets will be managed and distributed according to the trust instructions. No guardian will be appointed by a court; no probate court will get involved.

Irrevocable trusts are different. Because they can't be annulled, they're considered to be stand-alone entities, distinct from the maker. Because assets transferred to irrevocable trusts are out of the maker's estate, irrevocable trusts are a prime means of reducing estate taxes.

Similarly, transferring assets to an irrevocable trust can cut your income taxes. Income earned by an irrevocable trust generally is taxed to the beneficiary, if distributed, or to the trust itself, if not distributed.

On the downside, getting assets into an irrevocable trust means coping with the gift tax. You may, if you work with a skilled attorney, use your $10,000/$20,000-per-recipient annual gift-tax exemption when making gifts to a trust. Or you can use your $600,000/$1,200,000 lifetime gift-tax exemption. You'll owe a gift tax on transfers to a trust in excess of these amounts.

Filling the Roles

Who can be the players in the trust game? You, with your concerns about wealth transfer, generally are the maker of the trust. If you and your spouse are both contributing assets, each of you will be a co-maker. The beneficiaries typically will be your children. However, in cases where your children already have ample wealth and solid careers, we recommend naming your grandchildren as beneficiaries. That can skip one extra level of estate tax (your children's) and generate a long-term wealth buildup.

Trustees will vary. In a revocable living trust, you usually act as trustee. Successor trustees may be your spouse, your grown children or a reliable financial adviser.

For irrevocable trusts, you or your spouse generally shouldn't serve as trustee. In most cases, your grown children may serve as trustees, as long as you have confidence in their judgment. That's the case even if they're the beneficiaries as well. As trustees, they generally have the authority to tap the trust assets if necessary. If there's a "sprinkle" provision in the trust, the trustee can distribute different amounts to different beneficiaries according to need.

If you're going to have substantial assets in the trust, you probably will want a trustee with some financial savvy. Even if the trustee will hire a money manager to make the actual investment selections, you'll want someone who can look over the manager's shoulder with some knowledge. Q-TIP trusts, especially, need a financially savvy trustee or co-trustee.

What about irrevocable life-insurance trusts, which are used frequently in wealth-transfer strategies? As long as all the money going into the trust is used to purchase life insurance, there's no need to spend hundreds or thousands of dollars per year on a professional trustee. Your grown child or children can manage nicely.

But, after the insurance proceeds are distributed, there may be over $1 million worth of assets in the trust. If you intend to keep the assets in the trust after the proceeds are received, you may want to provide for a professional co-trustee to step in then.

The trust departments of banks and brokerage firms may serve well as professional trustees. They're much more strictly regulated than brokerages or the other departments of banks; you won't see them making casino loans. They're expensive, typically charging around 1 percent of the assets in the trust per year (that's $10,000 per year on a $1 million trust fund). They also have deep pockets, so there will be someone to sue in case things go wrong. And they provide continuity, because a bank or brokerage firm isn't likely to die, as human trustees will.

There is one situation, as we'll see, where you can act as trustee for an irrevocable trust: the charitable remainder trust. The assets of these trusts have to go to charity, so you can't take out more than the income you've provided for yourself. During your lifetime, you can act as trustee and receive income from the trust; after your death, your spouse can act as trustee and receive income, if the trust documents provide for that. When all the income beneficiaries are dead, the assets go to the charity and there's no need to have a trustee any longer.

You may be tempted to transfer property to minors via your state's Uniform Gifts to Minors Act (UGMA) or Uniform Transfers to Minors Act (UTMA) rather than through a trust. Generally, that's cheap and simple to do. When the minor comes of age, at 18 or 21, UGMA and UTMA property goes to the child with no strings attached. You can attach strings if the property is held in trust.

Paying the Price

What do trusts cost? It's hard to generalize. The same trust may cost more when drawn up by a Park Avenue law firm with 50 names on the letterhead than when drawn up by a single practitioner in Indianapolis. Similarly, a "plain vanilla" trust will be much less expensive than an elaborate variety where the lawyers put in dozens of hours to customize it to your situation.

As a general rule, expect to spend at least $500 just for breathing the word *trust* to a lawyer. Most wealth-transfer trusts can be drawn up for $2,000 or less (charitable remainder trusts may be a bit more expensive). Ask about price before you give an attorney the go-ahead. If it seems as if it will cost you more than $3,000 and you have no exotica you want to include, it may pay you to shop around before making a commitment.

Accounting for Trusts

After you've paid for establishing a trust, there will be ongoing administrative effort and expense. According to Michael Shaw, partner-in-charge, financial services, in the Los Angeles office of the accounting firm Coopers & Lybrand, any trust with over $600 worth of gross income must file a tax return using Form 1041. Even if it's a *simple trust*, meaning that all the income must be distributed, and the trust retains no income, the form must be filed.

With a *complex trust*, income may be retained by the trust or distributed. On income that's not distributed, tax may be owed—on some types of income. If income wouldn't be taxable to an individual—municipal bond income, inside buildup of life insurance or (in some cases) an annuity—then income tax won't be owed. But the trust will owe tax on income from taxable sources. If it seems that the trust will owe $500 or more in taxes, quarterly estimated tax returns must be filed.

In some instances, it pays to have income retained in the trust. Here are the tax rates for 1991:

Personal Income (Joint Return)	Tax Rate	Trust Income
up to $34,000	15%	up to $ 3,450
up to $82,150	28%	up to $10,350
over $82,150	31%	over $10,350

As you can see, income over $82,150 on a joint return will be taxed at 31 percent (plus state and local income taxes). These taxpayers will do better if they leave extra taxable income inside the trust, where it will be taxed at a much lower rate—15 percent, if the trust's retained income is $3,450 or less.

Beyond tax returns, what kinds of records does a trustee need to keep? Careful ones. The trustee probably will want to hire an accountant for all but the simplest trusts, but the accountant shouldn't be relied upon for everything. The trustee, with fiduciary responsibility, should keep careful records of all transactions. This will help the accountant prepare tax returns; in case of a challenge by the beneficiary or other parties, the trustee will need to be able to show how he or she handled the trust funds.

According to Shaw, the more complicated the investment strategy, the more books and records need to be kept. Simple strategies will demand less paperwork. If all the assets are placed with one money manager, for example, that money manager will have to keep thorough records. If the proceeds are all invested in life-insurance policies or annuity contracts, there will be less administration for the trustee to worry about.

- Trusts are legal fictions created to hold property.
- Trusts are created by a maker, a settlor, a trustor, a grantor or a creator.
- Trust assets are managed by trustees.
- Ultimately, trust income and trust assets are distributed to beneficiaries.
- Trusts that can be altered are called revocable.
- Revocable trusts don't save taxes but they can enable property to bypass probate.
- You probably can act as maker, trustee and beneficiary of a revocable trust.
- Irrevocable trusts can't be canceled.
- Assets transferred to irrevocable trusts are out of your control and out of your taxable estate as well as beyond the reach of probate.
- You or your spouse generally shouldn't serve as trustee for irrevocable trusts. Your grown children often are suitable trustees.
- Trusts are excellent vehicles for transferring wealth to minors and incompetent adults.

- If substantial assets are held in trust, the trustee or co-trustee should have some knowledge of financial matters and investing.
- Trusts have to file tax returns if they have substantial gross income; if there is retained taxable income, income tax will be owed.
- Besides filing tax returns, trustees need to keep careful records of all trust fund transactions.
- Some trustees may prefer to turn over control of the assets to a money manager or insurance company to reduce the administrative burden.

An Oldie but Goodie

Previously we explained how estates of up to $1.2 million can escape estate tax. In essence, $600,000 can be left to the children at the first death, but in trust so that the surviving spouse has use of the income. The other $600,000 can be held by the surviving spouse, to be passed to the children at his or her death free of estate tax.

This strategy works fine if there's no growth in the estate between the two deaths. But that's not always the case.

- Suppose a good portion of the estate consists of real estate. Perhaps the first spouse dies when real-estate markets are depressed, so the properties get a low value for estate-tax purposes. When the second spouse dies, 5 or 10 years later, real-estate markets may have rebounded and the properties may have doubled in value.
- Suppose the estate consists largely of shares in a closely held corporation. Thanks to good management by the second generation, the business booms and the shares gain greatly in value in the interim years.
- Suppose the money is invested in stocks and bonds that grow faster in value and generate more interest than the widow or widower manages to spend.

In all these situations, the estate will grow from tax-exempt into taxable territory.

Say Richard dies at age 75, leaving Liz a 72-year-old widow. At Richard's death, $600,000 goes into a children's trust while Liz has $600,000 of her own assets, in trust or held outright. During her lifetime, Liz takes $50,000 a year from each side: the children's trust and her own assets. After income taxes, she may have $60,000 per year to spend.

Liz dies at age 80. In the intervening eight years, even after her living expenses, the assets grow in value by around 7 percent per year, to $1 million on each side. At Liz's death, the children receive the $1 million in their trust fund free of estate taxes. But Liz's $1 million estate now is over the $600,000 limit. When that passes to her children, they'll owe around $150,000 in estate tax.

How can this tax be avoided? By using a strategy known as the *shrinking trust principal.* This technique has been around since the 1960s, and it still works today.

Smaller Is Better

Here's how estate tax can be avoided. Instead of taking income from both sides, Liz could take all the money she uses from her own assets. If her $600,000 worth of assets throws off $50,000 per year in cash income and she takes out $100,000, her assets might shrink to $550,000. The next year, if her assets generate $45,000 in cash, she'll have to invade principal for $55,000. And so on. She might, for example, sell her stock or real estate to the children's trust to raise cash, as long as she receives a fair price on all transactions.

She can do this for as long as her assets hold out. Suppose she dies with only $300,000 in her estate. That's well below the $600,000 limit, so no estate tax will be due.

At the same time, the children's trust will be growing because Liz isn't withdrawing any money. If she dies with only $300,000 in assets, the trust may hold $1.7 million in assets. Those assets, though, are outside her estate. At her death, they will pass to the children, free of estate tax.

Without Shrinking Trust Strategy	Children's Trust	Liz's Assets
Original principal	$600,000	$600,000
Annual withdrawals	$50,000	$50,000
Principal eight years later	$1,000,000	$1,000,000
Estate tax at Liz's death	$0	$150,000

With Shrinking Trust Strategy	Children's Trust	Liz's Assets
Original principal	$600,000	$600,000
Annual withdrawals	$0	$100,000
Principal eight years later	$1,700,000	$300,000
Estate tax at Liz's death	$0	$0

What if Liz lives so long that she spends down virtually all her assets? That's no problem. By then, the children's trust may have grown to $2 million. Liz still is entitled to all the income from this trust, so she should be able to live comfortably. (In most cases, the widow or widower will be able to "invade" the principal of the children's trust if an emergency arises.)

There are many variations on this strategy, but the concept remains the same. After the first spouse's death, the widow or the widower should spend his or her assets first, reducing the eventual estate-tax bill. Assets in the children's trust should be allowed to grow because they're outside the estate of the surviving spouse. Care should be taken when drawing up such trusts so that this strategy can be pursued without adverse income-tax consequences.

- After one spouse dies, up to $600,000 often is left to the children in trust, with the surviving spouse entitled to the income from that trust. Other assets typically are left to the surviving spouse, which avoids estate tax.

- At the death of the second spouse, all his or her assets will be subject to estate tax. This can be painful, especially if the survivor's assets have grown in the intervening years.
- To minimize or avoid estate tax at the second death, the surviving spouse should tap his or her own assets rather than the children's trust fund. This will shrink the widow or widower's estate. The children's trust can grow if it's not tapped and pass to the children free of estate tax.
- If the surviving spouse runs through all his or her assets, the enlarged children's trust then can be tapped for living expenses.

8

Cleaning Up with Q-TIPs

Up until now, we've given the impression that wealth transfer is fairly straightforward. The first spouse who dies leaves $600,000 to the children, perhaps in trust, to use the estate-tax exemption. The rest goes to the surviving spouse. When the second spouse dies, all the rest of the marital assets can go to the children.

But not everyone can follow this simple strategy. Suppose, as is often the case, the first spouse to die is the one with the greater amount of assets. After that death, if anything goes outright to the surviving spouse, then the survivor has control over those assets. The survivor may squander the wealth earned by the other spouse or leave the assets to people the breadwinner wouldn't have chosen.

Suppose the wealthy spouse foresees this problem, so he or she leaves assets directly to heirs besides the spouse. Not only would this leave the surviving spouse short of funds, it may trigger a large estate tax right away.

Have Your Cake and Eat It

Fortunately, there's a way the wealthier, likely-to-die-first spouse can have the best of all worlds. It's called a *Q-TIP*, and it's become a mainstay of wealth transfer. Before explaining how a Q-TIP works, let's look at the most common application: a second marriage.

Ken is a successful business owner in his late 60s. He was married and divorced, with three children from that marriage. His second wife, Barbara, is 55—only 10 years older than Ken, Jr., Ken's oldest child. Barbara has two children from her first marriage.

Ken expects to die before Barbara and to leave an estate worth around $2 million. Suppose he follows traditional estate planning and leaves $600,000 to his children and $1.4 million to Barbara. At her death,

53

she can leave that $1.4 million—Ken's $1.4 million—to her own children, leaving Ken's children nothing beyond that first $600,000.

That's where a Q-TIP comes in. Q-TIP property usually is held in a trust. Instead of leaving $1.4 million outright to Barbara, Ken leaves $1.4 million to a Q-TIP trust.

With a Q-TIP, Barbara gets all the income from the $1.4 million as long as she lives. Under some circumstances, the trustee can let her dip into trust principal. At her death, the trust funds go where Ken has directed them: to his children. So he is certain that his money will wind up where he wants it.

In addition, if the Q-TIP is drawn up properly, that $1.4 million will qualify for the unlimited marital deduction. No estate tax will be due until Barbara's death, when the money will pass to Ken's kids.

My Ball, My Rules

The Q-TIP acronym stands for Qualified Terminable Interest Property. As long as the income from the *property* (anything left in a Q-TIP) is solely for the surviving spouse for his or her lifetime, that property will qualify for the unlimited marital deduction. Therefore, estate taxes will be deferred. That's the case even though the surviving spouse doesn't have a *power of appointment* over those assets. That is, the survivor has no say in where the assets eventually will go. Instead, the first spouse to die sets the rules, confident that they'll be carried out according to his or her wishes.

You can see why Q-TIPs are popular in second marriages when each spouse has children from previous marriages. But you can use a Q-TIP even if you're still married to your high school sweetheart and the passion is just as intense as it was when you learned the magic of photosynthesis together.

Suppose you have a massive heart attack and die tomorrow. Your spouse, whom you find vibrant and attractive, likely will appeal to someone else and eventually remarry. Depending on your stage in life, your surviving spouse may start a second family or marry into one that's ready-made.

Again, a Q-TIP can help. The Q-TIP can provide lifetime income for your spouse, yet make sure that the assets you leave behind will find their way to your own children, not the children or stepchildren of your spouse's next marriage. If your widow, for example, marries a man who has six of his own children, you might find yourself sending a hockey team of strangers to Harvard. A Q-TIP can ease your mind.

Taking the Pressure Off

By the same token, what if you're the one who has always handled the family's financial decisions? If you die first, your widow or widower may not be equipped to handle large sums of money. There are lots of hustlers out there, from religious frauds to churning stockbrokers, looking for prey. If your money is in a Q-TIP with a competent trustee, your surviving spouse will always have enough to live on and your children can be sure they'll eventually come into their legacy.

It may sound like a Q-TIP is strictly for the selfish: I made the money, so I'll direct where it will go, even from beyond the grave. Actually, though, a Q-TIP takes the pressure off your surviving spouse. Children or stepchildren or new lovers or swindlers: they all can be put off, with no hard feelings, if your widow or widower explains that the money is locked into a Q-TIP.

Q-TIPs can avoid family troubles too. Suppose your spouse has consistently favored one child over the other. After you're gone, he or she has a club to hold over the one who always comes in second. "You only called me once last week, your sister called me three times, so I'm going to leave everything to her."

Sound petty? Of course. Unfortunately, such situations arise more often than people want to admit. Especially if the surviving spouse grows older and falls victim to Alzheimer's disease. You can't prevent hard feelings after your death, but you can at least be sure that your money won't be used as an intrafamilial weapon, thanks to a Q-TIP.

Avoiding the Death Watch

Let's see how Ken, whom we used in our example above, handled a problem that comes up fairly frequently. As we said, his second wife, Barbara, is 55, just 10 years older than Ken, Jr. If they both live to their life expectancies, Barbara will die just a few years before Junior—Junior won't have much time to enjoy his share of the $1.4 million, even though he and his siblings are the Q-TIP beneficiaries.

In these circumstances, Junior might spend much of his adult life sticking pins in a voodoo doll, hoping for his stepmother to die. You can see how a situation like that may poison family relations for years after your death.

Ken came to grips with this problem by buying two life-insurance policies. One is the second-to-die policy that most married couples can use to cover estate tax. When both Ken and Barbara die, Ken's three children will receive enough life-insurance proceeds to cover the tax payments.

In addition, Ken took out a single-life policy on his own life, payable to his three children. At his death, they'll receive $1 million right away. Thus, they won't have to go through life waiting for Barbara to die to get their inheritance.

Obviously, buying two large insurance policies is expensive, and Ken fears that transferring all that wealth from his estate will leave Barbara with not enough to live on. So here's how he revised his wealth-transfer plan:

1. He bought a single-life policy on himself for $1 million, payable to his kids, as mentioned.

2. He's leaving $600,000 to his children and using his estate-tax exemption. However, he's leaving the money in trust, with income going to Barbara during her lifetime. (The kids, with $1 million in hand, won't need the income from the $600,000.)

3. The rest of his estate, which he now estimates at $1.2 million after life-insurance costs, is left to a Q-TIP trust. This qualifies for the marital deduction, so no estate tax is due. Barbara will get lifetime income, but at her death the assets will pass to Ken's three children. Thus, Barbara will get income from two trusts, totaling $1.8 million. She'll be able to live well, perhaps saving money she can pass to her own children, but Ken's assets will eventually pass to his own kids.

4. Ken bought a $250,000 second-to-die policy, which should cover the estate tax due on Barbara's death.

5. Both life-insurance policies are held in tax-free inheritance trusts, which will avoid estate tax on the policies themselves. In fact, Ken has set up a separate trust for each policy to avoid confusion.

The result: Ken's kids will have an immediate $1 million, Ken's widow will have lifetime income from a $1.8 million estate, the entire $1.8 million will eventually go to Ken's kids, and no one in the family will have to pay any estate tax out of estate assets.

- If you leave property to your spouse, that will defer federal estate tax. However, your spouse will have the power to distribute your wealth, during his or her lifetime or at death.
- This problem can be avoided by using a Q-TIP, which qualifies for a marital exemption from estate tax; your surviving spouse gets lifetime income; you get to say where your wealth will wind up.
- Q-TIPs are most commonly used in second marriages, when you want your assets to go to your own kids, not those of your new spouse.
- Q-TIPs also are worthwhile in first marriages to guard against problems that may arise if you die and your spouse remarries.
- Even if there are no second marriages, a Q-TIP can protect your widow or widower from con artists.
- Q-TIPs can relieve the pressures of intrafamily disputes after your death.
- Unfortunately, Q-TIPs may give your children an incentive to see your surviving spouse die. Sophisticated wealth creation and transfer is needed to keep the vultures from circling.

Shrewd Tips for Q-TIPs

Some estate planning specialists believe that almost every married couple should have a Q-TIP as part of a wealth-transfer plan. Unfortunately, not every lawyer knows the "p's and q's" of drawing up a proper Q-TIP.

What kinds of property go into a Q-TIP? Property from which the surviving spouse can receive *beneficial enjoyment* during his or her lifetime. The easiest assets to handle are income-producing ones, such as

CDs, bonds, or dividend-paying stocks. The income that's produced must go to the surviving spouse.

If you hold shares in a closely held business, that probably can go into a Q-TIP. The profits from the business (probably in the form of dividends to stockholders) can be distributed according to the amount of the company held by the Q-TIP.

In the past few years, many small corporations have been organized as S corporations, because such corporations avoid the corporate income tax. Without going into all the details, be aware that you need to take special care before mixing an S corporation and a Q-TIP in the same alphabet soup. Only certain kinds of trusts are allowed to own shares in an S corporation, so your attorney must take pains to set up Q-TIP trusts so that they're eligible.

In some states, Q-TIP property may be in a *life estate,* which usually means that a spouse is entitled to the use (including the income) of a property for the rest of his or her lifetime. Practically speaking, life estates usually are used for real estate. Your spouse may receive a life estate in your residence, if you own it outright, but that residence might go to your children at your spouse's death.

Some kinds of assets just won't work in a Q-TIP—raw land, for example, that's being held in the hope it will appreciate eventually. If the land isn't generating cash, it won't be acceptable. The same holds true for stamp collections, antiques, cars, etc.

What happens if you leave unacceptable property to a Q-TIP? Your executor may bail you out. When it's time to file the estate-tax return, usually nine months after your death, your executor can make a "partial Q-TIP" election. That is, only qualified property will go into the Q-TIP.

Another option is to rely on the trustee. If the raw land or stamp collection is sold and the proceeds reinvested in income-producing property, the Q-TIP is likely to stand up.

What happens if these lines of defense fail, however, and ineligible property winds up in a Q-TIP? The IRS could say that the Q-TIP is invalid, so the marital deduction doesn't apply and estate taxes will be payable immediately rather than at your spouse's death. So you should have a Q-TIP plan in mind, one that's shared by your attorney, your executor and your trustee.

There are some other technicalities to watch out for. Suppose a Q-TIP earns income that's paid regularly (perhaps quarterly) to the surviving spouse. What if the spouse should die with income still in the trust, not yet distributed? To avoid problems with the IRS—and a possible disallowance of Q-TIP status—you should specify that any such undistributed income goes to your surviving spouse, to be included in that spouse's estate.

Judgment Days

There also is the human side to consider. Q-TIPs often give the trustee the power to invade the principal on behalf of the surviving spouse, if necessary. But what's necessary? Generally, there won't be much argument if money is needed for medical bills or college costs.

On the other hand, suppose a surviving spouse, with two children, remarries into a family with four children. Can the Q-TIP be tapped for a larger house? Or to build an extension onto the present house? Your two kids may benefit from living in the bigger house, but the five newcomers also will benefit from your wealth.

You can't be expected to foresee every contingency. You can, though, choose a trustee your surviving spouse will feel comfortable with if a request for money is necessary. A relative with sound business judgment may be a good choice. You might pick co-trustees: a relative with common sense plus a local bank's trust department, for example. In any case, make sure all the family members know, while you're still alive, that the Q-TIP is in place and how it will work.

You can even give your spouse some flexibility if you wish. Let's say you leave $1 million in a Q-TIP, with your three children the ultimate beneficiaries. As long as you're comfortable with your family situation, you might give your spouse the authority to allocate the $1 million among your three children after his or her death according to their needs, with a $100,000 minimum. So the child who wins the lottery might be left $100,000, the child who's a successful architect might get $300,000 and the child who's an inner-city fire fighter might get $600,000.

Another variation is to put the Q-TIP in place while you're still alive. Take the case of Jane, who sold her computer software business for $3 million, and who now wants to go into some high-tech defense work. She put $2 million into a Q-TIP and set aside the other $1 million for her new venture, which is extremely risky. If the new business fails, the $2 million in the Q-TIP won't be vulnerable: she knows her husband will have the income and her kids eventually will inherit the money.

No matter what your needs, you probably can meet them with a Q-TIP, as long as that Q-TIP is in the hands of savvy wealth-transfer professionals.

- Q-TIP property should be income-producing.
- When setting up a Q-TIP, work with your executor and your trustee as well as your attorney. Your executor can exclude nonproducing property if necessary, and your trustee can sell nonproducing property to reinvest in income-producing assets.
- If ineligible assets wind up in a Q-TIP, you could lose the marital deduction, forcing your estate to pay taxes immediately.
- Go over the Q-TIP terms with your family, so they'll understand how it works.
- Pick at least one trustee with whom your spouse will feel comfortable, in case principal has to be tapped for extraordinary expenses.

9 A Trusted Way To Double Your Money

When Arthur was 65, his wife Wendy died, leaving her entire estate to Arthur. Wendy had been a successful fashion designer. She left him $3 million, mainly in her pension plan, real estate and shares of her former company. Thanks to the unlimited marital deduction, the entire $3 million passed to Arthur free of estate tax.

As so often seems to be the case, Arthur's inheritance was shortly followed by a visit from a friendly life-insurance agent. Upon Arthur's death, the agent pointed out, he would leave a $3 million estate to his children unprotected by an unlimited marital deduction. Therefore, the kids would owe $1.1 million in federal estate tax. The insurance agent, not surprisingly, recommended the purchase of a $1.1 million life-insurance policy to pay off the estate tax.

Arthur, who never had much experience handling money, bought the policy. He died a couple of years later, holding essentially the same assets as he had inherited from Wendy. Sure enough, the insurance company paid $1.1 million to Arthur's children.

Unfortunately, Arthur owned the insurance policy: he applied for it, he paid the premiums. Therefore, the IRS considered the $1.1 million in insurance proceeds to be part of Arthur's estate. Adding that to the other assets, Arthur now had a $4.1 million estate.

Wendy's assets, inherited by Arthur	$3.0 million
Life-insurance proceeds	$1.1 million
Total taxable estate	$4.1 million

The federal estate tax on $4.1 million is around $1.65 million. So, while Arthur's children could use the $1.1 million from the insurance company to pay estate taxes, they also had to sell some assets to come up with the other $550,000 to satisfy the IRS.

The bottom line: Arthur had paid for a $1.1 million insurance policy, but his children wound up paying around $550,000 in estate tax on the policy proceeds. They received only $550,000 worth of benefits from the $1.1 million policy. In technical tax lingo, the insurance policy was included in Arthur's estate, so it was subject to the estate tax.

Arthur was not alone. Of all the estate-tax revenues that the IRS collects, insurance policies are the biggest source—more than stocks, bonds, real estate, etc. Reportedly, 90 percent of all life-insurance policies are held in such a way that they're vulnerable to estate tax.

Disowning Your Insurance Policy

What's the answer? Change the ownership of the life-insurance policy so that it's not included in the estate of the person who dies. Then the insurance proceeds will be truly tax-free.

Note: Generally, life-insurance proceeds are exempt from income tax. It's the *estate tax* that you have to worry about.

How can you keep a life-insurance policy out of your estate and keep the proceeds fully tax-free? One solution is to have your children own the policy. In our example, Arthur's kids could have applied for a policy on Arthur's life. They could have paid the premiums and be the named beneficiaries so that they'd collect at Arthur's death. If the premiums were too expensive, Arthur could have made cash gifts to provide them with enough money.

There are some problems with letting your children own such life-insurance policies. Life-insurance policies often have a cash value of tens of thousands of dollars. After they've been in force for several years, the cash value may be in the hundreds of thousands. If the children own the policy, it's too easy for them to take money out via loans or withdrawals. Then the money won't be there when it's needed.

Suppose you trust your children absolutely. You know they won't take money out of the policy. There's still a chance they'll get into a divorce fight, next year or 10 years from now. An insurance policy held by one spouse becomes a marital asset, and your son- or daughter-in-law may demand half the value.

There are other drawbacks to holding a large insurance policy as a personal asset. Suppose one of your children is involved in an accident and is held liable for damages. Or suppose there's a business failure and creditors are lined up, demanding to be paid off. In either case, the policy may be seized; it won't be available for paying estate tax.

In cases where your children are still minors, there's another drawback: the policy would have to be owned by a custodian or guardian.

What about situations where there's a married couple? Does it make sense for one spouse to own an insurance policy on the other's life? That works fine if your primary goal is family protection, but not if the goal is wealth transfer. By the time both spouses have died, the insurance proceeds will be included in the parents' estates and be subject to estate tax.

Policy of Trust

If life insurance shouldn't be owned by either spouse, and if there are risks in having it owned by the children, who should hold the policy? Your best choice may be an *irrevocable life-insurance trust,* also known as a *tax-free inheritance trust.*

Here's how this strategy works: You, the parent with estate-tax concerns, work with an attorney to set up a trust. The trust is *irrevocable.* That means that you can't change your mind later and terminate the trust or alter its terms.

You can't be the trustee, but your child or children can. (If necessary, you can name a financial professional as co-trustee.) Thus your children will have effective control over the assets of the trust—the life-insurance policy—without the risks of direct ownership.

The trust applies for a life-insurance policy and pays the annual premiums. Thus the trust is the owner of the policy. When the parent or parents die, the proceeds will not be included in the taxable estate.

Then what? The trustee (often a child of the insured individual) makes the decision. Usually the trustee will use the funds to buy illiquid assets, such as corporate stock or real estate, from the estate. This purchase is a *tax-neutral exchange,* meaning that no tax is due because of this asset shift from one pocket to another. A second possibility is for the trust to loan money to the estate, secured by the estate's assets. In either case, the estate will have liquidity—cash it can use to pay estate taxes.

Then the trustee can distribute the trust's assets to the trust's beneficiaries—probably the children of the insured parent. If there are reasons for keeping the assets in trust, the trustee can do so, maintaining control over those assets.

The outcome: The heirs keep full control over the family assets while all the life-insurance proceeds are used to pay estate tax and other death costs.

More than Double Your Money

An example can show how much money a tax-free inheritance trust may save. Let's say Bob and Carol, a married couple each aged 65, purchase a $1 million *second-to-die* life-insurance policy (see Chapter 20) through a tax-free inheritance trust. They pay an $18,000 annual premium for approximately 10 years, after which the policy is fully paid for. They have bought $1 million worth of coverage for around $180,000.

If Bob and Carol had not purchased the life-insurance policy, they might have spent it all on new cars, trips to Europe, etc. They might have invested the $180,000 in CDs and spent the interest. They might have invested in stocks or bonds and enjoyed compound growth. After income tax, that $180,000 might have grown to $200,000, $250,000, even $300,000.

Bob and Carol might have had anywhere from zero to $300,000 in their estate, piled on top of all their other assets. Estate tax and various costs could eat up around 50 percent. Therefore, the couple would wind up passing as little as zero, or perhaps as much as $150,000, to their children.

Instead, they transferred $180,000 worth of assets to a tax-free inheritance trust. When Bob and Carol die, their children will receive $1 million in life-insurance proceeds. That's 7 times what the children would have had otherwise—or 10 times or 20 times—the amount depending on how Bob and Carol would have handled their money. Here's the result, assuming the money not spent on life insurance would have been banked and the interest spent:

	Without Tax-Free Inheritance Trust	With Tax-Free Inheritance Trust
While Bob and Carol live	$180,000 is kept in estate	$180,000 is trans-ferred from estate
After Bob and Carol die	$90,000 is paid for taxes, etc.	$1 million is col-lected, tax-free
Bob and Carol's children receive	$90,000	$1 million

Leveraging Your Life Insurance

In essence, Bob and Carol are using leverage to increase what they can pass on to their children. Just as you might have been able to live in a $100,000 house with a $20,000 down payment by taking out a mortgage, so you can pass on $1 million worth of wealth to your family with $180,000 in payments over 10 years by using life insurance and a tax-free inheritance trust.

Using leverage, though, usually means taking risks. If you buy a $100,000 house with an $80,000 mortgage, you risk losing your house if you can't make the monthly payments.

Leveraging your estate with life insurance and a trust doesn't pose the same level of risk. What could go wrong? The insurance company might run into financial distress and not be able to honor its commitments. That's not likely, thanks to state insurance funds. You can reduce the risk even further if you stick with insurance companies that are at least 100 years old, have over $1 billion in assets and have an A+ ranking from A.M. Best Co., which rates insurers. For absolute peace of mind, choose an insurer that also has an AAA rating for claims-paying ability from Standard & Poor's, Moody's or Duff & Phelps. (For more details, see Chapter 18.)

A lesser risk is that interest rates will fall and your premiums won't earn as much as projected. Instead of making $18,000 payments for 10 years, Bob and Carol may have to pay for 11 years, or 12, or even 15, to get a $1 million policy.

Let's say that they have to pay for 20 years, surely an ultraconservative position. That's $360,000 in premiums. Assuming Bob and Carol would have held onto that money for 20 years, it would be in their taxable estate and reduced by 50 percent to $180,000.

So, even in this "worst case" example, transferring $360,000 to a tax-free inheritance trust gives your family more than five to one on your money.

Let's say, on the other hand, that Bob and Carol are scrupulous investors. Instead of putting their money in the bank and spending the interest, they invest the $18,000 each year in tax-exempt municipal bonds and reinvest all the interest. They'd have to live for around 25 years, until they're 90, earning 6.5 to 7 percent on their munis, to come out with the million dollars they can leave to their family via life insurance and a tax-free inheritance trust.

Why does the life insurance–insurance trust strategy work so well? First, you double your money by removing it from your taxable estate and putting it into a tax-free inheritance trust. Second, the life-insurance industry has several tax advantages that are effectively passed through to policyholders. When you pay premiums to a life-insurance company, your money is invested in taxable bonds and mortgages that pay higher yields than municipal bonds, yet you avoid the income tax.

Not Just Second-To-Die Insurance

Do you have to use second-to-die life insurance covering a married couple in a tax-free inheritance trust? Not at all. If you're divorced or already widowed, you can do the same thing with a single-life policy, one that will pay off after you die. Set up a trust and have it buy a policy on your life, naming your children as beneficiaries. The premium will be higher, because only one life is covered, so you'll get less leverage, but the technique still works. If one spouse is insurable but the other spouse isn't because of health problems, a second-to-die policy often can be obtained at some cost savings over a policy on the one insurable spouse.

Take the case of Daniel, who is divorced and remarried to a much younger spouse. He'd like to leave half of his $4 million estate to his children outright and the other half to a Q-TIP trust for his wife and children (see Chapter 8). Some estate tax will be owed after his death, some after his wife's death. So he buys two policies, one on his life and one on his wife's, and puts each of them into a separate tax-free inheritance trust. Again, the life-insurance proceeds will be there when they're needed.

You don't even need to use life insurance at all—that's why we prefer the term *tax-free inheritance trust* rather than *life-insurance trust*. Suppose, for example, that life insurance can't be obtained because either or both spouses are in poor health. You still can set up a trust and transfer assets to it. Inside the trust, the assets can grow. If the money is invested in municipal bonds or modified endowments, the earnings may not be taxed. You may not accumulate as much money as you would with life insurance, but you'll have an untaxed pool of funds that can be used to pay estate tax.

- A wealth-transfer plan may call for estate taxes to be paid with life-insurance proceeds.
- If you own a life-insurance policy and pay the premiums, the proceeds will be included in your estate. About half the proceeds will be lost to estate taxes and related costs.
- You can avoid this 50 percent bite by keeping life insurance outside your estate.
- Your children can own the life insurance, but they may be tempted to take money out of the policy. The policy may also be vulnerable in case of a divorce, damages award or bankruptcy.
- These problems can be avoided if an irrevocable life-insurance trust or a tax-free inheritance trust holds the policy. Your children, as trustees, still can be in control.
- A tax-free inheritance trust can hold a policy that insures one life or two.
- If insurance isn't available because of poor health, this type of trust can hold other assets, such as municipal bonds or annuities, and escape estate tax.
- Properly implemented, a tax-free inheritance trust can increase the amount of money you leave to your children 5 or 10 times with little risk.

10 Making Sure an Inheritance Trust Is Truly Tax-Free

Dr. Stan is 52, with an 18-year-old daughter from a marriage that ended in a divorce. Now he runs a cancer research clinic and has amassed an estate of around $2.5 million, largely in his pension fund.

Because he knows that his pension fund will be heavily taxed upon his death, he has set up a private foundation that will inherit his entire estate and continue his cancer research. With the estate going to a private foundation set up for charitable purposes, estate tax will be avoided.

But what about his daughter? Dr. Stan has bought a $2 million policy on his own life, held in a tax-free inheritance trust. He'll likely pay $25,000 per year for the next 15 years, or $375,000 in all. For this $375,000—which might have been reduced to around $190,000 by estate taxes and fees—he can be sure his daughter will inherit $2 million tax-free.

In addition, the terms of the foundation call for his daughter to be the paid administrator. Depending upon its size and on future interest rates, his daughter may earn $25,000 or more every year for her entire lifetime for deciding how to pay for cancer research. In fact, Dr. Stan's as yet unborn grandchildren may someday inherit this $25,000+ annual salary.

Putting the Pieces Together

Of all the people who have life insurance, only 2 to 5 percent are like Dr. Stan—they've discovered the benefits of holding their insurance in a tax-free inheritance trust. In the last chapter we described those benefits. Now, we'll go into the nuts and bolts, the points you need to discuss with your attorney when you set up the trust.

First, never be a "learning experience" for your lawyer. Work only with an attorney who's experienced in setting up these trusts. (See

Chapter 7 on how to choose an attorney to handle your wealth transfer.) Find out, at the start, how much he or she will charge to establish the trust. Generally, the fee should be between $500 and $1,500, depending upon the attorney's expertise and the complexity of your trust.

What about ongoing fees? They should be minimal or nonexistent, especially if the trust holds no assets besides a life-insurance policy.

Be certain the formalities are followed. If you write a check to the trust each year for the exact amount of the life-insurance proceeds, and the trustee must sign your check over to the insurance company, the IRS likely will try to challenge the trust's ownership of the policy. That's what happened in several court cases, and the IRS lost. As a result, the life insurance was not included in the estate of the person who was insured and no estate taxes were payable. However, why tempt the IRS?

Instead, the money should be paid to the trust and deposited in the trust's bank account. After a while, the trustee can pay the life-insurance premiums. The terms of the trust shouldn't explicitly oblige the trustee to pay for life insurance.

A "Crummey" Case That's a Gift to Taxpayers

Getting money into the trust so the trustee can afford to pay the premiums must be done with care. As we've mentioned, each individual can give up to $10,000 per year to an unlimited number of recipients without incurring a federal gift tax. Married couples can give each recipient up to $20,000 per year.

This gift-tax exemption applies only to *present interests.* George gives Reggie $10,000 in cash, which Reggie can spend tomorrow on a trip to Spain. That's a present interest. If the gift can't be used until a future date, that's a *future interest,* with no exemption from the gift tax.

Ordinarily, gifts in trust are considered gifts of future interest. Such gifts will lead to a gift tax unless you do it right.

What's the right way? Include a *demand right,* frequently called a *Crummey power,* in honor of the taxpayer who beat the IRS in a landmark case. In essence, if you make a gift that the trust beneficiary can demand right away, it's a present interest, even if the right to use that power later expires.

For example, Jack establishes a tax-free inheritance trust. Mac, his grown son, is the beneficiary. On August 4, Jack gives $5,000 to the trust. The same day, Jack's banker, acting as trustee, writes a letter to Mac telling him that he can withdraw the $5,000 anytime he wants in the next 30 days. Thus, Mac has a present interest and the gift is eligible for exclusion from the gift tax. (Even if Mac is the trustee as well as the beneficiary, he should write a letter to himself, explaining the withdrawal right.)

Thirty days go by and Mac doesn't withdraw any of the money. Now his Crummey power, or demand right, has lapsed. So the trustee uses the money to pay the life-insurance premium.

You may think, *Suppose I do this with my son and he takes the $5,000? He wants to buy a new car.* Well, you can let him know that if he exercises his demand right and takes the money, there may not be any future gifts for him to demand. The life insurance will lapse and he'll wind up facing a huge estate-tax bill with no insurance proceeds to pay it with.

Earlier, we mentioned that the gift-tax exclusion applies to gifts of up to $10,000 per year per recipient. That's not exactly true when it comes to gifts paid to trusts. In many situations, there's a $5,000 annual limit per beneficiary. If the premium requires a $10,000 annual gift, you might give $5,000 directly to the trust and another $5,000 to each beneficiary, who can in turn give the $5,000 to the trust. Be sure to work with a knowledgeable tax lawyer.

You don't have to make the demand right a limited one. Some people we know well trust their children absolutely, so they use *tunnel trusts* in which the children can withdraw the money anytime they want to. The insurance policy is held in trust not to keep it out of the children's hands but to protect it from spouses, creditors, taxes, etc.

Older May Not Mean Better

You may well have a life-insurance policy that you bought many years ago when your children were first born. By now, this policy may be fully paid up, with substantial cash value. Why not simply transfer that policy into a tax-free inheritance trust?

There are several reasons it may be wise not to do so. One, gifts in trust are gifts of future interest, not present interest, so you'd have to set up a Crummey power anyway. Two, old life-insurance policies with large cash values may exceed the annual gift-tax limitations.

Perhaps most important, if you die within three years of giving your life-insurance policy to a tax-free inheritance trust, it may not be tax-free. The insurance proceeds usually will be included in your taxable estate. As healthy as you are, there are no guarantees you'll live another three days, let alone three years. Why take a chance with thousands of dollars that could go to your children?

If you have an existing policy, largely paid for, you probably can borrow from the cash value tax-free. That money can be given to your tax-free inheritance trust, which can purchase a new policy not subject to the three-year rule.

What if you're not insurable? In recent years, you've developed a health problem, so insurers won't issue a new policy. In that case, if you own your old policy, you may have no choice but to transfer your old policy to your tax-free inheritance trust.

You'll have to consult your tax pro on this, but you may be able to borrow heavily from your old policy, reducing the cash value to only a few thousand dollars. Then you can transfer the policy to the trust without incurring a gift tax. Over the years, you can repay the loan, rebuilding the policy's cash value and the death benefits it will pay. (Tell your insurance agent that you want to be certain any policy loans don't exceed cumulative net premiums; if you go over that limit, you may owe taxes.)

Turning a Single-Premium Policy into a Home Run

Before the tax laws were changed in 1988, single-premium life-insurance policies were popular investments. You could buy a paid-up policy with one payment, yet have tax-free access to your money. If you bought one of those policies before June 21, 1988, you might consider emulating Charles and Diane, who enhanced their single-premium policy with a tax-free inheritance trust.

Charles and Diane are high-income professionals in their 50s. Their single-premium policy, which will pay $225,000 when they die, has a cash value of $75,000. So they decided to borrow $6,500 per year, tax-free, and transfer the money to a tax-free inheritance trust. The trust can use the money to purchase a $750,000 second-to-die insurance policy.

After 10 years and $65,000 worth of loans, the second-to-die policy likely will be paid for. They'll have taken $65,000 from their life-insurance cash value, which they probably won't need, and leveraged that money into $750,000 their children eventually will receive free of income and estate tax.

Avoiding the IRS "Triple Threat"

As you can tell from the above examples, there are many ways in which tax-free inheritance trusts can be used. Take the case of Molly, a self-employed professional who has built up $1 million in her Keogh plan. Molly still works and has no intention of retiring, so her income is ample for her needs. Her plan is to keep all the money in her Keogh plan until age 70½, when she must start taking distributions. Even at that age, she plans to withdraw the minimum, perhaps 6 percent per year. She thinks that in this way she'll leave most of her pension plan, chock full of cash, to her children.

Molly doesn't realize what's going to happen to her pension fund when she dies. First, all the income taxes that she's avoided over the years must be paid. Depending on which state she lives in, that could be as much as 40 percent right off the top. Then whatever is left will be piled on top of her other assets and subject to the estate tax, which can lop off as much as another 50 percent.

Finally, there's a newly created 15 percent surtax on "too-large" retirement funds (see Chapter 16). Any excess over a certain amount (the amount depends on your age at death) will be hit by the 15 percent tax. If you die at an age when $650,000 is the limit and you have a $1 million retirement fund, the tax will top $50,000, for a further 5 percent bite.

Molly's $1 million Keogh might provide less than $300,000 altogether to her children because of this triple threat.

What can she do? She can start to take withdrawals before they're required. As long as she waits until age 59½, she can take money out of a retirement plan without paying a 10 percent penalty tax. (Even if you are younger than 59½, you can avoid the 10 percent penalty tax by opting for lifetime income.)

She might take out, say, 8 to 10 percent of her plan each year. As long as her plan earns that much from stocks and bonds and CDs, it won't shrink despite the early withdrawals.

Let's say Molly takes out $90,000 each year from a $1 million Keogh plan. Even if she has to pay 40 percent on income tax, she'll wind up with $54,000 per year.

Balance in Molly's Keogh plan	$1,000,000
Annual withdrawals @ 9%	$90,000
Income tax on withdrawals @ 40%	($36,000)
Distributions to Molly, after-tax	$54,000

From that $54,000, Molly will be able to pay the annual premiums on a $1 million life-insurance policy, which she can hold in a tax-free inheritance trust. The exact amount of the premium will depend on Molly's age, when she applies for the policy, and whether it's a single-life or a second-to-die policy. In any case, there certainly will be more than enough from her $54,000. If Molly doesn't need the money currently, the excess can be given to her children or grandchildren to trim her future estate-tax bill.

Thanks to the life-insurance policy and the tax-free inheritance trust, her family is assured of receiving $1 million after tax, the amount in her retirement plan. No matter how heavily that plan is taxed at her death, the $1 million will be there.

From a Trust to a Dynasty

For another innovative example of how to use a tax-free inheritance trust, consider the case of Max, a successful business owner whose four grown children also have ample funds. He'd like to provide for his grandchildren, so he buys $4 million worth of life insurance, splitting the coverage between two insurance companies for added safety. He holds the policies in a tax-free inheritance trust. When Max and his wife die, the trust will collect $4 million.

Max has made other plans to cover his estate-tax liability so that $4 million can stay in the trust. At that point, though, after Max and his wife die, the first trust will *burst* into four *dynasty* trusts, one for each of their children, who act together as trustees.

During the children's lifetime, they can have *sprinkle* powers. That is, they can have the income for any reason if they need the money and if the principal can be invaded for certain major expenses. They can use trust funds for grandchildren's educational expenses, medical bills, down payment on a house, seed money to start a business, etc. In the meantime, the money in the trust funds continues to grow, outside the estates of Max and his wife and outside their four children's estates, so there will be no estate taxes. Assuming a 7 percent annual return and no extraordinary expenses, the $4 million will grow to more than $15 million in 20 years.

In essence, Max is using a tax-free inheritance trust to avoid the generation-skipping transfer and estate taxes, which can take a total of up to 80 percent of any money left to grandchildren. We call this added flexibility to the tax-free inheritance trust The Wealth Trust™. Careful attention must be paid to the trustees' powers. At the very least, they should be able to vote on income for other beneficiaries but not themselves. Usually a cotrustee may vote on the trustee's income. (For more on the generation-skipping tax, see Chapter 12).

Live the Good Life Without Making Your Kids Pay for It

Jane and Ted are both doctors in their early 50s. They'd like to retire early and spend as much time as possible camping and fishing. So far, they have about $1.2 million in assets, and they doubt they'll be able to accumulate much more, given their plans. Nevertheless, they'd like to leave their children in a comfortable financial position.

Therefore Jane and Ted set up a tax-free inheritance trust and use it to purchase a $1 million life-insurance policy. Because the policy will cover two lives, and because they're relatively young, the policy can be bought for only $6,000 a year in premiums, paid for approximately 10 years, for a total of $60,000.

Now Jane and Ted can retire whenever they want, camping and fishing to their heart's content. No matter what they do, even if they go through all their assets, they know their kids will eventually receive $1 million worth of life-insurance proceeds tax-free. Again, we see how $60,000 can be leveraged into $1 million tax-free. What other investment can pay off like that?

Remember that the IRS hates to lose hundreds of thousands of dollars, so make sure your tax-free inheritance trust is drawn up by a first-class estate-planning attorney, and that you and your trustees adhere strictly to the letter and the spirit of the law.

- Tax-free inheritance trusts can shelter huge amounts of money, but be sure to work with an experienced attorney.
- Expect startup fees of $500 to $1,500 in most cases, with minimal ongoing expenses.
- The trust beneficiaries must have the right to get at the trust's money (a Crummey power) before it is spent on insurance. You can use whatever persuasion you can think of to dissuade your beneficiaries from taking the money out, but you shouldn't absolutely forbid them in writing.
- If you're not insurable, an old life-insurance policy may be transferred into a tax-free inheritance trust, but you'll lose the tax benefit if you die within three years.
- Qualified retirement plans may be savaged by a triple tax. Life insurance held in a tax-free inheritance trust can give your heirs full value.
- A tax-free inheritance trust also may be used to avoid the punitive tax on transfers to grandchildren by adding the Wealth Trust™ option.
- Using a tax-free inheritance trust can ensure a sizable transfer to your children while leaving you free to retire early and spend your money as you'd like.

11

Give and Take

When he was a young physician, Dr. Ron invested $20,000 to help start a medical supply company. Now that company is publicly traded and Dr. Ron's shares are worth $1 million. The shares pay no dividends and Dr. Ron, in retirement, would like to increase his current income.

He could sell his shares and buy bonds, but about one-third of the proceeds from the stock sale would be eaten up by a tax on capital gains. Instead, Dr. Ron has chosen a strategy that would:

1. Eliminate his income-tax and estate-tax liability relating to those shares
2. Pay him and his wife a lifetime income with growth potential, based on the full market value of the shares
3. Generate a large tax deduction that he can use right away
4. Leave substantial funds to his children tax-free
5. Give something back to his community (and gain recognition for doing so)

What is this strategy? Dr. Ron established a *charitable remainder trust* (CRT), which may well be the best way to dispose of highly appreciated assets. He named himself as the sole trustee, so he was in control of the trust's assets.

Let's see how a CRT works, step by step.

Tax Reduction

Dr. Ron's *basis* in that stock was $20,000, the amount he invested. If he had sold those shares for $1 million, he'd have had a taxable gain of $980,000. Assuming a tax rate (federal and state) around 35 percent, he'd have owed around $340,000 in taxes. That would have left him with $660,000 to reinvest.

When you give away assets to charity, no gift tax is involved. In this case, Dr. Ron gave $1 million worth of stock to a CRT, removing $1 million from his estate without incurring a gift tax.

Moreover, a CRT is a tax-exempt entity. It can sell the stock for $1 million and owe no taxes. Then it can reinvest the proceeds in virtually anything—stocks, bonds, CDs, etc. In Dr. Ron's case, he chose an annuity, which we'll describe in Chapter 17.

Lifetime Income

A charitable remainder trust pays income to its beneficiary or beneficiaries, named by the donor when setting up the trust. This income can be for a fixed term, up to 20 years, or for the beneficiary's lifetime. Beneficiaries can be virtually anyone. For his trust, Dr. Ron chose to receive income for his lifetime and his wife's lifetime—probably the most common choice of beneficiaries.

A CRT can be either an *annuity trust* or a *unitrust*. The difference is whether you want a fixed return or if you're willing to take a chance on a variable return.

The annuity trust pays a return that is fixed, but at least 5 percent of the original trust amount. If Dr. Ron's CRT starts out with $1 million, he can elect to receive $50,000 per year, or any amount over that. He locks himself into $50,000 per year or $80,000 or whatever.

The unitrust pays a percentage of the trust assets each year, with 5 percent the minimum. If you choose an 8 percent unitrust, for example, you'd receive $80,000 the first year on a $1 million trust. If the trust earns more than $80,000, the principal will increase and so will your 8 percent payout. But if the trust earns less than $80,000, next year's payout will be smaller. And so on, in each succeeding year. (Unlike an annuity trust, a unitrust remains open, so you can make additional donations in later years.)

Unitrusts have more risk than annuity trusts, but there's also the potential for growth, if the assets are well managed.

In our example, Dr. Ron's CRT is managed by one of America's top investment professionals, so Dr. Ron feels comfortable choosing a unitrust and taking a 10 percent payout.

At 10 percent, he'll start off receiving $100,000 per year. Assuming his tax rate is 35 percent, he'll wind up with $65,000. If he had just sold the shares directly, he would have netted $660,000, after taxes, so a 10 percent return would be only $66,000 per year, or $43,000 after tax. He's ahead by $22,000 per year, more than 50 percent.

	Without Charitable Remainder Trust	With Charitable Remainder Trust
Dr. Ron sells shares for	$1,000,000	$1,000,000
Taxable gain	$980,000	$980,000
Tax on gain	$340,000	None*
After-tax proceeds	$660,000	$1,000,000
Annual income @ 10%	$66,000	$100,000
After-tax income	$43,000	$65,000

*Trust is tax-exempt.

Tax Deductions

Dr. Ron is giving $1 million worth of stock to charity, so he will get a charitable deduction. However, he won't get a full $1 million writeoff because the charities won't get the money right away.

Instead, the IRS uses life expectancy tables to estimate when Dr. Ron and his wife (both in their late 60s) will die, leaving the trust fund to charity. Then the IRS makes some more complicated calculations, estimating how much the trust will earn and how much it will pay out. There are tables for this calculation, too, from which the IRS comes up with a projected amount that will eventually go to charity. Say, for example, the IRS projects that $2 million will go to charity in 2011.

Then the IRS puts a *present value* on that projected future donation. How much needs to be invested now, at expected rates of return, to reach $2 million by 2011?

In our example, Dr. Ron and his wife get a tax deduction of about $220,000 for donating $1 million worth of stock. There are restrictions on how fast charitable deductions can be taken, but they expect to use the full writeoff in six years.

In a 35-percent tax bracket, a $220,000 writeoff will save them $77,000 in tax payments. That's like putting $77,000 in their pocket over the next six years.

Family Protection

So far, the big losers in this transaction are Dr. Ron's children. If he had simply sold the shares, he would have had $660,000 to reinvest. Assuming he and his wife would die holding those assets and a 50 percent estate tax, their children would inherit $330,000. Now the charity will get everything and the children will inherit nothing.

As compensation, life insurance can be taken out. Here, Dr. Ron and his wife purchase a policy that will pay $1 million to their children after both of their deaths. By holding this policy in a tax-free inheritance trust (see Chapter 10), the entire $1 million can go to their children.

The policy's expected cost is $250,000 paid over ten years. Of that $250,000, $77,000 is coming from their income-tax savings, that is, from the charitable deduction. So they have to come up with $173,000 over ten years, or roughly $17,000 per year.

	Without Charitable Remainder Trust	With Charitable Remainder Trust
After-tax annual income	$43,000	$65,000
Cost of life insurance		$250,000
Tax savings		($77,000)
Net insurance cost		$173,000
Annual insurance cost (10 years)		$17,000
Net annual income (after insurance cost)	$43,000	$48,000
Assets in estate	$660,000	$0
Life insurance proceeds	$0	$1,000,000
Estate tax @ 50%	$330,000	$0
Amount to children	$330,000	$1,000,000

So here's the bottom line. Dr. Ron and his wife get $48,000 per year in spendable income, rather than $43,000 per year. (If either one lives for more than 10 years, after which the insurance premiums are scheduled to vanish, the annual after-tax income will jump to $65,000 per year.) In addition, the children could wind up with as much as three times as much as they would have had if the stock had been sold outright.

As you can see, there is a wide variety of ways to rearrange the results. Suppose Dr. Ron and his wife purchased an insurance policy for only $330,000, to produce the amount the children would otherwise have inherited if the CRT had not been used. In that case, the tax savings would have paid for most of the costs of the policy, leaving Dr. Ron and his wife nearly $62,000 per year in after-tax income.

Contribution, Recognition

When you set up a CRT, you pick the charity or charities that ultimately will benefit. For those of us who have achieved some material success in this lifetime, charitable giving is a way of showing appreciation.

Although we'd like to think that all giving is motivated by noble ideals, there's another side to the coin. Big givers often get recognition, even if your gift won't be delivered for several years. This recognition may boost your ego or even boost your business as word of your beneficence spreads. For Dr. Ron, half of his $1 million trust is slated to go to his medical school, which has rewarded him by naming a teaching chair in his honor.

- If you establish a charitable remainder trust (CRT), you can transfer virtually any asset to it. The CRT will pay income to beneficiaries you name, usually yourself and your spouse; after the payment period, the money left in the trust will go to a charity or charities you select.
- Transferring highly appreciated assets to a CRT eliminates your obligation to pay taxes on the profits.
- Property you transfer to a CRT will be outside your taxable estate.

- You can choose either a fixed-income annuity trust or a unitrust with the potential for higher or lower distributions.
- You will get a partial tax deduction for the property you donate. The older you are, and the less income you take, the greater the tax deduction to which you're entitled.
- If you purchase life insurance payable to your children and held in a tax-free inheritance trust, you can compensate for the assets you've given away.
- Often, the end result is higher income to you and a greater transfer of wealth to your children, compared with a straight sale of appreciated assets.
- Besides the financial gain, there's the satisfaction of contributing to a charity, school, house of worship, etc. There may be recognition for you as a major donor.

Keeping Your Charity Sweet

Earlier in this chapter, we illustrated how it can pay to donate highly appreciated stock to a charitable remainder trust. CRTs work well with all types of appreciated assets, not just corporate stock. Real estate is an example, but if you donate real estate to a charitable trust, there are some special points to keep in mind.

Take the case of Ted and Alice, a recently retired couple in their mid-60s. Besides social security, they have little retirement income. However, they own a house in southern California near the Pacific Coast, which they bought for $50,000 in the mid-1970s. By 1990, the mortgage was fully paid up and the house was worth over $600,000.

The federal tax code has a provision for homeowners over age 55: they can avoid taxes on $125,000 worth of gain when they sell their principal residence. Ted and Alice were looking at a $550,000 profit. Even after their $125,000 break, they'd owe tax on $425,000. That tax might be $150,000, leaving them only $450,000 to use for a new home and retirement income. Suppose they buy a new home for $200,000: that would leave them only $250,000 to invest and an annual income probably less than $25,000.

Instead, Ted and Alice established a CRT for a gift of their house. Whenever real estate or other assets that are hard to value are involved, the donor should name an unrelated party as co-trustee; the co-trustee can have the assets appraised without being accused of a conflict of interest. Ted and Alice's house was appraised at $600,000, which became the value used for the donation to the trust.

Then Ted and Alice gave a two-thirds interest in the house to the trust, keeping one-third for themselves. As two-thirds owner, the trust listed the house and handled the sale for $600,000. Of that total, $400,000 went to the trust while $200,000 went to Ted and Alice.

Why did they do it that way? Ted and Alice already had decided to move to a less expensive area of California, where they could buy a comfortable townhouse for $200,000. So they took their $200,000 and *rolled it over* to the purchase of their new home, avoiding any current tax and preserving their $125,000 tax exemption, which they can use later.

The trust received the other $400,000, which Ted (acting as co-trustee) invested conservatively in a mutual fund that owns government-backed Ginnie Maes. Ted and Alice elected an annuity remainder trust, taking out a flat $40,000 each year. Thus they have locked in an annual income of $40,000 (60 percent higher than what they would have had otherwise to supplement their social security) in addition to owning a paid-up house.

They also receive a tax deduction of around $80,000 for the $400,000 donation to the CRT, which will benefit their church and the American Cancer Society. Ted and Alice decided to use this money to buy life insurance payable to their children after they both die. The $80,000 writeoff will save them about $25,000 in taxes. Adding an estimated $40,000 from their income over 10 years, they can buy three $100,000 policies, one for each of their children. The policies will be held in a tax-free inheritance trust.

Thus their children eventually will receive $300,000 in life-insurance proceeds, plus the $200,000 townhouse, for a total of $500,000. That's more than the children would have received if Ted and Alice had simply sold their house and received $450,000 after-tax. In addition, Ted and Alice will have a comfortable retirement thanks to the extra income, instead of struggling to survive.

Charity Can Begin at Home

So far, we have looked at a couple of "mainstream" charitable remainder trusts, with the assets eventually going to a *public charity,* which might include a college or a religious organization. In some situations, though, you might want to set up a CRT for a donation to a private foundation rather than to a public charity. (See Chapter 15 for a discussion of private foundations.)

Take the example of Robert, a real estate developer who has done very well, building up a huge estate. Among his assets are a debt-free shopping center valued at $4 million; if he sold it outright, he'd have a $3 million taxable gain. Therefore, selling this shopping center means mailing over $800,000 to the IRS.

Instead, Robert established a CRT and donated the shopping center. The trust sold the real estate and reinvested the entire $4 million in income-producing assets for distribution to Robert and his wife.

In Robert's case, the trust assets eventually will go to a private foundation that he has established, rather than to a public charity. What difference does this make?

For one, Robert's charitable deduction may be reduced. Often, deductions to private foundations are limited to 20 percent of a donor's adjusted gross income, compared to the 30 percent of adjusted gross income allowed for conventional charitable contributions.

With a private foundation, though, Robert gets to name the salaried administrator. His children, perhaps his grandchildren and future descendants, can eventually work as the manager of this foundation. They'll make sure enough money is distributed to worthy causes and fill out the appropriate tax returns. For that, they'll receive annual salaries that might be $50,000, $75,000 or more (depending upon the nature of the work they perform), possibly in perpetuity.

Turning a Gift into a Pension Plan

Another sophisticated use of a CRT may appeal to anyone who's looking for a way to build up a larger retirement fund. Perhaps your qualified plans are already *fully funded,* under current law, so further contributions aren't allowed. Or you own a closely held business and you're looking for a way to provide for your own retirement without going through the expense and aggravation of maintaining a qualified plan.

You might, in these situations, set up a CRT with a unitrust payout with the stipulation that distributions can't exceed income. So if the money you contribute is invested in zero-coupon tax-exempt bonds, for example, the trust will have no taxable income and may not have to make distributions. Over the years, you can continue to make contributions to the trust, where the money will compound tax-exempt.

When you reach retirement, the CRT can sell its tax-exempt bonds and reinvest in taxable securities. Then the unitrust distributions can begin. In fact, a *catch-up provision* can be included that will increase distributions at first to make up for all the distributions not previously made because of insufficient income.

In addition to this pay-now, collect-later plan, which has no IRA- or Keogh-type limitations on contributions, you'd get a partial tax deduction each year for contributing to a CRT. If you're 55 years old, name yourself as the income beneficiary and choose a 10 percent unitrust payout, you might get a $2,000 deduction on a $10,000 contribution.

As you might expect, not every lawyer who has just passed the bar exam can set up a CRT-as-retirement-plan. Check the experience of your attorney before embarking upon any complicated trust strategy. (See Afterword.)

The Fine Points

Charitable remainder trusts offer so many possibilities for planning that they may seem too good to be true. If you have highly appreciated assets, they're certainly worth considering. Nevertheless, CRTs aren't for everyone.

All CRTs must be irrevocable. What's more, gifts to the trust are irrevocable. Once you put assets into the trust, you assume they'll be sold and the proceeds reinvested in income-producing securities. If the property is not sold immediately, you may lose control without obtaining the income you desire.

Thus, setting up a CRT is not a step to be taken lightly. You're giving up full control over those assets, which may be real estate you've owned for years or stock in a closely held business you run. If you're not ready to walk away, don't give those assets to a CRT.

By the same token, you can't "invade" the trust principal to get extra funds, even if you're the trustee. You can't borrow from the fund. In essence, you're limited to the annual income you've agreed on. If there's a chance that won't be enough for you, back away.

The property you contribute to a CRT shouldn't be burdened with debt, such as a mortgage on real estate. If it is, you stand to lose your tax deduction. (You may even have to recognize a taxable gain.)

In general, income from a CRT must be taxable. There are some situations in which a trust can invest in tax-exempt bonds, for example, and flow through that tax-exempt income to the beneficiaries. But that won't work if you're donating appreciated property to avoid capital gains tax until your total income from the trust has equaled your capital gain. After that, you can receive tax-free income. But if you're a true tax-ophobe who insists upon tax-exempt rather than taxable income, you may have trouble with a CRT.

Un-Charitable Thoughts

Perhaps the greatest problem with CRTs is that they're *too good.* Now promoters are hawking CRTs the way they might sell penny stocks or gold mines. These promoters want to get the fees involved in managing the trust funds, sales commissions for the life insurance and up-front kickbacks from the named charities.

CRTs need expert preparation if they're to deliver all the promised benefits. Someone who was selling tax shelters a few years ago is not likely to have the desired expertise. You may, in fact, fall victim to a scam if you give money to one of these kickback artists. How can you avoid the pitfalls?

Don't do business with a stranger who calls you on the phone or sends you a letter. You probably don't need to work with a so-called professional administrative firm. If you trust your accountant, attorney or financial planner to handle your overall finances, then he or she likely will be able to administer a CRT. What if you don't have a trusted adviser? The *advanced underwriting* departments of major insurance companies have experts that will help you make sure all the i's are dotted and t's crossed.

Don't let someone else name your charity. If you think about it, you probably can come up with organizations you'd like to help. The chance to receive some recognition and some benefits from that recognition may be a factor in making your choices.

You probably don't want to let the charity, or any other outsider, act as trustee (unless, as we've explained, a co-trustee is needed to appraise hard-to-value assets). When you act as trustee, you have some control and you can direct the way the trust fund is invested. You don't, for example, want some super-cautious charity putting your money into a passbook savings account.

In general, even though a CRT is irrevocable, the choice of a charitable beneficiary is not. Say you name Alma Mater when you set up the trust but in later years you become disenchanted with Alma Mater's policies and politics. You can change your mind and name a school for handicapped children, a local hospital, etc.

The choice of charitable beneficiary can be made irrevocable by stating as much in the trust documents. If you do that, ask the beneficiary to pay for setting up the trust. CRTs often are more complex than other types of trusts, so costs might be a bit higher: expect to spend $1,500 to $2,500 to create a CRT. If a charity knows it's going to come into hundreds of thousands of dollars down the line, it may well be willing to pay a couple of thousand dollars now.

What about *pooled income funds*? These are CRTs run by the charities themselves. (Colleges and private high schools are particularly active here.) You give them the money, take a partial writeoff and receive a lifetime income.

Pooled income funds may work if you want to give away a relatively small amount. It doesn't make sense spending $1,500 to set up a trust if you're giving away only $5,000 or $10,000. Also, if you're uncomfortable handling money, you may prefer turning over the responsibility to the charity. However, most people like to stay in control of their own income stream. If you prefer making your own financial decisions and you're thinking about a sizable donation, you're better off establishing your own charitable remainder trust, working with expert advisers.

- If you're donating hard-to-value assets to a charitable remainder trust, name an independent co-trustee to get an appraisal.
- Donating assets to a private foundation may cut your charitable deduction, but it enables you to provide ongoing salaried jobs for your children and grandchildren after your death.
- If your pension plan is overfunded or if you don't want the hassles of a qualified plan, a CRT may provide extra retirement income.
- Gifts to CRTs are irrevocable. Don't donate assets you can't afford to give away.
- Don't donate assets that are burdened with debt.
- If you donate appreciated assets to a CRT to avoid capital gains taxes, you'll have to wait—perhaps for years—before you can receive tax-exempt income.
- Be wary of promoters calling you with "deals" on CRTs.
- Your own financial advisers can administer a CRT, provided they're competent and experienced. You probably should act as trustee to keep control.
- You can change your choice of charitable beneficiaries. If you make the choice irrevocable, ask the charity to pay the start-up costs.
- Pooled income funds can make sense for small contributions or for people who prefer not to be responsible for investing the trust funds.

Putting Charity First

In the last few sections, we've described charitable remainder trusts: you give assets to a charity, you collect an income and the remainder goes to charity.

The mirror image is the *charitable lead trust.* With a CLT, you once again give assets to a trust. Here, though, the charity or charities get income for a fixed number of years. After that period, the assets are returned to the *remaindermen,* usually the donor or members of the family.

When does a CLT make sense? If you have an extremely large estate and you don't need all the income it generates, a CLT may be a means of fulfilling charitable obligations and passing assets to your children with little or no estate or gift tax.

Suppose, for example, you give $1 million to a CLT and elect to pay out 8 percent for 10 years. Each year, $80,000 will go to your college, local hospital, etc. At the end of 10 years, whatever is left in the trust will go to your children.

No estate taxes are due, even if you have died in the interim. Gift taxes, however, may be payable. The gift taxes depend on IRS valuation tables in effect at the time of the transfer to the CLT. You might, in the above example, wind up with a taxable gift of $500,000. Assuming a 50 percent bracket, you'd owe $250,000 in gift tax. If you had kept the assets in your estate until you died, your family would owe a full $500,000 in estate tax—so you wind up saving $250,000 in taxes.

	Without Charitable Lead Trust	With Charitable Lead Trust
Value of assets	$1,000,000	$1,000,000
Paid to charity	*	$800,000 in 10 years
Remainder to heirs	$0	$1,000,000
Gift tax	$0	($250,000)
In taxable estate	$1,000,000	$0
Estate tax	($500,000)	$0
Net to heirs	$500,000	$750,000

*At your discretion

It's possible to eliminate all gift and estate tax. In the above example, paying 9 percent to charity for 15 years may allow you to pass the remainder to your children free of all taxes.

The best candidates for a CLT may be those individuals who are "expected" to make regular charitable contributions to various organizations. With a CLT, you can meet all those commitments and transfer assets outside your estate at the same time. If the assets in the trust appreciate, or if the income received is greater than the income paid out, the growth in trust assets is similarly sheltered from estate and gift tax. (You won't have to pay income tax on any buildup, either.)

But CLTs are not as popular as CRTs because they don't offer as many benefits. The income-tax deduction is limited, and if you take it, you're liable for taxes on trust income, so many people elect not to take the deduction.

Again, CLTs are irrevocable and must be drawn up by an experienced attorney.

- If you give assets to a charitable lead trust, charities you name will receive income for a given time period.
- At the end of the time period, the assets can pass to your children.
- No estate tax will be payable; gift tax will be reduced or eliminated.
- The more money that goes to charity, the less the gift tax you'll have to pay.
- CLTs are best suited for individuals with large estates, no pressing need for current income and major commitments for charitable giving.

12 Bridging the Generation Gap

For nearly 200 years, the United States has had a variety of estate and inheritance taxes; our present system traces its roots to a 75-year-old law. Just as the federal government has been trying to raise revenues by taxing wealth, so the truly wealthy have been devising ways to avoid these taxes.

Historically, one of the most popular strategies was "generation skipping." Here's how it worked:

At his death, Cornelius set up a trust, naming his grandchildren as beneficiaries. His wife and, after her death, their children were entitled to the income from the trust. After all their children died, the grandchildren inherited the trust principal.

Suppose this trust was set up in 1916, when the federal estate-tax law was introduced, and that Cornelius died shortly thereafter when the top federal estate-tax rate was 10 percent. If Cornelius had a $10 million estate, $1 million went to the federal government while $9 million went into the trust. If that money earned 4 percent, a reasonable return back then, the trust income was $360,000. Cornelius's wife and children, with $360,000 to spend each year in the 1920s and 1930s, could live lavishly if they desired.

When the last of his children died in the 1940s, Cornelius's grandchildren received all $9 million, not diminished by any further estate tax. Not until their deaths, many more years in the future, would further estate tax be owed. Thus, the estate tax could be avoided and family wealth could be kept intact.

This is a simplified version of the generation-skipping strategies employed until 1976, when Congress decided to raise revenues by going after generation skips. That law was modified in 1986, resulting in the present rules.

In essence, generation skipping usually doesn't pay any more because such transactions are taxed twice. If you set up the kind of trust described above, there will be an estate tax at your death and another estate tax when your children die:

Original estate	$5,000,000
Amount subject to generation-skipping tax	$1,000,000
Tax at your death (@ 55%)	($550,000)
Net after taxes	$450,000
Generation-skipping tax (assume 55% rate at your child's death)	($247,500)
Net after taxes	$202,500

Here, $1 million is reduced to $202,500 through two rounds of estate tax. That's a loss of nearly 80 percent.

There are some exceptions to this rule. Through 1989, grandparents could make direct transfers of up to $2 million per grandchild. That provision has expired; now each individual has a $1 million exemption from the generation-skipping tax, so a married couple can leave a total of up to $2 million to their grandchildren free of double taxation.

Remember, these exemptions are only from the double tax. You'll still owe regular federal estate and gift tax on these transfers.

All in the Family

Is there a way to keep more wealth in your family? Yes, if you plan well. For estates of $3 million and more, there is a strategy that provides for your children and leaves assets to your grandchildren while reducing estate tax.

Let's take the example of Arnold and Sylvia. Starting from almost nothing, they built up an empire of real-estate investments worth around $5 million. Now their properties generate high income from rents, while there is almost no mortgage interest to pay.

Arnold and Sylvia don't want to sell their properties. They have a low *cost basis*. They'd owe over $1 million in income tax.

They could, if they want, hold onto their properties until death. Under current tax law, all assets (stocks, real estate, rare coins etc.) get a *stepped-up basis* at death. This means that if your heirs sell your properties right away, they would owe no income tax.

There's still the estate tax to pay. On a $5 million estate, that will be over $2 million. To raise $2 million, the couple's three children would have to sell substantial amounts of their real estate. Even in the best real-estate markets, that would take time; in a weak market, that might involve selling properties at distress prices. Besides, Arnold and Sylvia have worked so hard to build up a quality real-estate portfolio that they want to keep the properties in the family.

Therefore, Arnold and Sylvia have followed the advice we've set out in this book. They've set up a tax-free inheritance trust and made cash gifts to the trust, which purchased a $2 million life-insurance policy that will pay off after both of their deaths. Their oldest son, Randy, is the trustee of the tax-free inheritance trust. When the insurance proceeds are collected, he'll buy $2 million worth of real estate from his parents' estate. That money will be used by the executor to pay the estate taxes.

Normally, the tax-free inheritance trust would then distribute all its assets to Arnold and Sylvia's three children, leaving them with all $5 million worth of real estate. In this case, though, the wealth transfer involves three generations, not just two.

The $2 million in real estate, now held by the tax-free inheritance trust, will not be distributed. Instead, it will stay in trust for the benefit of the grandchildren.

This will leave Arnold and Sylvia's three children with "only" $3 million worth of real estate held outright. As we said above, this is high-quality, income-producing real estate, so they should be able to live very comfortably on the income alone. If necessary, they can sell off properties or borrow against them to raise cash.

As for the tax-free inheritance trust, now holding $2 million in real estate, it will sunburst into three separate trusts. Why three? Because Arnold and Sylvia have three children. In one trust, the *vested,* or main, beneficiaries will be Randy's children; in another trust, his brother Peter's children will be the main beneficiaries; in the third trust, their sister

Nancy's children will be the main beneficiaries. In each trust, the parents of the main beneficiaries (Arnold and Sylvia's children) will be secondary beneficiaries.

Once the three trusts are set up, the real estate will be divided among them, nearly $700,000 apiece. Trustees will be *crossed.* That is, Randy will be trustee for the trust that benefits Peter and Peter's children; Peter will be trustee for Nancy and Nancy's children; and Nancy will be trustee for Randy and Randy's children.

As the grandchildren go through life, their trustee can dip into their funds for education, health care, housing and business opportunities if necessary. In case of emergency, the trust funds can be used to help Arnold and Sylvia's children. Otherwise, cash from the real estate will be reinvested, and the properties can be expected to appreciate long-term. When Arnold and Sylvia's children die, the proceeds will pass to the grandchildren tax-free. If you assume total returns of 9 percent per year (after-tax cash flow plus appreciation) and a time period of 24 years, Arnold and Sylvia's grandchildren will receive a total of around $16 million down the line from an original $2 million in assets. No estate tax will have to be paid until the grandchildren's deaths.

So this strategy "kills two birds with one stone," or, in this case, one tax-free inheritance trust. The trust provides the money to pay Arnold and Sylvia's estate tax without having to dispose of assets, and it provides a means of passing money to their grandchildren without incurring the generation-skipping transfer tax (or an intermediate round of estate taxes.)

Leveraging Your Exemption

Why is the $16 million, in our example, exempt from the generation-skipping tax? Because, when Arthur and Sylvia set up the original trust to buy the life insurance, they made gifts to the trust to pay the premiums. Those gifts were on behalf of their grandchildren, the primary beneficiaries of the trust. Therefore, Arnold and Sylvia filed gift-tax returns, using up part of their $2 million exemption from the generation-skipping tax. From that point on, all the money received by the trust remained outside the reach of the generation-skipping tax.

Figure 12-1
Per Stirpes and Per Capita Distribution

Sealors: Arnold/Sylvia

	INCOME TO **RANDY** FOR HIS LIFETIME	INCOME TO **PETER** FOR HIS LIFETIME	INCOME TO **NANCY** FOR HER LIFETIME
Optional methods of distribution to children	Corpus to grand-children at Randy's death via options below	Corpus to grand-children at Peter's death via options below	Corpus to grand-children at Nancy's death via options below

PER STIRPES

Optional allocations of corpus to grand-children

$^1/_6$ $\quad$ $^1/_6$

RANDY'S CHILDREN

$^1/_3$

PETER'S CHILD

$^1/_{12}$ $\quad$ $^1/_{12}$
$^1/_{12}$ $\quad$ $^1/_{12}$

NANCY'S CHILDREN

Optional methods of distribution to grand-children

Outright; free of trust

Continuing trust; income and corpus to grandchild until attaining specified age or ages

figure 12-1, cont.

INCOME AVAILABLE TO RANDY, PETER AND NANCY AS NECESSARY	INCOME AVAILABLE TO RANDY, PETER AND NANCY AS NECESSARY		
Corpus to grand-children at death of last child via options below	Corpus to grandchildren at Randy's death via options below	Corpus to grandchildren at Peter's death via options below	Corpus to grandchildren at Nancy's death via options below

PER CAPITA

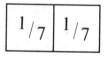

RANDY'S
CHILDREN

PETER'S CHILD

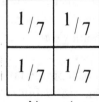

NANCY'S
CHILDREN

Trust for the lifetime of the grandchild;
income and corpus distributed as necessary
at death of grandchild,
corpus distributed as grandchild directs,
or failing direction as settlor directs*

* In order to avoid double taxation, the corpus must be included as part of grandchild's estate

Suppose, for example, that Arnold and Sylvia used up $500,000 worth of their exemption to fund the life-insurance premiums. That would leave them with $1.5 million worth of exemption from the generation-skipping tax.

The approach Arnold and Sylvia are using isn't the only way to cope with the generation-skipping tax. For example, there is no need for their trust to divide into separate subtrusts for each child. The trust could stay intact with generally the same result.

So why sunburst? Because this technique gets money into the hands of the grandchildren faster. As we've seen, the real estate will be divided into three sections. Under the terms of the subtrusts, whenever one of Arnold and Sylvia's children dies, one of the trusts will terminate and the assets will be distributed. (In some states, this method may reduce inheritance taxes.) Thus, some money is distributed then, while the remainder stays in trust.

Suppose Randy dies first, 20 years after his parents both die. The trust of which he is the secondary beneficiary, and his children are the main beneficiaries, will terminate and the assets will go to Arnold and Sylvia's grandchildren.

Which grandchildren? The assets could go only to Randy's two children. This, in effect, would reward them for having their father die first.

Or one-third of the assets could go to Randy's two children, one-third to Peter's child, and one-third to Nancy's four children. That would penalize Nancy's children, because their mother had more children than her siblings.

The most common practice is to have the assets distributed *per capita* to all seven grandchildren in equal amounts. The same will happen at Peter's death and at Nancy's, until all the assets are distributed evenly to the third generation.

Another alternative would be to have the original trust sunburst into subtrusts for each grandchild, but that would complicate matters, because grandchildren might be born after the trust is set up, or even after Arnold and Sylvia die and the main trust splits into subtrusts.

This sunburst strategy is by no means the only one to use. If a family prefers to keep the assets in trust for as long as possible, the original trust could stay in place with distributions delayed until all three of Arnold and Sylvia's children have died. (See Figure 12-1.) As yet another alternative, distributions can be delayed until 21 years after the death of all the grandchildren who are alive when the trust is established. With this approach, you can provide for your great-grandchildren!

Big Game

This strategy, as we said, may be considered for estates of $3 million and up. That way, you can leave at least $2 million to your children, which should be more than adequate, and $1 million or more to your grandchildren. Practically speaking, generation skipping works best for larger estates of $5 million, $10 million and up.

In large estates, though, the amount of life insurance to be acquired may need to be huge if it's to cover the estate-tax bill and leave your children well off. In such a case, you might want to make a taxable gift to pay the premium. You can give up to $600,000 free of the federal gift tax. For $600,000 in total premiums, you might be able to buy anywhere from $3 million to $8 million worth of second-to-die life insurance, the amount depending upon the ages of yourself and your spouse. That will leverage the amount you'll leave to your grandchildren anywhere between 5 to 1 and 13 to 1.

If you give $600,000 to a tax-free inheritance trust on behalf of your grandchildren, in a single payment or a series of annual gifts, that will cut into your exemption from the generation-skipping tax. That still would leave you with $400,000 that's exempt from the generation-skipping tax, or $1.4 million in the case of a married couple. If the estate is large enough, you can put that $400,000 or $1.4 million into a separate trust payable to your grandchildren, but with your children having access to the principal. Again, you'll accomplish the prime goal of generation skipping: keeping wealth intact as it passes across two generations, with one layer of estate tax rather than two.

Introducing the Wealth Trust

You can see the power of giving cash or property to your grandchildren. By transferring anywhere from $200,000 to $500,000 to a trust, you can buy a $2 million life-insurance policy that someday will enrich the trust and your grandchildren, the ultimate beneficiaries. That $2 million, or even larger amounts, can grow unimpaired by estate taxes until your grandchildren die, which might not be for decades. In the meantime, the trustees can tap the trust funds in case of real needs.

With two simple steps you can make any irrevocable trust into *wealth trusts*. First, include a provision enabling the trustee to buy and hold residential real estate. And give the trustee the discretionary power—but not the obligation—to let the beneficiary use the trust property or properties.

Second, add a provision enabling the trustee, with the consent of the beneficiary, to make distributions to pay the premiums of life insurance covering the grandchildren (and thus help with future estate taxes). Assuming the grandchildren are very young, such insurance will be relatively inexpensive.

After the trust is amply funded, the trustee may buy a townhouse in Palm Desert, California, a condo in Boca Raton, Florida, or other desirable locations. The trust provisions can permit the beneficiaries to live in the house rent-free. Or the beneficiaries can use the real estate for vacations. As yet another option, the trustees may buy "inexpensive" starter homes for a number of grandchildren.

If the beneficiaries don't want to live in the trust's properties, the trust can rent it for income. When a particular piece of real estate no longer is suitable, because of size or location, the trustee can implement a *1031 exchange,* tax-free, for a more desirable piece of property.

While all this is going on, the real estate may appreciate, to the ultimate profit of the beneficiaries and their own heirs. If the trust follows the three basic rules of buying real estate—location, location, location— the property likely will gain value in the long run.

In essence, the idea is to relieve your descendants of the need to buy houses, which can be a tremendous financial burden. Once that obligation is shifted to a wealth trust, your beneficiaries and their families will have much more disposable income available for other purposes.

Wealth trusts also offer asset protection. No matter how fine a family you have, the odds are that at least one of your children or grandchildren will suffer a broken marriage. In most states, if the house or vacation home is owned by the trust, with the beneficiary using it at the discretion of the trustee, the house won't be considered marital property subject to a divorce settlement. Similarly, homes held in this type of trust won't be exposed to other creditors.

If you're buying a pair of slacks and a jacket is included in the purchase price, you might as well take the jacket—you may want to wear it someday. The same thing is true of trusts. When you set one up, you may as well include the power to purchase residential real estate. Someday it may make a lot of sense.

Wealth trusts may be the best way to provide for grandchildren. Some people don't like the idea of leaving a grandchild a large sum of money, or even a regular income, fearing their incentive will be stunted. That won't be a problem if you set up a trust to provide a grandchild with the use of a house or condo. Your grandchild will have one major financial load lifted, but he or she still will have to work to earn money for food, clothing and other living expenses. What better legacy can you provide?

- The truly wealthy have used generation skipping for decades. The goal is to pass wealth from grandparent to grandchildren, incurring only one level of estate tax yet giving all generations use of the money.
- Recent tax-law changes have imposed a double tax on generation-skipping transfers. As much as 80 percent can be lost to the IRS.
- Each individual has a $1 million exemption ($2 million for married couples) from the generation-skipping tax.
- If you expect to have an estate of at least $3 million, it may make sense to use your $1 million or $2 million exemption to make lifetime gifts to a tax-free inheritance trust. This trust can buy life insurance. (If you're not insurable, the trust can make other investments.)
- After the tax-free inheritance trust provides cash to help pay estate taxes, it can stay intact rather than terminate. The grandchildren may be beneficiaries, with your children having

access in case of emergencies. No more estate tax needs to be paid until your grandchildren's (or even until your great-grandchildren's) deaths.

- To get money to your grandchildren more rapidly, the original tax-free inheritance trust may sunburst into subtrusts, to be terminated with each of your children's deaths.
- Wealth trusts give the trustee the power to buy residential real estate. This can provide the trust beneficiaries rent-free housing as well as asset protection.

Trust Funds Without Growing Pains

Throughout this section, we've discussed wealth-transfer strategies that use trusts. Tax-free inheritance trusts, which are frequently used, often hold no assets except life insurance. Those trusts are relatively easy to manage.

But other types of trusts are more demanding. Suppose, for example, you set up gifting trusts for your children. Each year, you and your spouse give $20,000 to each child. What will be done with the money?

There's also the question of what will happen in the future. At some point, life insurance held in trust will mature—those proceeds may have to be reinvested. Or suppose you set up a Q-TIP trust for your spouse, to be funded at your death. How should that money be invested to provide best for your surviving spouse and your children?

The responsibility lies with the trustee or co-trustees. In some circumstances (notably, charitable remainder trusts), you can be the trustee. In most types of trusts, though, someone else has to be the trustee in order to remove the trust assets from your taxable estate. When someone else acts as trustee, you lose control of the investment decisions. (As a practical matter, when the trustee is your grown child or a financial adviser, you can indicate how you'd like the money invested, although you can't make the ultimate decisions.)

No matter who the trustee is, he or she becomes a *fiduciary*. That means the trustee is responsible for investing wisely on behalf of the trust beneficiaries. The general rule is that investments must be prudent, rather than speculative. A trustee who invests in a start-up business that turns sour, for example, may find himself or herself personally responsible for any losses suffered by the trust. The same rules govern pension-fund investing, so trustees should approach their investments as they would approach investments for a retirement plan.

The outcome of this *prudent-man rule* is that trustees tend to invest in stocks, bonds and cash equivalents. (Real estate is usually difficult to hold in a trust portfolio, although mortgages may have a place.) Liquidity is important: an investment that's not quoted every day in *The Wall Street Journal* may not be appropriate for trust funds.

The limitations still leave a wide range of possible investment vehicles. In fact, it's not really fair to expect a trustee to pick individual stocks and bonds unless he or she is an investment professional.

A Proactive Approach

One possible approach for a trustee is to place money directly with a professional money manager. That professional will have discretion for switching money among stocks, bonds and cash equivalents as well as for picking individual securities. Some investment pros have records of earning 15 or 20 percent per year long term.

If you have only $100,000 or $200,000 to invest, you're unlikely to be accepted as a client of a first-class money manager. Most top pros want at least $500,000 before they'll manage your money. Superstars may require a $5 million minimum to handle an account.

What if you have a smaller amount to invest? Working with a major brokerage firm, you can put your money into a *wrap account*. That is, a Merrill Lynch or PaineWebber will take your $100,000 and $100,000 from the next person and so on, to come up with $5 million for a top pro to manage. You'll pay 2 to 3 percent of assets per year ($2,000 to $3,000 on a $100,000 account) to cover all fees and commissions. So, if your money manager can earn 15 percent per year, you'll wind up with 12 to 13 percent growth. That's truly exceptional, doubling your money every five or six years.

Building a Fund of Funds

Another solution is for the trustee to invest in a portfolio of no-load mutual funds. Mutual funds, you probably know, are pooled funds in which millions of dollars—even billions—are raised from investors who contribute as little as a few hundred dollars apiece. The money raised can be invested in stocks or bonds. Some mutual funds are general equity or fixed-income funds; some are extremely specialized, focusing on small-company growth stocks, for example, or intermediate-term municipal bonds. With a mutual fund investment, a trustee can put together a balanced portfolio, with diversified holdings and professional management. Most mutual funds offer automatic reinvestment of dividends, which trustees should elect unless the beneficiaries need income right away.

Mutual funds are divided between those that impose a sales charge (up to 8.5 percent) and those that have no initial load. Load funds have no guarantee of superior performance, so trustees usually are better off sticking with no-loads in order to have more money at work. Even if the sales load is only 4 percent, that means there's 96 percent to be invested, versus 100 percent in a no-load.

Trustees who want help with recordkeeping can buy many no-load funds through discount brokers such as Charles Schwab. They'll pay small sales commissions, but trustees may find it worth the expense because one monthly statement from the brokerage firm summarizes the position of all the mutual funds held by the trust.

How can you or your trustee pick the right mutual funds? Many publications, such as *Forbes, Business Week, Money* and *Barron's,* regularly carry rankings of mutual funds. Look for no-loads with excellent long-term performance. Mutual funds with less than a five-year history aren't proven, so they may not be appropriate for prudent investments. You can also subscribe to any of several newsletters that recommend mutual funds for investors. Excellent no-load funds are offered by many companies, including Fidelity Investments, Twentieth Century Investors Research, Vanguard Group, Stein Roe & Farnham, Scudder Stevens & Clark, Neuberger & Berger Management, T. Rowe Price Associates and Dreyfus Corp.

Trustees Need To Be Tax-Wise

Trustees should keep tax considerations in mind when they invest. Charitable remainder trusts, for example, are tax-exempt. The money that's paid out is generally taxable income to the recipient, but undistributed earnings escape taxation. Some trusts, often including offshore asset-protection trusts (see Chapter 14), are *grantor trusts,* meaning that all the trust's income is taxable to the individual who sets up the trust.

Most types of trusts, though, have their own tax brackets. If they invest in stocks or bonds or mutual funds, these trusts will owe income tax on dividends or interest or capital gains.

One way to avoid trust taxation is for the trustee to buy municipal bonds, which are exempt from income taxes. But the muni market is treacherous these days, with billions of dollars in defaults and downgrades in recent years. In addition, reinvesting the interest can be tricky.

Most trustees, therefore, will be better off with no-load muni funds, where there's professional management and the interest can be reinvested. On the other hand, no-load muni funds probably will deliver only around 6 or 7 percent per year over the long term. Other investments may do better, especially over a 20- or 30-year time horizon. The next section will explain how to fund trusts using annuities and other insurance-related vehicles.

- Money held in trust needs to be invested wisely if the trust is to fulfill its objectives. The same prudent-man approach used for pension-fund investing applies to trusts established for wealth transfer.
- Most trustees aren't equipped to pick individual securities. Professional money managers may be hired, if necessary, through pooled accounts set up by brokerage firms.
- Trustees can invest in a portfolio of no-load mutual funds. Buying through a discount broker will put all the funds on a single statement.
- To reduce income taxes, the trustee can invest in municipal bonds or muni bond funds. Long-term returns may be low compared with alternative investments.

Look Ma, No Work (And No Taxes)

Some trustees prefer to invest trust funds in annuities. There's no current tax to pay, there are no worries about reinvestment and long-term returns may beat muni funds. (Note: there may be situations in which a tax-deferred annuity actually is taxed inside an irrevocable trust, so you need to caution your tax pro to be extra careful in this area.)

An annuity, strictly speaking, is a contract calling for certain payments over a certain time period, possibly the recipient's lifetime (see Chapter 17 on private annuities). A pure annuity is an *immediate annuity.* Here, you give a lump sum to another party (usually an insurance company), which sends you a check every month for the rest of your life, or perhaps the life of yourself and your spouse.

A variation on the immediate annuity is the *deferred annuity.* Here, you pay the insurance company *before* you want your income. Suppose you want to retire at age 65, so you buy a deferred annuity at age 55. A deferred annuity can be purchased with a single lump sum or with a series of smaller premium payments. Those premiums will compound tax-free until you *annuitize* the contract and begin taking monthly payments.

How will the compounding work? The answer depends on whether you purchase a fixed or variable annuity. A *fixed annuity* is like investing in a series of CDs. Usually, the interest rate you receive is changed each year to reflect current interest rates. The taxes are deferred until you take your money out.

A *variable annuity,* like a variable life-insurance policy, offers you a family of mutual funds inside an annuity "wrapper" that shelters you from taxes until you annuitize the contract. Long-term, a variable annuity should outperform a fixed annuity if a substantial amount is invested in stock funds. The greater the investment buildup inside the annuity, the more money you'll eventually take out. Remember, however, that the outstanding performance of stocks in the past is not a guarantee of future success; variable annuities pose more risks than fixed annuities.

If the income isn't needed right away, a tax-deferred annuity can increase the size of the trust fund, provided the provisions of the tax code are strictly followed. Also, an annuity means less work and less responsibility for the trustee. The money is placed in the hands of investment professionals. The trustee doesn't have to make investment decisions.

Some trustees like annuities that have special features, such as a guarantee of 100 percent gain in ten years. Another investment vehicle, available either as a variable annuity or as an unsheltered group of no-load mutual funds, holds mainly equities while the investor is working, and then switches to a bond emphasis in his or her retirement years for less risk and greater income.

Take the case of Mary, who is remarried to a younger husband, Michael. Mary will leave most of her considerable estate to her children, but she also wants to provide for Michael after her death. She doesn't want to use a Q-TIP trust because Michael may live for many years, delaying wealth transfer to her own children.

Therefore, Mary has set up a trust with Michael acting as the trustee as well as the beneficiary. She gave Michael $500,000, which he used to buy three single-premium deferred annuities, all variable. Among the three contracts, Mary has identified 10 different top-flight investment managers, each of whom was allocated $50,000.

Now Michael has a diversified portfolio managed by 10 different pros, invested in everything from utility stocks to overseas bonds. Michael pays no taxes and doesn't have to worry about reinvesting interest or dividends. After Mary dies and her estate passes to her children, Michael will have access to a large trust fund, which he can tap at will.

Exit Strategies

If trust funds are invested in annuities, the trustee's main decision is how to take the money out when the time comes. The traditional method is to annuitize: cut a deal with the insurance company to take monthly payments. If that's the case, each payment you receive will be part taxable, part tax-free return of principal as shown in Tables 12-1 and 12-2.

Suppose the annuity calls for a payment of $870 per month. The insurance company will help you calculate how much is taxable. If the taxable portion is $453, and the recipient is in a 33 percent tax bracket, then $151 will go to the IRS while the recipient keeps $719, or 83 percent of each payment.

If the trustee decides to annuitize a contract, there are several options to choose among. Should he or she select a *single-life annuity*? The

Table 12-1
Sample Annuity Payouts (Single)

Purchase Payment $100,000.00   Mode of Payment: Monthly
Male age 65   Life type: Single

	Primary	Exclusion Ratio	Excludable Monthly Benefit
Life	$870.00	47.90%	$416.73
5 year certain and life	$857.00	47.90%	$410.50
10 year certain and life	$828.00	47.30%	$391.64
15 year certain and life	$793.00	46.20%	$366.37
20 year certain and life	$759.00	45.00%	$341.55

Table 12-2
Sample Annuity Payouts (Joint and Survivor)

Purchase Payment $100,000.00   Mode of Payment: Monthly
Male age 65, Female age 60   Life type: Joint and Survivor

	Primary	Secondary	Exclusion Ratio	Excludable Monthly Benefit
Life	$712.00	$712.00	46.10%	$328.23
5 year certain and life	$712.00	$712.00	42.40%	$301.89
10 year certain and life	$711.00	$711.00	42.50%	$302.18
15 year certain and life	$709.00	$709.00	42.20%	$299.20
20 year certain and life	$705.00	$705.00	41.50%	$292.57

NOTES:
- Tables 12-1 and 12-2 are illustrations only. The figures can change from company to company and as interest rates rise and fall.
- Excludable monthly benefits are not subject to income tax.
- No cash surrender or loans available.
- The first annuity payment can often be deferred a number of months from the purchase date.

payments to investors are high, but they'll stop after the recipient dies, even if that's next week.

Another option is a *joint-and-survivor annuity*. The monthly income will be lower, but the payments will go on until two people die. If a married couple is involved, the choice may be between $870 per month as long as Fred lives, and $712 per month as long as either Fred or Ethel is still alive.

Yet another option is the *period certain*. That is, you can take a single-life annuity, but you're guaranteed at least 10 or 20 or 30 years of payments. If Fred dies halfway through a 20-year period certain, Ethel will collect the annuity for another 10 years. (See Table 12-2.)

Which works best? If the *annuitant* (annuity recipient) has no dependents, a single-life annuity can make sense. If dependents are involved, a joint-and-survivor or period certain annuity is a better choice in most cases: A single-life annuity is too risky.

One problem with the traditional method of annuitizing is that monthly payments are fixed. Receiving $870 a month may sound great in 1992. But by 2002 or 2012, that $870 will have a fraction of its 1992 purchasing power.

You can avoid this problem if it's a concern. One strategy is to choose a variable-payout annuity. (If your insurer doesn't offer a variable-payout annuity, you can switch to one that does, tax-free.) In this arrangement, your payout is a percentage of the annuity account, not a fixed dollar amount. So if your annuity account grows over the long term, your payout also can grow. Of course, there's a risk of loss here, too, since accounts can lose as well as gain.

Another option is not to annuitize your contract. Instead, you can take withdrawals whenever you need money, on your schedule. (Unless you withdraw exceptionally large amounts, you won't run into a surrender fee.) This gives you flexibility and extends your period of tax-free compounding. The downside? Taxation. Everything you withdraw will be fully taxed up to the amount of income earned inside an annuity. (Those earnings are equal to the account balance minus premiums paid.) Withdrawals before age 59½ usually will be subject to a 10 percent penalty tax. (Annuities bought before 1982 may receive more favorable tax treatment.)

Some sophisticated financial pros advise clients to defer annuitizing and extend the tax shelter. However, if the annuitant needs regular income for living expenses, annuitizing probably is the way to go.

Annuities with a Kicker

A variation on investing in annuities is buying a modified endowment contract, or MEC, which we explain in Chapter 21. MECs are usually single-premium; they can be fixed or variable, just like annuities. Investment buildup is slower: you might get 8 percent per year from a MEC versus 9 percent in an annuity. But MECs also provide an income-tax-free death benefit, and there are fewer tax problems with trust ownership.

Therefore, trustees who are concerned about protecting someone should consider a MEC instead of an annuity. MECs offer the same advantages as a trust vehicle—no current taxation, ease of administration, professional investment management. Indeed, there may be fewer tax concerns. And, with a MEC, if the covered individual dies during the buildup stage, his or her beneficiaries will receive more money than will annuity beneficiaries in the same situation.

If family protection isn't a concern and your main objective is to provide a stream of income at some future date, an annuity will beat a MEC, because the buildup will be faster.

Pay Longer, Borrow Later

MECs generally involve a sizable single premium, so they don't qualify for tax-free policy loans. If you extend the pay-in period, probably to at least five years, you can buy a life-insurance policy with which tax-free loans are possible. We've mentioned life insurance as a means of covering estate taxes, but there are other creative ways in which life insurance can be used in wealth transfer.

Take the case of Phil, a widower in his 70s. He's in poor health, so he can't get life insurance, which means he can't provide as well as he would like to for his children and grandchildren.

So Phil has set up trusts for each of his two children and four grandchildren. Each year he gives $10,000 to each trust; the trusts each buy permanent life insurance, with payments scheduled over seven years. In each policy, one of Phil's two children is insured (they're in good health) and his grandchildren are the beneficiaries.

Thus, Phil is removing $60,000 each year from his estate. If he dies before the policies are paid for, his will contains provisions saying that the premiums will continue.

Therefore, even though Phil's children will have to pay estate taxes, they'll also have access to three life insurance policies apiece. As trustees, they can borrow against the cash values, tax-free, if necessary. When Phil's children die, his grandchildren will receive the death benefits.

This type of insurance commonly is used by major corporations as a means of providing deferred compensation to top employees. When they retire, their employer can tap the cash value for retirement income; at their death, their dependents will receive taxable death benefits. These companies employ some of the top accountants in the United States. If they think life insurance makes sense for deferred income and family protection, it's worth considering as an investment vehicle for trust funds.

- Deferred annuities offer trustees a way to invest while minimizing taxes and recordkeeping responsibilities. Expert tax advice is needed to mix annuities with irrevocable trusts.
- Buying a fixed annuity is like investing in series of CDs and deferring income taxes.
- Buying a variable annuity is like investing in a family of mutual funds and deferring income taxes.
- When you annuitize a contract, a single-life annuity will work if the recipient has no dependents. Otherwise, you should choose a joint-and-survivor or period-certain payout.
- Compared with a deferred annuity, a modified endowment contract (MEC) has a slower investment buildup but a greater death benefit, so it may be appropriate if family protection is a concern. Also, a MEC may avoid tax problems that an annuity might present.
- Life insurance policies paid for over a few years usually offer tax-free policy loans. They may be suitable for providing deferred income as well as family protection.

III

BEYOND
TRUSTS

13 Keeping Good Company

When you run your own business as a one-man or one-woman show, you probably have a *sole proprietorship*. As your business grows and more people get involved, you might organize your business either as a partnership or as a corporation.

Many entrepreneurs choose to incorporate, often because of perceived income-tax advantages. Indeed, there are some tax benefits to incorporation. Some expenses, such as medical reimbursement plans, may be easier for a corporation to deduct. The same holds true for auto and entertainment deductions. You have to be careful, though, to keep records and pay the company back for expenses that are personal rather than legitimate business expenses.

If you play it straight, you can, for example, buy a computer and lease it to your corporation. You get to take deductions for depreciation to offset the income you receive, while your corporation deducts the lease payments. (You must, though, set reasonable lease rates, taxable to you.)

Aren't there headaches involved with running a corporation? Payroll deductions and other recordkeeping burdens? If necessary, you can lease your employees. That is, your workers are actually employees of a leasing agency, which shuffles all the papers and provides the fringe benefits. Your corporation makes deductible lease payments to the agency. As long as the leasing agency follows all the rules on withholding, payroll taxes, etc., the arrangement will hold up.

Tax angles are fine and should be discussed thoroughly with a professional. For the purpose of this book—wealth transfer—the main advantage of incorporation is the so-called *corporate shield*. That is, shareholders generally are not personally liable for the obligations of the corporation.

You probably recall when an Exxon tanker was responsible for a huge oil spill in Alaska, and you may have read about all the lawsuits that followed. With all these claims being pressed, nobody bothered John and Mary Smith, who owned 100 shares of Exxon and who were, therefore, co-owners of Exxon.

The reason? The corporate shield of *limited liability* that protects the personal assets of corporate owners. In today's litigious society, you can't afford the exposure you have as a partner or a sole proprietor.

Your catering business probably isn't going to spill crude oil into Alaskan waters. But you might, for example, hire an employee who gets into a dispute with a customer who's female or homosexual or disabled or a member of an ethnic minority. You may not have been directly involved, yet you may find yourself sued on charges of harassment, abuse or discrimination. Doing business as a corporation, rather than as a sole proprietorship or a partnership, will give you a greater chance of protecting your personal assets.

When Cash Really Counts

If you own all or part of a small business, a corporation or partnership or sole proprietorship, you have special wealth-transfer concerns. Perhaps most important, the IRS likely will put a substantial value on your business, leading to a heavy estate-tax burden.

For example, you have a moderately successful home-remodeling business, posting a profit of $150,000 per year. The IRS may say that your business is worth $2 million. At your death, if you want to pass it on to your son, he'll owe perhaps $600,000 in estate tax just on the value of your business, regardless of any other assets.

In this example, your death may hamper your company, if you've been the prime mover. Customers may be reluctant to continue doing business with your successor; your bank may shy away from lending money. A few hundred thousand dollars may be needed in working capital until new management proves its capabilities.

Owners of closely held companies often rely on life insurance to help them meet these burdens. Fortunately, if you control a company, you may be able to use *split-dollar* insurance to provide adequate coverage without having to use substantial amounts of your personal after-tax dollars.

Split-dollar comes in many varieties, but the underlying principle remains the same. You as an individual and the company split the cost of buying life insurance, and you also split the benefits. In perhaps the most common form, your company pays the premiums. If it's a cash-value policy, the company retains the cash value as a corporate asset, while you are personally covered by the death benefit.

But didn't we say costs were split? How can that be, if the company pays the premium?

In this case, where the company pays the premium on your life insurance, you're receiving a benefit. The IRS considers that to be taxable compensation and will demand that you pay tax, depending on your age and the amount of life-insurance coverage you receive. Special IRS tables determine how much taxable income you'll have to recognize, but that amount generally is far less than the premium itself.

For example, Larry is 64 while his wife, Dinah, is 58. The company that they jointly own is paying the premium for a $500,000 second-to-die life-insurance policy. According to IRS tables, they have to recognize $261 worth of taxable income this year. In a 35 percent tax bracket, they have to pay $91 in taxes this year: not a bad price for $500,000 worth of life insurance.

As they get older, they'll have to pay more, but the amount will still be modest compared to their insurance protection.

Suppose that in a few years they'll recognize $1,000 worth of taxable income: in a 35 percent income-tax bracket, they'd owe $350 in taxes. If they wish, their company can give them a bonus of $550. The $550 will be deductible for the company while they'll owe about $200 in tax on the $550 bonus. That will leave them around $350 to pay the tax on the life insurance they receive. Naturally, this strategy works best if the company is in a high tax bracket so the deduction is valuable.

Imputed income from company-purchased life insurance	$1,000	
Income tax @ 35%		$350

Bonus (deductible to company)	$550
Income tax on bonus @ 35%	($200)
Net bonus, after tax	$350

The only catch with this "double bonus" technique is that total compensation, including the bonus, can't be "excessive" by IRS standards. If so, the $550 bonus will be treated as a nondeductible dividend. The subject of excess compensation is beyond the scope of this book, but it's something that all small-business owners should discuss with their tax pro.

With the life insurance in place, you're covered. In case you die, the needed money will be there. Usually, in a split-dollar arrangement, at your death the company will get back whatever it paid in premiums and the rest will go to beneficiaries you select. If the insurance has cash value, the cash value will be on the corporate balance sheet, a reserve that can be tapped in case of emergency.

Take the case of Sam, a 49-year-old entrepreneur with a 46-year-old wife. He wanted $3 million worth of second-to-die life insurance to cover his estate-tax obligation. The premium was $33,000, payable for approximately 10 years, but Sam, like many business owners, doesn't have an extra $33,000 a year to pay for life insurance. So his company pays the premiums and keeps the cash value on its books. After 10 years, that cash value likely will exceed $330,000.

At some point, perhaps when he sells the business or retires, Sam will *roll out* the policy. That is, he'll pay his company the cash value and put the paid-up policy into a tax-free inheritance trust. In the meantime, Sam's company has both a sizable asset on its books and ample protection in case of Sam's premature death.

Estate Freezes Come In from the Cold

Owners of family businesses have a tool they may be able to use to reduce estate taxes if they intend to pass the business from one generation to the next. The *estate freeze,* as it's known, was once widely used, then not used at all after Congress changed the law. In late 1990, the law was changed once again: estate freezes are back, but with tough limitations.

To see how an estate freeze would work, consider the case of Mal, who owns 100 percent of the stock of a paint manufacturer. He intends to retire in a few years and pass control of the company to his son, Steve. The first step he takes is to hire an appraiser to value his paint company; the appraiser finds the company is worth $1 million.

Then Mal exchanges his stock for two new classes of stock, one class of preferred and one class of common. The next step is to put a value on the preferred shares. Say they will pay a cash dividend of $30,000 per year. IRS tables (which are revised periodically) might assign a value of $600,000 to those shares. If the company is worth $1 million and the preferred is worth $600,000, the common shares are therefore worth $400,000.

Appraised value of company	$1,000,000
Value of preferred shares, as per IRS tables	($600,000)
Value of common shares (i.e., the difference)	$400,000

Then Mal gives the common shares to Steve. Mal eventually retires, pocketing $30,000 a year from his preferred stock, in addition to his other sources of retirement income, and Steve takes over the business.

What does this accomplish? That depends on what Steve does with the paint company. Suppose Mal lives for another 20 years, during which time the company grows to a $4 million value. At his death, assuming no further transactions in the company's shares, Mal's interest in the company is "frozen" at $600,000, the value of his preferred shares. So Steve owes perhaps $300,000 in estate taxes, versus the $2 million he would have owed if he had inherited a $4 million company.

Mal's gift to Steve of common stock, worth $400,000, will be subtracted from his $600,000 estate–gift-tax exemption, so he doesn't have to pay a gift tax right away. That still leaves him with $200,000 worth of exemption remaining for other transfers.

What does the IRS think about estate freezes? Its main concern is that the senior generation (Mal, in our example) will improperly pump up the value of the preferred shares it retains. This would reduce the value of the common shares given to the junior generation (Steve) and reduce the gift-tax obligation.

Therefore, the new law says that the devices formerly used to inflate the value of the preferred stock—puts, calls, various rights—won't work any more. The preferred must have true value; in general, this means it must receive a cash dividend. So estate freezes will be most appropriate if (1) the senior generation is ready to step aside; (2) the company can afford to pay a meaningful dividend to the retired or semiretired owner of the preferred shares; and (3) if the company is likely to appreciate enough to make it worthwhile to get future appreciation outside the estate of the senior generation.

- Incorporating a business may provide tax advantages to its owners.
- For wealth creation and preservation, the main advantage of the corporate form is the corporate shield that protects personal assets from business-related claims.
- When a business owner dies, his or her family may have to pay massive estate taxes. The company may need extra working capital, too, while new management proves itself.
- Often, life insurance is relied upon to provide the needed cash.
- If you control a company, you can use split-dollar life insurance, with costs and benefits split between you and the company.
- Split-dollar insurance has many varieties; a sophisticated insurance agent may come up with the plan that works best for you.
- In 1990, the tax law was changed so that estate freezes are once again a viable planning tool for family businesses. An estate freeze transfers the future appreciation of a company to the next generation.

• The estate freeze rules are stringent. The best candidates are companies with high growth potential and excess cash flow.

Know How To Fold 'Em

Just because you have lots of life insurance doesn't mean you have a wealth-transfer plan for your company. You need a formal, written *business continuity plan*. You need to spell out who will run your business after you. If not, your company may not survive your departure and there won't be much wealth to transfer to your family.

The written plan generally is called a *buy-sell agreement*. A buy-sell agreement is a contract to transfer ownership of your company. You sell; the new owner buys. The buy-sell spells out who the parties are, when the transfer will take place and how much will be paid. Without a buy-sell, your family may one day be negotiating those points out of weakness.

If you have one primary co-owner, there's usually a mutual buy-sell. Whoever leaves first, the other buys him or her out. If there are three or four owners, the two or three survivors can take over from their former colleague. Buy-sells between co-owners may include a right of first refusal. Ava, Magda and Zsa Zsa are co-owners of an auto body shop. Ava, who wants to retire, agrees to sell her share to Mikhail, whom Magda and Zsa Zsa can't stand. The buy-sell may give Magda and Zsa Zsa the right to buy out Ava for the price that Mikhail agreed to pay.

Or suppose, as part of her wealth-transfer planning, Ava has been making gifts of her business interests to her children, $10,000 worth per year. The buy-sell may give Magda and Zsa Zsa the right to buy the shares given away, as well as the shares still held by Ava.

Sole Searching

If you're the sole owner of your company, with no obvious successor, you need to search for one. You might designate a key employee as successor or hire someone to be the crown prince(ss). If the key employee already is on board, that's generally preferable, because both parties know what they're getting. Some corporations use ESOPs *(employee stock ownership plans),* essentially selling the business to all its employees.

Otherwise, you may have to hunt for a competitor, a customer or a supplier to buy your company. If you don't find a successor, your family may wind up paying a huge estate-tax bill to inherit a company that has no future. The end result often is a liquidation, at a fraction of its former value.

Do you need a buy-sell if your child or grandchild will take over your company? Probably. Suppose you decide to simply hold onto your shares and leave them to your child in your will, with no buy-sell. You may saddle your estate with a large estate-tax bill and you may shortchange your other heirs.

Take the case of Harry, who owns a successful elevator-repair business and few other assets. Harry's two sons have been working in the business ever since they were in high school, and they expect to take over the company's ownership, but Harry's daughters have gone into other careers.

So Harry has entered into a buy-sell with his sons. At his death, the sons will buy Harry's share from the estate. That will put cash into the estate, not only to pay the estate tax but to provide for the daughters, who won't run the profitable business. Having a buy-sell in effect and known in advance to your family members can spare a lot of hard feelings later on.

Most buy-sells are like Harry's, taking effect at the owner's death. Increasingly, though, buy-sell agreements cover retirement as well. When you retire, not only may you want to stop working, you also may want to sell all or part of your interest in your company to raise cash. Typically, payment for a retirement buy-out is stretched over several years.

There's a trap here: What if you sell to Joe, with payment promised over five years, but Joe strips all the value out of the company after a year or two? You may have to come out of retirement and patch together a company that has lost its employees, its customers, its credibility.

It's not easy to guard against this problem, but it helps to know your buyer and it helps to have a buy-sell drawn up by a hard-nosed lawyer. You might want to insist upon regular financial reports during the buyout period so you can move to prevent a catastrophe before it gets out of hand.

Another possibility that's often not covered in a buy-sell, but should be, is your disability. What happens if you have a stroke and can't keep running your company? If it's in the buy-sell, your successor can take charge of the company and buy you out over an extended time period.

Although buy-sells are designed to set the rules in case of an owner's death, retirement or disability, that's not their only function. If partners decide to part ways, a buy-sell can set the terms and spare the turmoil. Or if your company has some junior shareholders or partners and they leave (voluntarily or involuntarily), a buy-sell can help facilitate a separation without litigation.

Don't Go by the Book

Perhaps the most difficult aspect of drawing up a buy-sell agreement is to set a price. Valuing a closely held business is more art than science. Yet, unless a purchase price can be agreed upon in advance, the whole deal may fall through.

Some buy-sells call for *book value* to be paid, but that often doesn't reflect the true worth of a business. Real estate, for example, may be worth far more than its book value, and intangibles (such as good will) aren't included. A more sophisticated method is to use an average of book value, a multiple of earnings and a multiple of sales.

If you ask an "expert," he or she will generally recommend that you have a third party perform the valuation. Some experts go as far as to say that the buyer and seller should each hire an appraiser, those two appraisers can agree between them on a third appraiser, and the average of the three appraisals will be the accepted price. (As you might expect, the experts making such recommendations usually are in the appraisal business.)

Some informal arrangements can be just as practical. Each year, for example, the co-owners may get together and decide on a value for the business. If necessary, they can increase the life-insurance coverage to keep up with the valuation. The buy-sell may say, for example, that the purchase price will be either the amount of life insurance or the book value, whichever is greater.

Making Sure the Price Is Right

If a buy-sell is between co-owners, or a sole owner and an unrelated successor, the agreed-upon price likely will be fair. The buyer wants to get as much as he or she can; the seller wants to pay as little as possible. Therefore, *arm's-length* buy-sells often can put a value on a closely held company for estate-tax purposes.

However, to the IRS, a buy-sell agreement in a family business is naturally suspect. Estee may think her business is worth $4 million, but she'll agree to sell it to son Ron for $2 million. If she dies, the difference between the market value and the buy-sell value means a dispute over as much as $1 million in estate taxes in a 50 percent bracket.

The 1990 tax act spells out the ground rules for buy-sells, especially those in family businesses. A buy-sell must be (1) bona fide; (2) not a device to transfer the business at less than full value; and (3) comparable to similar arrangements entered into at arm's length. If you follow those guidelines, your buy-sell valuation probably will be accepted for estate-tax purposes, saving your family heirs an expensive fight with the IRS.

After you've determined how much money will be needed to fund a buy-sell, you can arrange for the money to be there. If the prospective buyer has plenty of cash on hand, that's not a problem, but buying a small business generally requires amounts that can't be raised easily. So the seller may be covered by life insurance, with the proceeds going to the buyer. When the owner dies, the successor uses the insurance proceeds to pay for the buyout.

The Value of Cash Value

What kind of insurance should fund a buy-sell? In Chapter 19, we'll discuss the relative merits of term versus permanent life insurance. It should be noted, though, that permanent insurance, which is more expensive than term, offers a buildup of *cash value*. If you retire or become disabled, this cash value may be a source of funds for the buyout. With term insurance, no cash value is available, so retirement and disability buyouts must be funded from the company's cash flow, and may, in some cases, put a financial strain on the company or on the new owner.

If a family member or employee is relying on permanent insurance to buy you out, you might be able to pay a "double bonus" to the buyer to make the premiums affordable. (See the beginning of this chapter on how a double bonus plan can work.) The bonuses likely will be deductible, so this is a tax-efficient way of financing your own retirement or helping your family handle estate taxes.

On the technical side, your buy-sell will be either a *cross-purchase* or a *redemption plan.* In a cross-purchase, the buyer buys directly from the seller. In a redemption, the company buys the interests of the departing owner, so the remaining owners hold all the outstanding shares.

The end result is the same, but a redemption may be simpler to administer, especially if there are several owners involved. With a redemption plan, the life insurance is held in the company, so there's more assurance the money will be there for the buyout. Cross-purchase plans may offer some tax advantages, and they've been gaining in popularity.

If you can't decide which way to go, you may use a hybrid buy-sell. Typically, the new owner has the first option to buy directly from the owner who has died. If he or she doesn't exercise the option, the business has the obligation to buy. If the life-insurance proceeds to fund the buyout are in the wrong place, they can be loaned "from one pocket to the other." This strategy offers the company's new owner a chance to pick out whichever type of plan will work out best at the last possible moment, rather than making the decision years in advance.

- If you own a small company, you should have a buy-sell agreement. That will ensure that your company will continue after your departure, and that your family will be fairly compensated.
- A buy-sell is a written contract between a business owner and his or her successors. A proper buy-sell should identify the buyer, specify the events that will trigger a sale, and set the price to be paid.
- The usual buyers are the business owner's children or co-owners. If that's not feasible, a key employee may be the successor.

- Buy-sell agreements should cover retirement, disability and departure of an owner from the company in addition to the owner's death.
- Placing a value on a small company deserves careful consideration. If there are co-owners, the value can be set by mutual consent. If not, a third-party appraiser may be needed.
- In many cases, life insurance is used to provide the funding for the buy-sell.
- Cross-purchase and redemption buy-sells each have advantages; a hybrid buy-sell may permit the decision to be deferred until it's apparent which one will work best.

14 All in the Family

During the 1980s, you probably became familiar with the term *limited partnership*. First, many tax shelters were structured as private limited partnerships open to a few selected investors. Then, after the tax laws were changed, limited partnerships for the general public became a popular way to invest in real estate, cable TV, airplane leasing and so on.

But a limited partnership needn't be an investment vehicle: The *family limited partnership* is a powerful wealth-transfer tool. The very rich have known about this strategy for years, and now those whose wealth isn't quite as great are learning about the uses of the family limited partnership.

To start, let's describe the basic limited partnership. It's a partnership with two classes of partners: general and limited. General partners have complete control, while limited partners have no control at all. Limited partners, though, have the same kind of limited liability that's enjoyed by corporate stockholders.

General Partners	Limited Partners
Complete control	No control
Makes all decisions	No decisions
Receives a salary	No salary
Liable for partnership's debts	Protection against creditors

In a family partnership, the general partners usually are the spouses, or the one spouse with most of the assets, while the children or grandchildren may be limited partners. This structure enables the senior generation to transfer assets outside their taxable estates while retaining control over those assets.

Suppose, for example, you hold a portfolio of stocks and bonds worth $1 million. You could, if you wished, transfer those stocks and bonds to your children, using your $10,000 or $20,000 annual exclusion from the federal gift tax. However, once those securities are transferred, they're out of your control.

You could, it's true, give the securities to a trust set up for your children. However, if you're the trustee, with control over the assets, and the beneficiaries are family members, the transfer may not be recognized for estate-tax purposes. The trust assets may be included in your taxable estate.

You could transfer your stocks and bonds to a trust, naming your eldest child as trustee. In this case, however, you could say "It's time to sell stocks and buy bonds," but your child, as trustee, might not go along. As trustee, he or she now has control.

Instead, you create a family limited partnership with 100 shares (perhaps 99 LP shares and 1 GP share): each share will own 1 percent of the assets in the partnership. You retitle the securities so that the stocks and bonds are owned by the Smith Family Limited Partnership. As long as you, the owner of the stocks, hold 100 percent of the partnership shares, no gift tax is involved.

Then you begin to give away shares of the limited partnership. You and your spouse could transfer $20,000 worth of shares in the family limited partnership each year to each child free of gift tax. Or, you could make larger, taxable gifts to the limited partners to get appreciating assets outside your estate. Up to $1.2 million can be given away without incurring a federal gift tax.

You might wind up with only 1 percent of the assets in an extreme example, while your children hold the other 99 percent. As long as your 1 percent is a general partner's interest and the other shares are all limited partners' interests, you still control all the assets. As you can see, a family limited partnership can be a valuable tool in the case of a closely held business or investment real estate.

As general partner, you make all the operating decisions. But your control goes beyond that. As the manager, you're entitled to a salary. You decide how much to pay yourself, as long as it's "reasonable" for the work involved. In the case of an operating business or investment property, where difficult management decisions are involved, you may be entitled to as much as 50 percent of the partnership's income as your salary.

Moreover, you (as general partner) decide how much money to distribute each year. Your Smith Family Partnership may own a shopping center, for example, where income is $50,000 per year. You might decide to pay yourself a $20,000 salary for managing the partnership. As for the other $30,000, you might distribute it all. Or you might decide to distribute none of it and reinvest all $30,000. Or anything in between.

You Run the Show

So the general partner has a real choke hold over the limited partners. Take the case of Lois, who wanted a divorce from Hi. Their assets were all in a family limited partnership, with Hi as the sole general partner. Lois wanted a generous property settlement and Hi turned over 99 percent—all the limited partnership interests.

Hi kept the 1 percent general partner's interest. As general partner, he decided not to pay any distributions to the limited partner (Lois).

Adding insult to injury, in a limited partnership all income *flows through* to the individual who owns the interest. Thus, Lois, as 99 percent owner of the partnership, had to report 99 percent of the partnership's income. She owed the income tax, even though she received none of the cash flow. That's the kind of power a general partner has in a limited partnership.

Now we don't suggest you behave like hardcase Hi. We do think you should be aware of the problem of *phantom income,* as described above. You should distribute at least enough cash to your family members so they'll be able to cover their tax obligation.

Give Your Kids the Business

The wealth-transfer advantages of a family limited partnership are apparent. If you have a family business worth $2 million, for example, you and your spouse might give away 60 percent ($1.2 million worth) of the shares to your children through a family limited partnership. Suppose the business doubles in value over the next 10 years, to $4 million.

The 60 percent of the shares held by the children now will be worth $2.4 million. If you give away other shares in the interim, you might wind up with 75 percent, 80 percent or more of the business in your children's hands, outside your estate, while you retain control through your general partner's interest.

Valuing a family limited partnership can be tricky. Suppose you and your spouse die while holding only 20 percent of the shares of a $4 million business through a family limited partnership, but that your 20 percent includes the general partner's interest. Some tax pros suggest that your 20 percent interest is worth less than $800,000 (20 percent of $4 million) because a *minority discount* applies. The IRS, on the other hand, may contend that your share of the business really is worth more than $800,000 because of your control.

How can you cope with this issue? Steven A. Sciarretta, a Boca Raton, Florida, attorney who specializes in estate planning, has this idea: Create three general partnership interests. You and your spouse each can hold one of these interests; the third can be donated to a charitable remainder trust. Now, with only one of three general partnership interests, your estate won't include a controlling interest.

As we mentioned in Chapter 11, a gift to a charitable remainder trust removes assets from your estate. Because such trusts are irrevocable and a charity is the beneficiary, you can be the trustee, remaining in control while you're alive. (You'll want an independent co-trustee to appraise the general partnership interest that you donate.) At your death, the charity can be permitted—but not obligated—to sell that general partnership interest to your estate, keeping the business in the family.

Naturally, you'll want to work with an experienced attorney when setting up a family limited partnership, whether or not you decide to combine it with a charitable remainder trust. Expect to spend several thousand dollars on startup fees for a family limited partnership, plus substantial annual costs of preparing tax returns.

Don't Downplay Asset Protection

Some attorneys have begun to use family partnerships (all general partners, not a limited partnership) for holding life-insurance policies. Your children, for example, can be the partners, which removes the life insurance from your estate. According to the advocates of this strategy, it's easier to handle gifts this way for the purpose of paying the insurance premiums.

We're not convinced that this is the way to go. You're giving up the protection of an irrevocable life insurance trust, probably exposing the insurance policy to your children's creditors. For a life insurance policy, we recommend the tax-free inheritance trust with someone besides yourself as trustee; you'll have to let someone else take control to avoid estate taxes on the policy.

Don't confuse a *regular family partnership,* consisting of all general partners, with the family limited partnership described in this chapter. A family limited partnership can let you reduce your estate-tax burden while still retaining control over your assets. (For a look at how family limited partnerships can also protect your assets against creditors, see the section "How Limited Is Limited?" in this chapter.)

- A limited partnership consists of limited and general partners. The general partners make all the decisions.
- You may transfer all or part of your assets into a family limited partnership. You (or you and your spouse) can be the general partner; your children may be limited partners.
- You can give away your assets to the limited partners, removing as much as 99 percent of your assets from your taxable estate.
- Even if you retain only 1 percent, you still have total control if you're the general partner.
- This control extends to the salary the partnership pays the general partner and to the distributions made (or not made) to the limited partners.
- Family limited partnerships are well suited for transferring small businesses and real estate to the next generation.
- Valuation is tricky and may require an outside appraisal. The donation of your general partnership interest to a charitable remainder trust, handled by a savvy attorney, may be one way of avoiding a valuation dispute with the IRS.

American Belt, Offshore Suspenders

One of the prime requisites of a wealth-transfer plan is that there must be some wealth to transfer. In the United States in the 1990s, that means avoiding civil litigation and the incredible awards for damages that often result.

That's not always possible. If you're a doctor, for example, you expose yourself to malpractice suits every time you see a patient, and malpractice awards now average around $1 million. Attorneys, accountants and business owners face similar threats. In fact, almost anyone who has substantial assets is likely to find those assets the target of a lawsuit some day.

You can—and should—protect yourself with liability insurance. But insurance is expensive, and your coverage may not cover the largest awards. In some circumstances, you may not be able to acquire liability insurance at all.

In addition, your liability coverage might be "porous" because of exclusions—"you're insured if someone falls off the roof but not if he hits the ground." Your policy might be canceled, perhaps because a company is moving out of your state, and an incident may happen while you're between insurers. Or, in these days of financial distress, your insurer might go bankrupt, effectively leaving you without coverage.

Therefore, if you're truly concerned about asset protection, you can supplement your insurance with two more levels of security: a family limited partnership and an offshore trust.

How Limited Is Limited?

Earlier in this chapter, we described the use of a family limited partnership for wealth transfer: you can remove assets from your taxable estate while you retain control. As we mentioned, the limited partnership interests are shielded from liability, just as corporate stockholders are protected against corporate creditors.

If you set up a family limited partnership for your assets and assign 99 percent of those assets to the limited partners, you have 99 percent protection. Most states in the United States recognize limited partnerships and the protection they provide against creditors.

Typically, if a creditor wins a suit against a limited partnership, he or she is awarded a *charging order*. With a charging order, the creditor can't become a substitute limited partner, can't replace the general partner, can't force cash distributions or the sale of assets. All the creditor can do is wait for the assets to be distributed at the discretion of the general partner.

As we saw earlier in this chapter, a general partner can hold up distributions, sticking the creditor with a tax obligation (from the limited partnership's income) but no cash flow to pay the taxes. In fact, the IRS has ruled, in 1977, that creditors in possession of charging orders will be fully taxed, even if they receive no cash from a limited partnership.

So the establishment of a family limited partnership offers solid asset protection—creditors face daunting barriers to collection. However, the U.S. judicial system is increasingly tilting toward plaintiffs in damages awards. The courts are continually recognizing new "rights," of people bringing suits at the expense of people trying to hold onto their wealth. If you rely on a family limited partnership to protect your assets, you're open to the whims of the system, and to those of the particular judge hearing your case.

A court might find that a limited partnership should be created for a legitimate business purpose, not merely for protection from creditors. Using such reasoning, limited partnership laws might be disregarded. In fact, one court in California recently ruled that a creditor could seize and sell a limited partnership interest. This ruling is very narrow, meaning that it won't apply to many other cases, but it may signal a trend toward the weakening of limited partnership protection.

Put an Ocean Between You and Your Creditors

If you want belt-and-suspenders protection, and a wider range of options when your assets are threatened, you can combine a family limited partnership with a *foreign situs trust*. That is, the partnership interests can be transferred to a trust set up in another jurisdiction under non-U.S. laws. Then any creditor has a formidable challenge: before he or she can collect, lawsuits must be pursued domestically and offshore, against the limited partnership and the foreign trust.

As we indicated, ownership of the assets might be held by the "Smith Family Limited Partnership." Nearly all this partnership, however, can be owned by the trust. Typically, transfers of limited partnership interests to the trust are *incomplete gifts*—strings are attached—so no gift tax is due.

Usually, all partnership income flows through from the partnership to the trust and then to the Smith family, as beneficiaries of the trust. So income tax is payable, as it would be ordinarily, and the entire transaction is tax-neutral. Indeed, if you go shopping for an offshore tax haven, just to cut income taxes, you're likely to run afoul of the IRS, far more powerful and persistent than any creditor or plaintiff's lawyer.

If you set up an offshore trust, what happens to your assets? They can stay right where they are in most cases, says Barry S. Engel of Engel & Rudman, a Denver law firm that specializes in asset protection. A brokerage account, for example, probably can stay in your broker's New York office. If you have real estate, though, or other assets that obviously are subject to a U.S. jurisdiction, you might want to borrow as much as possible against those assets and contribute the cash you receive to your partnership or trust.

With a foreign trust, it's important to choose the right location, one that's "asset-protection friendly," so that it's difficult for creditors to bring claims. Some foreign countries are not appropriate because they recognize judgments by U.S. courts.

A favorite for asset-protection trusts is the Isle of Man, a British possession in the Irish Sea, which provides unusually strong protection against litigation. Many Americans like the idea of a trust in Great Britain, with economic and political stability. In addition, Guernsey, Jersey and Gibraltar have recently moved to provide more asset protection and so have some areas of the Caribbean, including the Cayman Islands, the Bahamas and the British Virgin Islands.

In 1989, the Cook Islands in the Southwest Pacific passed trust legislation designed, among other things, to attract foreign situs asset-protection trusts. Engel and his firm were principal consultants in the drafting of this law. According to Engel, the Cook Islands law now provides more certainty and protection than any other jurisdiction.

Act Before the Iron Gets Hot

No matter what location you choose, the key to asset protection is to act when you don't need it. That is, set up your family limited partnership and asset-protection trust before your wealth is endangered. In fact, some law firms carefully screen clients and refuse to set up asset-protection trusts for those involved in malpractice suits or divorce actions. If you move assets merely to avoid litigation that's current or clearly visible, that likely will be considered a *fraudulent conveyance* and will not be honored.

In practice, the sooner you erect your barriers, the better. Some jurisdictions have time limits, after which your asset protection will be even stronger. In the Cook Islands, for example, if no creditor brings an action within one year of setting up the trust, the trust will be considered bona fide and not fraudulent.

Naturally, you'll need to work with a lawyer who's experienced in international asset protection and, just as naturally, such services aren't inexpensive. Expect to spend $15,000 just to create a garden-variety asset-protection trust, plus $2,000 or so each year for administration. If you have an extremely large and complex estate, you may want to set up separate trusts to protect different classes of assets, such as securities, real estate and an art collection.

Therefore, these trusts make sense mainly for those with high liability risks. With an offshore trust–limited partnership in place, you may be able to recoup some of the cost by cutting back on liability insurance. Also, some of your fees and related expenses may be tax-deductible.

Dealing from Strength

Remember, the use of a family partnership and offshore trust doesn't mean you can act illegally or recklessly with impunity from collection. Instead, it's a strategy that can give you tremendous bargaining power when you're involved in a legitimate dispute.

Take the case of Paul, a real-estate developer who had borrowed heavily using his property as security. When his real-estate venture soured, the lender refused to foreclose and take the illiquid property.

Instead, the lender wanted to go after Paul's liquid assets—stocks, bonds, etc.

Paul, however, had previously established a family limited partnership in the United States and an Isle of Man trust. He said to the lender, if you want my other assets, you'll have to incur enormous time and expense trying to recover from my limited partnership and my foreign trust, with no certainty that you'll wind up with anything. Faced with this reality, the lender settled for the property that secured the loan.

Or take the case of Dr. Lou, who didn't carry malpractice insurance because he thought it was a "magnet" for lawsuits. Then he encountered the threat of a lawsuit against his personal assets.

Dr. Lou negotiated with the plaintiff's lawyer. Why risk your 40 percent contingency fee, the doctor argued. All my assets are protected by a limited partnership and an offshore trust, and 75 percent of my wages are exempt from any judgment under state law. The lawyer, figuring that 40 percent of something beat a possible 0 percent of a bigger claim, settled for a relatively small sum.

So a family limited partnership, combined with an offshore trust, won't make you completely judgment-proof. Nothing can in the United States today. But this powerful combination can enhance your bargaining position and make the playing field more level.

We can't emphasize how important it is to work with a knowledgeable lawyer in this area. Ask if he or she has ever put together this asset-protection combination; get references and check them.

On the other hand, don't be scared away by the idea of going offshore. A well-planned trust is not hard to administer. "Of all the offshore trusts I've set up," says Engel, "no client has ever come back and said, 'Gee, what did I get myself into?'"

- You may have wealth today but not tomorrow if you wind up on the wrong end of a huge liability award.
- If your assets are held in a family limited partnership, with 99 percent assigned to the limited partnership interests, you have strong protection against creditors. Creditors have few rights to assets held by limited partners.

- As an added protection, an offshore asset-protection trust makes it even more difficult for creditors to take property from you.
- The Isle of Man, in the Irish Sea, and the Cook Islands, in the South Pacific, are excellent jurisdictions for asset-protection trusts.
- The combination of a family limited partnership and an offshore trust may not give you absolute protection, but it puts you in a strong negotiating position when disputes arise.
- To avoid charges of fraud, your asset-protection strategy should be in place before you're faced with litigation.
- Asset protection should not be undertaken lightly. Make an effort to be certain your lawyer is experienced in this area.

15 Henry Ford, John D. Rockefeller— And You

Press accounts of American "greed" make it seem that we're all strictly out for Number One, in a desperate race to wind up with the highest numbers on our personal balance sheets. But that's not the case. The United States leads the world, far and away, in contributions to charities, schools, hospitals, religious organizations, etc.

Think about it. You're probably motivated by economic concerns; who isn't? But at the same time, you likely write a check to your alma mater, to cancer research, to a school for handicapped children, to an international relief agency. Therefore, when it comes to wealth transfer, you may well want to provide for others besides your family.

When you consider charitable contributions, you probably think of all those organizations that fill your mailbox every day, soliciting contributions. Those are *public charities.* Most organizations set up for religious, educational, scientific or benevolent purposes qualify as public charities, as long as they don't try to influence legislation, spread propaganda or benefit a specific individual.

But you don't have to make your donations through a public charity. You've probably heard of the Ford Foundation or the Rockefeller Foundation. Those are *private foundations,* essentially, personal charities. You don't have to be a Ford or a Rockefeller—you may have a relatively modest estate—to benefit from a private foundation.

Free To Change Your Mind

What are the advantages of a private foundation? Mainly, control. Suppose you give $500,000 to the Red Cross. That's it. The Red Cross can do whatever it likes with your $500,000. If the Red Cross does something five years from now that you don't care for, you can't ask for a refund.

Suppose that one month after your gift to the Red Cross, you learn that Mount Sinai Medical Center has made a breakthrough in AIDS research that you'd like to support. Unfortunately you can't, because you've already contributed so generously to the Red Cross.

A private foundation can help you deal with this problem. Instead of giving $500,000 to the Red Cross, you give $500,000 to the Jane Johnson Foundation. You get an immediate tax deduction and you remove the $500,000 from your taxable estate, just as you would with a gift to the Red Cross.

With a private foundation, though, you can name yourself as trustee or executive director and stay in control. You might, for example, invest in 8.5 percent Treasury bonds and thus earn $42,500 per year (tax-exempt, because of your foundation's charitable status). The $42,500 can be contributed to the Red Cross each year.

If you eventually lose your love for the Red Cross, or want to sponsor AIDS research instead, that's easy enough to do. As executive director, you merely decide to send your $42,500 somewhere else in a given year. Or you decide to split the $42,500 contribution among several charities.

Forget-Me-Not

Besides control, there are other advantages to establishing a private foundation. Recognition, for example. If you give $500,000 to a public charity in a lump sum, you'll get 10 minutes of effusive thanks and then nothing. With a private foundation, and the power to distribute the proceeds in any direction each year, you'll get your 10 minutes of glory every year.

Moreover, you'll have a chance to provide meaningful employment— and substantial compensation—to your children, grandchildren and more distant descendants. You can name them as replacement trustees or directors to succeed you after your death.

A private foundation must distribute at least 5 percent of its assets each year. Let's say you leave $2 million to a private foundation and that the foundation earns 9 percent per year, or $180,000. Of that $180,000, $100,000 (5 percent of $2 million) must go to recognized charities. The other $80,000 can go to legitimate expenses, including salaries for your descendants.

If you leave $2 million to a private foundation, you likely will have substantial other assets, so your children won't go hungry. Still, as the saying goes: You can never be too rich, too thin or have too much income.

Building a Good Foundation for Your Business

What other benefits are there to a private foundation? If you donate appreciated assets, you won't have to pay tax on the accumulated gains. (That's similar to making a gift to a charitable remainder trust, as we've seen in Chapter 7.)

There may be special benefits for small-business owners. To reduce estate tax, you might contribute nonvoting stock to your private foundation. This will get some of the company's value out of your taxable estate without relinquishing control.

Suppose SignWrite Co. is in the business of producing telecommunications equipment for deaf people. The SignWrite Foundation could be established and nonvoting shares of SignWrite could be given to it. The owners of SignWrite have full control and a smaller estate tax burden. Through dividends from SignWrite Co., the SignWrite Foundation could receive enough cash to make its charitable contributions.

For those charitable contributions, the SignWrite Foundation supports research into communications for the hearing-impaired. It gives scholarships to hearing-impaired students. It buys equipment for donations to inner-city schools that otherwise wouldn't be able to provide for the hearing-impaired. Thus, SignWrite increases its visibility and goodwill among professionals dealing with the hearing-impaired, the ones who'll make the decisions on which equipment will be purchased. (It must be noted, though, that there are limits on how much stock a private foundation can hold in one particular company, how long it can hold that stock and what kinds of business interests a foundation can own.)

Win with This Triple Play

A private foundation may mix nicely with other planning strategies we've already discussed: the tax-free inheritance trust and the charitable remainder trust.

Take the example of Sam, who inherited a huge block of blue-chip stocks from his parents. After Sam receives the stock, it has appreciated from $1 million to $5 million in value, so Sam would owe well over $1 million in capital-gains taxes if he were to sell his shares. If he decides not to sell, his children could owe $2.75 million in estate tax at a 55 percent rate.

So Sam has created a charitable remainder trust, to which he donated the $5 million worth of stock. Acting as trustee, Sam has sold all the stock. Because the trust is tax-exempt, it avoided that huge capital-gains tax. Then Sam reinvested that $5 million in 30-year Treasury bonds, locking in a yield over 8 percent. Charitable remainder trusts, as we mentioned, turn over all their assets to a charity after the income recipients (Sam and Sue) die. Thus, Sam and his wife Sue will get over $400,000 per year in annual income for the rest of their lives. That's around $260,000 per year after income taxes. After Sam and his wife die, the $5 million will go to the Sam Smith Foundation, which he has created.

The foundation's 5 percent charitable obligation will be $250,000 per year. That will leave an extra $150,000 per year to pay the foundation's expenses, including salaries to the directors, Sam's children. It's likely that $75,000 or more will be available indefinitely as annual salaries.

The only problem, as you can see, is that Sam's children stand to lose $2.25 million. That is, if Sam and Sue hold onto the shares until they die, the children will inherit $5 million worth of stock and owe perhaps $2.75 million in estate tax, leaving them with $2.25 million.

So Sam has established a tax-free inheritance trust and named his children as trustees. The children have bought $2 million worth of insurance, payable to them after Sam and Sue die. Thus they'll eventually receive $2 million tax-free.

Where will the trust get the money to pay the insurance premiums? Don't forget, Sam gets a tax deduction from his donation to the charitable remainder trust. Considering his age and that of his spouse, his tax deduction will be $1.5 million, which he can take over the next six years. In a 35 percent tax bracket, a $1.5 million deduction will be worth $525,000 in tax savings. That $525,000, paid over 10 years of insurance premiums, should be enough to purchase a $2 million second-to-die life insurance policy.

So here's how the strategies compare:

1. Do nothing; hold onto $5 million worth of stock

Income to Sam and Sue (dividends @ 4%)	$200,000/year
After-tax income (35% bracket)	$130,000/year
Estate value of stock (assumes no appreciation)	$5,000,000
Estate taxes (55 percent estate-tax bracket)	($2,750,000)
Inheritance for children ($5,000,000 – $2,750,000)	$2,250,000

2. Sell stock; pay capital-gains tax; reinvest remainder in Treasury bonds

Value of stock	$5,000,000
Capital gain	$4,000,000
(appreciation since Sam's inheritance)	
Capital-gains tax (35% of $4,000,000)	($1,400,000)
After-tax proceeds ($5,000,000 – $1,400,000)	$3,600,000
Income to Sam and Sue (in 8% Treasury bonds)	$288,000/year
After-tax income (exempt from state taxes)	$200,000/year
Estate value of bonds	$3,600,000
Estate tax (@ 55%)	($1,980,000)
Inheritance for children ($3,600,000 – $1,980,000)	$1,620,000

3. "Triple Play" Strategy: Tax-Free Inheritance Trust—Charitable Remainder Trust— Private Foundation

Value of stock donated to charitable remainder trust	$5,000,000
Tax on sale of stock	$0
After-tax proceeds to be reinvested	$5,000,000
Income to Sam and Sue (in 8% Treasury bonds)	$400,000/year
After-tax income (@ 35% tax rate)	$260,000/year

Tax deduction for contribution	$1,500,000
Tax savings (@ 35%)	$525,000
Insurance coverage purchased by tax savings	$2,000,000
Tax-free insurance proceeds to children	$2,000,000
Children's salary from private foundation	$75,000/year

Comparing Strategy 3 with Strategy 1, you can see that Sam and Sue will receive twice as much lifetime income with our "triple play" while their children receive almost as much of an inheritance. Compared with Strategy 2, the triple play provides higher income to Sam and Sue as well as more of an inheritance for their children.

You might say that Sam and Sue are giving up growth potential if they switch from stocks to bonds. That's true. But they're also eliminating the risk that the market will crash and the stock will fall in value. Or they could take some of the extra income (Strategy 3 versus Strategy 1) and increase the insurance coverage to $3 million or $4 million to offset lost potential appreciation.

Besides, look at the extra benefits from our triple play. For an indefinite time period, Sam's legacy will provide $250,000 per year to deserving charities. What's more, his children and their children and their children, etc. will have the responsibility of deciding how the largess will be provided. That's a lifetime of meaningful work, in addition to perhaps $75,000 in annual salary they'll receive for performing this work.

Build Your Foundation with Care

Private foundations have their uses, as we've seen, especially if you combine one with a tax-free inheritance trust and a charitable remainder trust. However, they're not for everyone. What are some of the drawbacks?

They're expensive to establish. The up-front legal costs likely will run from $3,500 to $7,000. And they must be legitimate. That is, you must make regular contributions for qualified purposes, and you need to keep books and records to show how you arrived at your decisions and how you used the money.

There are strict rules against *self-dealing*, too. For example, the Smith Family Foundation can't be established for the purpose of sending little

Smiths to prep school and college. All salaries should be earned, with enough documentation to show that the work actually was performed.

If you give money to a private foundation, either directly or through a charitable remainder trust, the tax benefits will be less than what they would be if you had contributed to a public charity. Suppose your adjusted gross income (AGI) is $100,000 per year. You can deduct gifts of appreciated property to public charities up to 30 percent of AGI. Gifts to private foundations are limited to 20 percent of AGI, or $20,000 in this example. In either case you have up to six years to use the writeoff, but, if you donate large sums to a private foundation and you have a relatively low AGI, you may lose some of your tax benefit.

In our example above, Sam gets a $1.5 tax deduction for the remainder value of his stock. He can spread that over six years at $250,000 per year. But unless his AGI is at least $1.25 million per year, he won't be able to use his full deduction. (If that's a concern, Sam might make a partial donation of his stock.)

So you have to proceed carefully to make sure a private foundation works for you. In general, you need a donation of at least $2 million to make it worthwhile to set up a private foundation.

- Not all charitable contributions need go to public charities. You can establish a private foundation to serve as your family's personal charity.
- With a private foundation, you retain control over charitable beneficiaries during your lifetime, and your heirs have that control in the future.
- You can arrange for your children, grandchildren, etc. to be salaried employees of your private foundation indefinitely.
- Business owners may reduce estate tax and promote their companies through a private foundation.
- Private foundations can be particularly powerful when combined with a tax-free inheritance trust and a charitable remainder trust.
- Private foundations are expensive to create and require careful administration.

- There are strict rules against using a private foundation primarily to benefit members of your own family.
- Tax benefits are lower for contributions to a private foundation than for gifts to public charities.

16 The 15 Percent Solution

Virtually every week, some bureaucrat or legislator in Washington bemoans the low savings rate in the United States. Back in 1986, however, Washington passed a punitive tax on savers. Now, if you save "too much," you'll face a triple tax when you transfer wealth to your family.

Here's how it works: You probably know that retirement plan distributions are subject to income tax. Moreover, if you take *excess distributions* from qualified retirement plans, you'll be hit with a 15 percent excise tax on top of the regular income tax. At present anything over $150,000 in one year, or over $750,000 in a lump sum, is an excess distribution. (There may be limited exceptions if you made a "grandfather" election after the law was passed.) In a few years, indexing will kick in, raising the $150,000 and $750,000 limits each year.

Suppose you take $200,000 out of your retirement plans in 1992. The entire $200,000 will be subject to income tax, perhaps at an effective rate of 35 percent, including state and local taxes. In addition, $50,000—the excess over $150,000—will be taxed an extra 15 percent.

Retirement plan distribution in 1992	$200,000	
Income tax @ 35%		$70,000
Excess distribution		
($200,000 – $150,000 allowance)	$50,000	
Excise tax @ 15%		$7,500
Total tax		$77,500
After-tax distribution	$122,500	

Your natural reaction may be to avoid this 15 percent surtax. You don't need $200,000 per year to live, so you withdraw only $150,000 per year. Now you're paying only income taxes.

With this approach, though, your retirement plans (IRAs, Keoghs, corporate plans) will continue to grow, tax-deferred. After your death and the death of your spouse, the "excess" amount—calculated according to actuarial tables—will be taxed at 15 percent. If you die at age 70, for example, anything in your qualified plans over $961,000 will be subject to the 15 percent excise tax. (The exact number changes from month to month as the IRS publishes new tables reflecting current interest rates.)

Now your family faces a triple tax. Your estate will owe a 15 percent excise tax on the "excess" buildup. Your net pension principal after the excise tax will be included in your estate and be subject to estate tax of around 50 percent. Finally, your estate will owe the income taxes you've deferred by putting money into a retirement plan.

Suppose you retire at age 65 and have a spouse who's 61. At that point, you have $750,000 in your qualified plan. You die first and your spouse lives until age 85. Assuming your retirement plans grow at just 3 percent after distributions, your spouse will leave a balance of $1.5 million. Now the IRS will step in:

Balance in qualified retirement plans	$1,500,000	
Amount subject to excise tax ($1.5 million – $579,000)	$921,000	
Excise tax @ 15%		$138,150
Amount subject to estate tax ($1.5 million – $138,150 in excise tax)	$1,361,850	
Estate tax @ 50%		$680,925
Amount subject to income tax ($1.5 million – $680,925 in estate tax)	$819,075	
Income tax @ 35%		$286,676
Total taxes		$1,105,751
After-tax distribution to heirs	$349,249	

That's right. Incredible as it seems, your reward for saving diligently over the decades will be to see 74 percent of your retirement plan taxed away! Your family will wind up with only 26 percent: $349,249 out of $1.5 million.

With dollars like these at stake, the pension fund triple tax is a formidable threat. You have a great deal of discretion when taking money out of a large qualified plan, so what's the best way to do it?

Don't focus solely on tax savings. Suppose you have a large qualified plan and you begin taking annual $150,000 distributions from your plan early, perhaps starting at age 60. You'd pay no excise tax while you're alive and you'd reduce your plan so that your family will owe little or no excise tax at your spouse's death. Also, a smaller pension principal means less estate tax to pay.

But that's letting the tail wag the dog. By taking early distributions from the retirement plan to cut taxes, you're stunting your plan's (tax-free) growth. The estate—even the after-tax estate—likely will be smaller than it might have been if the retirement plan had been allowed more years of compounding.

Suppose in our example you and your surviving spouse took large distributions and managed to reduce the retirement plan to $579,000, so no 15 percent excise tax will be due:

Balance in qualified retirement plans	$579,000	
Amount subject to excise tax	$0	
Excise tax		$0
Amount subject to estate tax	$579,000	
Estate tax @ 50%		$289,500
Amount subject to income tax ($579,000 – $289,500)	$289,500	
Income tax @ 35%		$101,325
Total tax		$390,825
After-tax distribution to heirs ($579,000 – $390,825)	$188,175	

Now the total tax bill would be reduced from $1.1 million to $390,825. That may sound good, until you realize that your family would wind up with $188,175 rather than $349,000. You'd truly be cutting off your nose to spite your face.

Moreover, if you take large amounts out of your retirement plan to avoid the excise tax, any distributed money left in your hands will be included in your taxable estate, subject to estate tax.

Does that mean your best strategy is to do nothing—let your retirement plan grow until age 70½, when you're required to take distributions, and then take the minimum distributions? Not really. You're almost certain to pile up hefty excise, income and estate taxes that way.

There's another problem with this do-nothing strategy. If most of your assets are tied up in retirement plans, you or your spouse may not have assets available to leave to your children at the first death. So you might not be able to use your $600,000 estate-tax exemption fully.

Coping with Tax Complification

Coping with such complexities of the federal tax code isn't simple, but here are some tips for dealing with this triple tax threat:

1. Retirement plans are primarily for retirement income. If you're dependent upon distributions for a comfortable lifestyle, don't stint. Take out enough so that you'll have enough to live on after tax. (If you take out $60,000, for example, you'll still have $39,000 to spend after paying a 35 percent income tax.)
2. Make sure that each spouse has enough assets outside of retirement plans to leave $600,000 to nonspousal beneficiaries (probably your children). If your spouse doesn't have enough assets, you might begin retirement plan distributions in your 60s in order to move enough assets outside your retirement plan to your spouse, so you both can fully use your $600,000 estate-tax exemptions. (Distributions before age 59½ should be avoided, because there's a 10 percent penalty tax.)
3. What if you have enough money outside your retirement plan to make those $600,000 bequests and you don't need the retirement plan distributions for income? One strategy is to take early distributions, pay just the income tax, but give the money to your children. You and

your spouse can give up to $20,000 per year to each of your children, and, if desired, to each child's spouse and each grandchild. If done correctly, this will help thin down your retirement plan so you'll avoid the 15 percent excise tax. The gifts will move the money out of your estate and reduce your estate-tax obligation.

What about the tax-deferred growth you give up, by moving money out of your retirement plan? If they don't need the money for living expenses, your children can invest those $20,000 gifts in tax-free bonds, annuities or their own retirement plans. You may want to make gifts in trust, to encourage long-term accumulation.

4. Buy second-to-die life insurance with retirement plan distributions after paying the income tax. These policies, which pay off after the death of both spouses, are relatively inexpensive. Counting the life-insurance proceeds (tax free, if held in a tax-free inheritance trust) your total estate may be maximized.

   In our example, with a 65-year-old husband and a 61-year-old spouse, they could take out $40,000 per year, pay the tax and invest part of the remainder (about $20,000) in a second-to-die policy for around 10 years. That would provide $1 million to be passed on to their children free of all taxes, in addition to whatever they get from the couple's retirement plan.

5. Don't assume that there's a "magic bullet" when it comes to reducing this tax triple threat. Go over the different scenarios carefully with your CPA or financial planner. Insist that your adviser use a sophisticated computer spreadsheet that compares various alternative strategies and comes up with the one likely to provide the most wealth for you to transfer to your family.

- Whenever you take money out of a qualified plan, you have to pay income taxes. (There's an exception if it's money that you have contributed yourself without getting a tax deduction.)
- After you and your spouse die, any money left in retirement plans will be subject to estate taxes.
- After paying estate tax, the money left in a retirement plan will be subject to income taxes.

- "Excess" retirement plan amounts (as determined by IRS tables) are also subject to a 15 percent excise tax.
- Altogether, 75 percent (or more) of the balance in your retirement plan may be lost in taxes.
- Planning for this triple taxation is extremely difficult. Your prime goal should be maximizing the amount that goes to you and your family. Leave too much in a retirement plan and you'll pay punitive taxes; take too much out and you'll stunt the fund's tax-deferred growth.
- A computer spreadsheet may be used to find the best strategy.
- Enough money should be withdrawn from your plan so that each spouse can use the $600,000 estate-tax exemption.
- Money withdrawn from a retirement plan, if not needed for living expenses, may be given to family members to avoid estate tax, or invested in life insurance to increase your total estate.

17

Gambling with Death

Robert is the owner of a small business worth $2 million, which he plans to leave to his daughter Randi. If he leaves it to her in his will, she could owe around $1 million in estate tax at a 50 percent rate.

Another possibility (see Chapter 13) would be for Robert and Randi to enter into a buy-sell agreement. At Robert's death, Randi would be obligated to buy the company from his estate, which would be obligated to sell to her. In either case, Randi may rely upon life-insurance proceeds to raise the money that will be needed.

But what if Robert is in poor health and is *uninsurable?* (That is, no insurance company can be found to provide adequate coverage at reasonable rates.) How will Randi come up with $1 million?

One strategy that might work in this case is a *private annuity* between Robert and Randi. A private annuity is similar to the commercial annuities offered by life-insurance companies, brokers, mutual funds and so on. A pays money to B; B promises a lifetime income to A.

Here, rather than money, Robert transfers his company to Randi and Randi promises a lifetime income to Robert. What happens? If it's done right, Robert can transfer his entire company to Randi with no gift or estate tax.

On the Table

There are two keys to a private annuity. First, all property must be transferred at fair market value, as attested by an independent appraisal. Second, the transaction must conform to tables published by the IRS. These tables, which change periodically, reflect the age of the donor and the interest-rate environment at the time of the transfer. From these tables, Robert and Randi can determine a "fair" level of annuity payments.

The older Robert is, the shorter his life expectancy. Because Randi's payments are expected to be spread over fewer years, each payment will have to be greater. (Conversely, the younger Robert is, the smaller each payment will have to be.)

Similarly, the higher the prevailing level of interest rates at the time of the transfer, the greater the annuity payments Robert will receive.

As an example, suppose Robert's age is 65 when he gives Randi a company valued at $2 million. Robert's life expectancy is 20 years; assume current IRS tables mandate a 10 percent interest rate. Therefore, Randi must promise to pay Robert $280,848 per year for the rest of his life.

If such a bargain is struck and it's carried out, Robert can transfer his company to Randi with no gift tax and no estate tax while deferring income tax on his capital gain. In addition, Robert will receive substantial lifetime income.

Long-Term Hitch

As we've described them so far, private annuities sound great. Yet they're used infrequently. Why aren't they used more often in wealth transfer?

For one thing, the cash requirements can be great. In this example, Randi has to come up with $280,848 per year. Possibly the company can generate that much income, plus enough for her to live on. But that's not certain. The problem is even greater if a private annuity involves a transfer of assets (real estate, for example) that has a low yield. Then where will the money come from?

Suppose, in our example, Randi only pays Robert $120,000 per year, not $280,848. By the IRS annuity table, her payment would be adequate for an $854,500 asset transfer. The excess $1,145,500 ($2 million minus $854,500) will be treated as a taxable gift.

Randi will have other problems, too. Of all the payments she makes, nothing will be deductible. If Robert lives to be 100 or more, Randi is obliged to keep paying him $280,848 every year. Moreover, all those $280,848 payments will pile up in Robert's estate. Unless he spends the money or gives it away, Randi may wind up paying estate tax when her father dies.

For Robert, the deal is not without perils, either. The $280,848 he receives each year may be heavily taxed. Assuming his basis in the company's shares is $100,000, only $5,000 of each payment will be a tax-free return of capital. Each year he'll owe tax on a $95,000 capital gain and $180,848 in taxable interest income.

Also, for a private annuity to work it must be unsecured. Therefore, if Randi doesn't make the requisite payments, Robert is out of luck. Suppose Randi makes three $280,000 payments and then stops. The IRS likely will treat the transaction as a sale for $842,544. The difference between the $842,544 Randi paid and the $2 million the company is worth may be a $1,157,456 taxable gift, generating a gift-tax obligation for Robert.

Last, the transaction will be set aside if the donor has a terminal illness at the time of the transfer, as noted above.

So when can a private annuity make sense?

1. If the asset to be transferred generates substantial cash flow
2. If the person making the transfer is in poor health, with a life expectancy shorter than the tables suggest, but certainly never where death is imminent
3. If there's substantial trust between donor and recipient

If all those ifs are in place, a private annuity may work. Randi pays Robert for a few years, Robert dies and Randi owns the company with no further obligations.

- A private annuity is a contract between parties. One gives an asset to the other; the recipient promises to pay the donor a lifetime income.
- When the donor dies, no further payments are due.
- Assets may be transferred without paying gift or income tax.
- The recipient is obligated to make substantial payments to the donor, no matter how long the donor lives.
- If the recipient defaults, the donor is stuck with no asset, no income and perhaps a sizable gift-tax obligation.

- Private annuities work best between family members, where there is mutual trust. The best situations may be those where a parent or grandparent is in poor health, so probably won't live very long, but does not yet have a terminal illness.

POLICY MATTERS

18 The Short-Term View

We've mentioned life insurance more than a few times so far in this book as a wealth-transfer tool. In our strategies, life insurance often provides much of the wealth you'll transfer to your family. Life insurance isn't always the answer, but it's too important to ignore.

The premise of life insurance is simple. You pay money to a life-insurance company to buy a policy. When the insured individual dies, the insurance company pays money to the beneficiary or beneficiaries you've named. Despite all the efforts in recent years to dress up life insurance in more fashionable garb, the essence hasn't changed.

On the surface, this is a strange bargain. You're paying money that you could be spending or investing right now. You won't enjoy that money: your beneficiaries will collect after you're dead. So why bother?

Because life insurance serves a purpose. When you die, your income (among other functions) will stop. Life insurance is a means of taking care of anyone who depends on your income.

Let's look at John, a bachelor with no living relations except his parents, who enjoy a comfortable income. If John dies, he'll be missed by parents and friends, but no one will suffer financial hardship. There's no need for his life to be insured.

John marries Joan. They're both well-educated, successful professionals. Again, if one dies, the other will grieve. But the survivor will keep working and earning a living. There's still no reason to buy life insurance.

Enter the twins, Jim and Jan. Now, what happens if John dies? Sure, Joan may keep working, but who'll pay for the housekeepers and the baby-sitters and the day-care centers the twins will need? Where will all the money come from for clothes and schools and phone calls? And what happens if John and Joan die together, leaving two orphans?

Unless either John or Joan comes from a wealthy family who can raise the twins with no financial strain, they now need life insurance. If Joan or John dies, the survivor will receive a chunk of cash when it's most needed, with no delays for probate. The life-insurance proceeds, along with the earned interest, can ease the burden during the years ahead.

Pure Insurance

Therefore, if you have dependents, you probably need life insurance. How much? That's a subject beyond the scope of this book. In general, you need to sit down with a paper and pencil to figure out how much your family will need to replace your lost income.

Once you come up with a number, you have to decide which type of insurance to buy. In most cases, our prototypical couple with young children and decades of high expenses ahead of them will be better off buying *term insurance,* the purest kind.

Term insurance is life insurance stripped down to or close to the bare minimum. You pay a premium to an insurance company for a certain term, or time period. If you die during that term, your family collects the *face value* of the policy. (If you've bought a $100,000 policy, your beneficiaries receive $100,000.) If you don't die, you pay another premium for another term. And so on. Often, the term is one year.

What's the advantage of term insurance? It's the cheapest form of insurance. A healthy 35-year-old male who doesn't smoke might buy $500,000 worth of term insurance for $530 in the first year, as shown in Table 18-1. This is certainly a modest amount to pay for so much peace of mind.

What's the disadvantage of term insurance? It gets more expensive as you grow older. As our 35-year-old hits 40, 45, 50, etc., he becomes more and more likely to die according to actuarial tables. Therefore, life insurers will charge him $650 per year, $880, etc. If he reaches 90, say, or 95, his term premium might be around $100,000 per year. What insurance company will bet that even the healthiest 95-year-old, eating yogurt and playing squash, will live out another year?

Table 18-1
Term Insurance Premiums,
$500,000 Face-Value Policy

Annual Policy Premium $530.00   Preferred nonsmoker
Male age 35   Dividends buy paid-up additions

Beg of Yr	Att Age	Current Premium	Guaranteed Maximum Annual Premium	Beg of Yr	Att Age	Current Premium	Guaranteed Maximum Annual Premium
1	35	530	530	34	68	7,355	22,165
2	36	550	1,450	35	69	8,205	24,350
3	37	570	1,555	36	70	9,150	26,830
4	38	595	1,675	37	71	10,215	29,635
5	39	620	1,805	38	72	11,410	32,760
6	40	650	1,955	39	73	12,750	36,220
7	41	685	2,125	40	74	14,235	39,990
8	42	730	2,305	41	75	15,880	44,085
9	43	775	2,500	42	76	17,700	48,575
10	44	835	2,710	43	77	19,730	53,840
11	45	880	2,935	44	78	22,375	61,420
12	46	940	3,175	45	79	26,225	70,605
13	47	1,015	3,430	46	80	31,430	79,815
14	48	1,095	3,705	47	81	37,350	85,290
15	49	1,185	4,010	48	82	43,055	87,485
16	50	1,290	4,355	49	83	48,420	87,485
17	51	1,395	4,745	50	84	53,795	87,485
18	52	1,520	5,185	51	85	59,545	88,055
19	53	1,670	5,680	52	86	65,625	89,990
20	54	1,845	6,225	53	87	72,000	94,050
21	55	2,040	6,815	54	88	78,875	99,920
22	56	2,240	7,445	55	89	86,515	106,900
23	57	2,440	8,120	56	90	95,205	114,395
24	58	2,645	8,850	57	91	105,270	122,505
25	59	2,855	9,645	58	92	118,075	131,795
26	60	3,100	10,535	59	93	136,655	143,455
27	61	3,385	11,535	60	94	136,655	159,825
28	62	3,740	12,660	61	95	136,655	185,375
29	63	4,165	13,925	62	96	136,655	227,700
30	64	4,670	15,320	63	97	136,655	295,125
31	65	5,245	16,835	64	98	136,655	372,315
32	66	5,885	18,465	65	99	136,655	495,610
33	67	6,590	20,230				

NOTE: This table is an illustration only. The figures can change from company to company and as interest rates rise and fall.

Suppose you're 90 and the term premium is $95,000 per year, so you don't pay it. Now if you die, there is no insurance in force and your beneficiaries receive nothing.

You can see where term insurance makes sense. John and Joan don't expect to have any children except their twins. In 20 or 25 years, the twins will be through with their education and earning their own living if all goes well. They'll no longer be dependents. Because their insurance need is for a finite term—or at least it seems so now—and their disposable income is limited, they're probably better off with term insurance.

Safety First

If term insurance suits your needs, how should you go about selecting the right policy? You can shop for the lowest-cost choice. In fact, there are several services that can survey the market for you via computer and tell you which term insurance policies will cost the least.

We don't think that's the way to go, at least not initially. Before you worry about saving $20 or $30 a year on term insurance, you want to be sure the insurance company will be around to pay off.

You've certainly read about the S&L fiasco. Insurance companies invest in many of the same vehicles as S&Ls: real estate, mortgages, corporate bonds. That doesn't mean the insurance industry will go the way of S&Ls. Many S&Ls were thinly capitalized and ineptly managed, to put it kindly (some would say fraudulently managed). Insurance companies, on the other hand, generally have deeper pockets and higher-quality portfolios.

There are exceptions to this rule, and some insurers may go under. Weak insurers may be the ones charging the lowest premiums to lure customers. Again, the risks are low, but why take a chance if you can reduce it?

Therefore, you should insist upon certain standards from your life insurance company. For example, your insurer should be over 100 years old and have at least $1 billion in assets.

If a company has been around for over 100 years, it has managed to survive depressions, recessions, crises and panics. It's likely to be around long enough to pay off on your policy.

Why is size so important? Because the bigger a company is, the less likely the government will let it go under. Back in the 1970s, for example, Washington led a bailout of GEICO, the huge Government Employees Insurance Company. So, although insurers such as Equitable Life Assurance Society are rumored to be in serious financial difficulty, a failure like that would be such a catastrophe that the politicians probably won't let it happen. (Continental Illinois Bank, another huge financial institution, also was rescued because it was judged "too big to fail." As of this writing, Executive Life Insurance is in trouble, but bailout efforts are under way.) Small insurers, though, enjoy no such security, so there's safety in numbers. Big numbers.

There may be safety in ratings, too. A.M. Best has long been known for rating insurance companies and their financial conditions. Recently, though, A.M. Best has been criticized for being too lenient. Some well-rated companies have run into trouble. Thus, you should run, not walk, from any insurer rated less than A+ from A.M. Best.

For extra safety, double-check even on companies rated A+ by A.M. Best. Standard & Poor's, Moody's and Duff & Phelps, best known for rating bonds, also rate insurance companies for their claims-paying ability. Look for an AA or AAA rating from one of these companies, in addition to an A+ from A.M. Best.

Once you have all the ingredients—longevity, size, top ratings—you can be reasonably sure of a life insurer's financial health. Then you can go shopping for the lowest price among the companies who meet all these criteria.

What else should you look for in a term policy? It should be *guaranteed renewable.* That is, as long as you keep paying the required premiums, the company can't arbitrarily cancel your policy.

Another desirable feature is *convertibility.* A convertible term policy can be converted to some form of permanent insurance (see the section "Pay Now Rather than Later," below), issued by the same company.

Why should you bother with convertible term? There may come a point in your life when you decide that permanent life insurance is better for you than term. Usually that means taking a physical exam.

Suppose your health has deteriorated over the years, to the point where you can't get insurance. With convertible term you have the right to convert to permanent life insurance at some cost. Considering that the cost of this conversion privilege is practically nil in most policies, it pays to add this sort of health insurance to your life insurance.

- Life insurance is a must if you have dependents who'll suffer financially in case of your death and the consequent loss of your income.
- Term insurance provides coverage for a specific time period. It's the cheapest form of life insurance.
- As you get older, term insurance becomes more expensive.
- If you see a time when your need for life insurance will drop or disappear altogether, term insurance probably is the best choice.
- Limit your selection to insurance companies that are at least 100 years old, have over $1 billion in assets, are rated A+ by A.M. Best and have either an AA or AAA rating from Standard & Poor's, Moody's or Duff & Phelps before shopping for price.
- Term policies should be guaranteed renewable and convertible to permanent life insurance.

Forever Yours

Do you remember the days when you first had children? Perhaps you went to work while your spouse stayed home with the kids. More likely than not, your spouse needed a station wagon to haul youngsters, friends, strollers, toys, spare clothing, shopping bags, etc.

When your kids grew older and the strollers disappeared, a four-door sedan probably replaced the station wagon. Now, with the kids out of the house, your spouse may ride around in a sleek BMW.

The car that met your needs yesterday may not be right for you today. The same goes for life insurance. The policy that worked for family protection when you owned a station wagon may not be suitable for wealth transfer now that you're in a BMW.

Pay Now Rather than Later

If term insurance as described in a previous section isn't the right answer, what is? The alternative to term insurance is *permanent life insurance.* While term insurance covers only a specific time period, permanent insurance endures until you die as long as you pay the required premiums.

How does permanent insurance work? As you remember, a 35-year-old man who wanted $500,000 worth of term life insurance might pay $530 per year, but his payment will increase each year to $700, $1,000, $2,000, etc., to the point where the premium can be tens of thousands of dollars per year when he becomes a "senior senior."

Permanent insurance, on the other hand, charges you a level premium, albeit one that's often much higher initially than a term premium. While our 35-year-old man can buy $500,000 worth of term insurance for $530 in the first year, to buy $500,000 worth of permanent insurance might cost $5,300 per year. That $5,300, though, is the price he'll pay year after year, with no escalations, as shown in Table 18-2.

In essence, you're playing a numbers game with the insurance company. The company may figure that you'll live another 40 years after age 35. If you pay $5,300 per year for 40 years, it will collect a total of $212,000. That $212,000, if invested well, will provide the company more than enough to pay your beneficiaries more than $500,000 when the time comes and still earn a profit, the insurer projects.

Therefore, the extra money you pay up front enables you to pay less in later years than with a term policy, and still keep your policy in force.

Cashing In

In our example, you'd pay an extra $4,770 in Year One (the $5,300 you pay minus the $530 actual cost of the insurance). What happens to that money, along with the extra $4,750 or so you pay in Year Two, etc.?

In the first year or two, much of that money goes to pay the agent's commission. After that, the excess you pay goes into a *cash value* that's a feature of permanent life insurance. Cash value is an investment account inside a permanent policy. If necessary, you can withdraw your cash value or borrow against it.

Table 18-2
Permanent Life Insurance
$500,000 Face-Value Policy

Annual Policy Premium $5,300.00   Preferred nonsmoker
Male age 35   Dividends buy paid-up additions

Beg of Yr	Att Age	End of Year Div- idend	Guar Cash Value	Cash Value of Addit Ins	Illust Cash Value	Incr in Illust Cash Value	Addi- tional Insur- ance	Illust Death Benefit
1	35	0	0	0	0	0	0	500,000
2	36	605	500	0	1,105	1,105	0	500,605
3	37	793	4,500	632	5,926	4,821	2,785	503,578
4	38	1,042	10,500	1,491	13,033	7,107	6,278	507,320
5	39	1,359	16,500	2,648	20,507	7,474	10,666	512,025
6	40	1,763	23,000	4,189	28,952	8,445	16,140	517,903
7	41	2,059	30,000	6,220	38,280	9,328	22,934	524,993
8	42	2,409	37,000	8,651	48,061	9,781	30,529	532,938
9	43	2,804	44,000	11,554	58,359	10,298	39,031	541,835
10	44	3,249	51,500	14,996	69,746	11,387	48,506	551,755
11	45	3,787	59,500	19,053	82,340	12,594	59,018	562,805
12	46	4,383	67,500	23,846	95,729	13,389	70,749	575,132
13	47	5,076	76,000	29,470	110,546	14,817	83,753	588,829
14	48	5,867	84,500	36,059	126,427	15,881	98,179	604,046
15	49	6,789	93,500	43,758	144,047	17,620	114,155	620,944
16	50	7,828	103,000	52,750	163,579	19,532	131,867	639,695
17	51	9,024	112,500	63,204	184,728	21,149	151,437	660,461
18	52	10,405	122,500	75,346	208,252	23,524	173,059	683,464
19	53	11,979	133,000	89,437	234,417	26,165	196,959	708,938
20	54	13,774	143,500	105,756	263,030	28,613	223,341	737,115
21	55	17,595	152,500	122,837	292,932	29,902	252,430	770,025
22	56	19,550	161,500	144,253	325,304	32,372	288,588	808,138
23	57	21,676	170,500	168,191	360,368	35,064	327,699	849,375
24	58	23,982	180,000	194,877	398,860	38,492	369,933	893,915
25	59	26,492	189,000	224,543	440,036	41,176	415,459	941,951
26	60	29,211	198,500	257,441	485,152	45,116	464,477	993,688
27	61	32,144	208,000	293,831	533,976	48,824	517,180	1,049,324
28	62	35,302	217,000	333,962	586,265	52,289	573,760	1,109,062
29	63	38,690	226,500	378,090	643,280	57,015	634,411	1,173,101
30	64	42,324	236,000	426,494	704,819	61,539	699,331	1,241,655

table 18-2, cont.

Beg of Yr	Att Age	End of Year Div- idend	Guar Cash Value	Cash Value of Addit Ins	Illust Cash Value	Incr in Illust Cash Value	Addi- tional Insur- ance	Illust Death Benefit
31	65	46,212	245,500	479,465	771,178	66,359	768,732	1,314,944
32	66	50,364	255,000	537,318	842,682	71,504	842,825	1,393,189
33	67	54,808	264,000	600,385	919,193	76,511	921,825	1,476,633
34	68	59,577	273,500	669,035	1,002,112	82,919	1,005,977	1,565,554
35	69	64,702	282,500	743,621	1,090,824	88,712	1,095,559	1,660,261
36	70	70,211	292,000	824,520	1,186,731	95,907	1,190,883	1,761,094
37	71	76,130	301,000	912,086	1,289,217	102,486	1,292,292	1,868,422
38	72	82,498	310,000	1,006,643	1,399,141	109,924	1,400,157	1,982,655
39	73	89,303	318,500	1,108,562	1,516,366	117,225	1,514,906	2,104,209
40	74	96,556	327,000	1,218,197	1,641,754	125,388	1,636,944	2,233,500

NOTE: This table is an illustration only. The figures can change from company to company and as interest rates rise and fall.

The cash value keeps your policy alive as you grow older. Suppose you reach the point where your term premium would have been $10,000 per year to maintain a $500,000 policy. Your premium has been frozen at $5,300 per year. Thus, the insurance company dips into your cash value for the other $4,700 needed to keep the policy in force.

The Premium Vanishes

Most insurance companies take the concept of cash value one step further. Instead of $5,300 per year for a $500,000 policy, a company might offer you the chance to pay $7,000 per year or more.

Why would you pay thousands of dollars more to buy the same insurance coverage? Because that gives you a faster buildup of cash value and enables your premium to "vanish" after a certain time period.

Let's say you pay $7,435 for 10 years. At that point, you might have $85,000 in cash value. If that $85,000 is invested in bonds earning 8.5 percent per year, the income would be over $7,000 a year: roughly, enough to pay your premiums. Thus, your obligation to write checks for further premiums would vanish. You'd pay no more premiums, yet your $500,000 life insurance would stay in force. (See Table 18-3.)

Naturally, many 35-year-olds prefer to pay a $7,435 premium for 10 years, rather than pay a $5,300 premium each year for the rest of their lives. Keep in mind, though, that vanishing-premium strategies are always based on projections of future events (interest rates, policy retention rates, mortality rates). Later we'll cover the subject of policy illustrations in some detail. For now, realize that vanishing-premium strategies are predictions, not guarantees. You may pay that $7,435 for 8 or 9 or 11 or 12 years, instead of the 10 years suggested by your agent.

Triple Shelter

A discussion of cash value also should cover the tax benefits of life insurance. All life insurance (term or permanent) delivers one tax shelter; permanent insurance offers two more, related to cash value.

The prime benefit of life insurance is that (with few exceptions) it's exempt from income tax. Suppose our 35-year-old pays his $600 term premium and dies the next week. His family collects $500,000. Some people might call that a $499,400 gain, but not the IRS. No income tax will be due. (As we've stressed throughout the book, that $500,000 in insurance proceeds will be subject to estate tax unless the proper steps have been taken.)

Permanent insurance, as we've said, includes cash value. In a given year, out of a $5,000 premium, $1,000 might go toward the cost of insurance while $4,000 goes into the cash value. That $4,000 will be invested, most likely in interest-paying bonds and mortgages. That interest won't be taxed; so the inside buildup compounds tax-free, as long as it's within an insurance policy.

If you die, the inside buildup is forgotten and your heirs receive the insurance proceeds, free of income tax. If you cash in *(surrender)* your policy, however, all the income taxes you've avoided will be taxed. This leads us to the third tax shelter: policy loans.

Most permanent life policies offer you a chance to borrow against your cash value instead of making taxable withdrawals. The proceeds from such loans are usually tax-free. (See Chapter 21, on modified endowment contracts, for a discussion of the new tax rules on policy loans.) Often the insurance companies let you borrow at below-market rates. What's more, the interest on the loans need not be paid in cash; instead, unpaid interest is added to your loan balance. (Whether or not you pay in cash, interest on policy loans generally isn't deductible.)

Let's say you borrow $50,000 from your cash value. Over the years, compound interest brings your debt balance to $80,000. When you die, the $80,000 loan balance is deducted from the $500,000 face value, and your family receives only $420,000 in insurance proceeds.

Bearing the Load

As a rule, commissions are higher for permanent insurance than for term insurance. Suppose you buy a $1 million second-to-die policy, agreeing to pay $20,000 a year for 10 years, or $200,000 altogether. Commissions vary from company to company and policy to policy, but the agent's commission might be 60 percent of the first year's premium, or $12,000. For the next nine years, the agent might get 4 percent of your premiums, or $800 per year, for servicing the policy. That's a total of $19,200 over the 10 years.

Altogether, then, 9.6 percent of your premiums go to the agent. Looking at it another way, 1.92 percent of the insurance you buy ($19,200 compared with $1 million) goes to commissions.

The question is, are you getting your money's worth for your $19,200? If you're not in for the long term, the answer is no. If you think there's any chance you'll cash your policy in before 10 years are up, don't buy permanent life insurance. Buy term insurance and pay lower premiums as well as lower sales commissions.

If you're in for the long haul, you need permanent insurance, and that means paying sales commissions such as those described above. Then the question isn't how much of a commission you're paying but what you are getting for your money. Is it worth paying $200,000 over the next 10 years to buy a $1 million policy for your children?

No matter what kind of insurance you buy, but especially for permanent insurance, you should make your agent earn his or her commission. Investigate an agent's knowledge and reputation thoroughly before making any commitment. And don't hesitate to request any help you need in dealing with your life insurance.

Table 18-3
Vanishing Premium Illustration
$500,000 Face-Value Policy

Annual Policy Premium $7,435.00   Preferred nonsmoker
Male age 35   Dividends buy paid-up additions

End of Yr	Att Age	Annual Premium	From Surrender of Additions	Annual Outlay	Ann Net Equity Incr	Net Equity	Guar Cash Value	Net Death Benefit
1	36	7,435	0	7,435	185	185	0	500,185
2	37	7,435	0	7,435	3,388	3,573	3,125	500,968
3	38	7,435	0	7,435	6,828	10,401	9,435	502,168
4	39	7,435	0	7,435	7,598	17,999	15,930	504,546
5	40	7,435	0	7,435	8,429	26,427	22,595	508,900
6	41	7,435	0	7,435	9,598	36,025	29,705	515,284
7	42	7,435	0	7,435	10,597	46,622	36,995	523,737
8	43	7,435	0	7,435	11,593	58,215	44,470	534,251
9	44	7,435	0	7,435	12,682	70,898	52,130	546,694
10	45	7,435	0	7,435	13,870	84,768	59,985	561,139
11	46	7,435	7,435	0	7,005	91,773	68,025	555,780
12	47	7,435	7,435	0	7,630	99,403	76,260	551,843
13	48	7,435	7,435	0	8,303	107,705	84,695	549,328
14	49	7,435	7,435	0	9,042	116,747	93,340	548,248
15	50	7,435	7,435	0	11,370	128,117	102,185	550,168
16	51	7,435	7,435	0	11,370	139,488	110,305	553,656
17	52	7,435	7,435	0	12,409	151,897	118,570	560,122
18	53	7,435	7,435	0	13,480	165,376	126,975	568,261
19	54	7,435	7,435	0	14,636	180,012	135,500	578,091
20	55	7,435	7,435	0	15,887	195,899	144,130	589,711
21	56	7,435	7,435	0	16,484	212,383	152,860	602,460
22	57	7,435	7,435	0	17,866	230,249	161,680	617,099
23	58	7,435	7,435	0	19,372	249,621	170,605	633,708
24	59	7,435	7,435	0	21,004	270,626	179,630	652,353
25	60	7,435	7,435	0	22,771	293,396	188,760	673,128
26	61	7,435	7,435	0	24,641	318,037	197,975	696,098
27	62	7,435	7,435	0	26,636	344,674	207,260	721,338
28	63	7,435	7,435	0	28,760	373,433	216,595	748,951
29	64	7,435	7,435	0	31,062	404,495	225,940	779,100
30	65	7,435	7,435	0	33,550	438,045	235,280	811,990

table 18-3, cont.

End of Yr	Att Age	Annual Premium	From Surrender of Additions	Annual Outlay	Ann Net Equity Incr	Net Equity	Guar Cash Value	Net Death Benefit
31	66	7,435	7,435	0	36,290	474,336	244,595	847,861
32	67	7,435	7,435	0	39,270	513,605	253,895	886,925
33	68	7,435	7,435	0	42,450	556,056	263,170	929,341
34	69	7,435	7,435	0	45,811	601,866	272,440	975,175
35	70	7,435	7,435	0	49,324	651,190	281,700	1,024,462
36	71	7,435	7,435	0	53,065	704,255	290,920	1,077,364
37	72	7,435	7,435	0	57,011	761,266	300,055	1,134,103
38	73	7,435	7,435	0	61,153	822,418	309,065	1,194,906
39	74	7,435	7,435	0	65,430	887,848	317,875	1,259,999
40	75	7,435	7,435	0	70,418	958,266	326,455	1,330,121
41	76	7,435	7,435	0	75,960	1,034,227	334,795	1,406,008
42	77	7,435	7,435	0	82,087	1,116,313	342,905	1,488,260
43	78	7,435	7,435	0	88,729	1,205,042	350,830	1,577,310
44	79	7,435	7,435	0	95,792	1,300,834	358,625	1,673,374
45	80	7,435	7,435	0	103,236	1,404,070	366,325	1,776,642
46	81	7,435	7,435	0	111,033	1,515,103	373,945	1,887,326
47	82	7,435	7,435	0	119,033	1,634,137	381,470	2,005,581
48	83	7,435	7,435	0	127,608	1,761,745	388,880	2,132,090
49	84	7,435	7,435	0	136,536	1,898,281	396,150	2,267,345
50	85	7,435	7,435	0	145,934	2,044,214	403,305	2,411,868
51	86	7,435	7,435	0	155,978	2,200,192	410,450	2,566,258
52	87	7,435	7,435	0	166,867	2,367,059	417,730	2,731,135
53	88	7,435	7,435	0	178,856	2,545,915	425,400	2,907,181
54	89	7,435	7,435	0	192,161	2,738,077	433,790	3,095,098
55	90	7,435	7,435	0	207,080	2,945,156	443,390	3,295,615
56	91	7,435	0	0	222,423	3,167,580	447,220	3,516,378
57	92	7,435	0	0	239,797	3,407,376	451,185	3,751,487
58	93	7,435	0	0	259,492	3,666,868	455,410	4,002,132
59	94	7,435	0	0	282,204	3,949,072	460,065	4,269,305
60	95	7,435	0	0	310,215	4,259,286	465,245	4,556,481

NOTE: This table is an illustration only. The figures can change from company to company and as interest rates rise and fall.

When Insurance Pays Dividends

One other aspect of permanent insurance needs to be covered. Some life insurance companies are structured as corporations, just like IBM or

AT&T. They're owned by shareholders. Other life insurers, though, are set up as *mutual companies*. In effect, they're owned by their policyholders.

Naturally, most life insurers show profits in most years. Stock companies pay out some of those profits in dividends to their shareholders, just as any corporation might.

What happens to mutual company profits? They're largely passed through to policyholders. The distributions are called dividends, but they're not dividends in the usual sense because they're usually not taxable. Instead, they're nontaxable partial refunds of premiums already paid.

Policyholders, if they want, can simply pocket the refunds. More commonly, they can apply the refunds to their policy. Thus, they can increase the amount of insurance they're carrying with no extra cost, or they can reduce future premiums while still maintaining their insurance coverage.

In our example, where a $500,000 permanent insurance policy costs $5,300 per year, if the insurer is a mutual company, additional dividends might reduce that premium to $5,200 in one year, or $5,100.

Dividends aren't guaranteed, no matter what has happened in the past. If a policy assumes a certain level of dividends and those dividends don't materialize, costs will be higher in order to maintain coverage.

Making Sure There's Wealth To Transfer

Permanent life insurance comes in many forms, as we'll see in the next few chapters. Generally, you'll want some kind of permanent insurance if your need is permanent. Certainly, wealth transfer is a permanent need, so insurance you carry for wealth transfer should be permanent.

Let's go back to the case of John and Joan, who used term protection to provide for their twins. By the time their twins finish school and go off on their own and are no longer dependents, John and Joan have managed to accumulate a $2 million estate. At this point, they don't want life insurance to provide clothes and tuition for the twins, but they want insurance to cover the estate-tax bill the twins likely will have to pay.

So they decide to keep paying term insurance premiums. Let's say John fools the actuaries and lives to 95. Term insurance premiums now become so high that the twins' inheritance is squandered on insurance costs. But if the payments stop before John dies, the twins will receive no insurance proceeds and will have to pay the estate tax out of their own pockets.

John and Joan are better off buying a new policy—a "BMW"—to lock in their costs with permanent insurance. If they start in their 50s or 60s, the annual premium likely will be reasonable, so they won't have to worry about living "too long."

In many cases, wealth-transfer strategies involve vanishing premiums. Starting at age 65, John and Joan might pay $350,000 in premiums over 10 years for a $2 million policy.

You may think, I don't want to pay $350,000 for life insurance. I don't want to enrich the insurance companies, who already own all the big buildings in town. However, at this stage, you're not buying insurance as much as you're transferring wealth. Over 10 years, John and Joan will shift $350,000 into a tax-free inheritance trust, following the strategies we've outlined. Thanks to that transfer, their children will get $2 million, a 6 to 1 return. So permanent life insurance, used in the right place at the right time, can be a source of wealth that your family can rely upon.

- As you get older, term insurance becomes prohibitively expensive.
- If you have a permanent insurance need—one that will last your entire life—you should have permanent life insurance.
- Initially, permanent insurance may be more expensive than term insurance, especially for the very young. However, permanent insurance is fixed-rate, so eventually it becomes less expensive than term.
- If you pay extra premiums, you may purchase a paid-up policy in 10 years or so.
- Permanent insurance includes a cash value, a savings account you can tap in emergencies.
- Virtually all life insurance proceeds are exempt from income tax. With permanent life insurance, the cash value buildup also is free of income tax, and policy loans may be tax-free besides.

- Because wealth transfer is an insurance need that won't disappear, wealth-transfer strategies usually involve permanent insurance.

19 The "Death" of Whole Life

Government isn't always the problem. No matter how obstructive and frustrating governments may be at times, federal or state or local, there's no denying that government has provided us with benefits: safety regulations, child labor laws, and—the modern life insurance policy.

In the 19th century, permanent life insurance was a real loser's game. You had to die to win. That is, permanent life insurance had no cash values. You could hold onto a policy for 10 years, 15 years or more, but if you stopped paying premiums, you'd collect nothing.

In the 1920s, though, the federal government stepped in with the requirement that permanent life insurance provide a cash value. Thereafter, for about 50 years, from the 1920s to the 1970s, *whole life* policies not only were the most popular type of permanent life insurance policy, they were an important savings vehicle for millions of Americans.

Whole life insurance was term insurance plus a guaranteed savings account. Your premiums were guaranteed; your cash value was guaranteed; your death benefits were guaranteed. Dividends, if they exceeded expectations, either reduced premiums or added insurance coverage.

If you decided you no longer wanted to pay your premiums, you (not the insurance company) were entitled to the cash value. You could pay the deferred taxes on the investment buildup and pocket the remaining cash. You could use the cash value to purchase a paid-up policy for a smaller amount of coverage. You could use the cash value to buy term insurance for a given number of years. This was a great improvement over the "bad old days" of no cash values, and whole life insurance worked well for half a century.

What killed whole life? Soaring inflation and volatile interest rates. For those 50 years, up until the early 1970s, insurance companies guaranteed that cash values would earn around 4 percent. Sometimes it was 3 percent, sometimes it was 5 percent, but the interest rate environment was relatively stable, so the insurance companies could deliver those returns with secure, long-term investments. Policyholders were satisfied with low-risk, tax-sheltered returns of around 4 percent per year.

Then came the early 1970s. From 1952 through 1972, the inflation rate was an average of 2.3 percent per year, with a peak of 6.1 percent in 1969. From 1973 through 1981, inflation averaged 9.2 percent per year, peaking at 13.3 percent in 1979.

As inflation soared, lenders demanded higher returns on their loans, so they'd have a "real" (after-inflation) profit. Interest rates went up and down like a yo-yo, but more up than down. Who wanted to be locked into 4 percent with a whole-life policy when they could earn 12 percent in a money-market fund? That's when investment advisers began telling clients to "buy term and invest the difference"—put the money that otherwise would have gone into permanent insurance into a CD or a money-market fund.

What's more, whole life policies allowed policyholders to borrow against their cash value, often at 5 percent or 6 percent. Therefore, many policyholders stripped out their cash value at 6 percent, to reinvest in a money fund at 12 percent.

This was great for investors but a disaster for the insurance companies. Every dollar they loaned to policyholders at 5 percent or 6 percent was a dollar they couldn't invest in money funds or bonds or mortgages earning 12 percent, 15 percent or more.

The Insurers Strike Back

So the insurance companies were forced to make their policies more competitive: they offered higher investment returns. Universal life and variable life, which we'll cover later, became "hot" items.

In the meantime, what happened to whole-life? It changed to adapt to the new era. Some companies continue to call the modified policies whole-life, while other insurers now use the expression *interest-sensitive life*.

What's different about interest-sensitive life? You start out with a low guaranteed rate, around 4 percent, just as in the old whole-life contracts. However, you're entitled to a *current rate* on your cash-value buildup, as long as that current rate exceeds the guaranteed rate. You might, for example, earn 8 percent or 9 percent on your cash value, even though the guaranteed rate is 4 percent.

Suppose, at the time you purchase an interest-sensitive insurance policy, the company expects to be able to earn 9 percent on cash value. Your agent will show you a computerized illustration. The illustration will show what will happen to cash values if the guaranteed rate, perhaps 4 percent, is paid all along. Another column of figures will show what will happen if the current rate—9 percent in this case—prevails over the life of the policy.

In truth, neither of these columns reflect what's likely to happen to cash value over the years. Suppose next year the current rate goes up to 10 percent. The money that the insurance company receives that year in premiums is invested at the higher rates and blended with all the other investments in the company's portfolio. The *portfolio rate,* as it's known, might move up to 9.2 percent or 9.3 percent.

A few years later, interest rates might drop off and the portfolio rate might fall to 8.7 percent or 8.8 percent.

Altogether, interest-sensitive life offers you a guaranteed amount of life insurance for a guaranteed level premium. Cash values aren't guaranteed, but changes in the interest rate are likely to be gradual.

Mastering the Universal

While interest-sensitive life insurance offers many guarantees, another type of life insurance emphasizes flexibility rather than guarantees: *universal life insurance.*

Universal life was introduced in the late 1970s, when inflation and interest rates were at their peaks. Premiums paid for these policies are considered "new money," not blended with old investments, so universal life started out offering 12 percent cash-value buildup and more. Actuaries originally called it "cannibal life," because it was so good that it was eating up all other types of life insurance.

In the beginning, universal life was offered only by a handful of small insurers. In fact, large insurers asked the IRS to rule that universal life was really a disguised money-market fund, not true life insurance. If that were the case, policyholders wouldn't be eligible for life insurance tax benefits (described in a previous section of this chapter). In the early 1980s, the IRS ruled that universal life really is life insurance, as long as certain guidelines are met. Since then, most major insurers offer universal life.

With whole life or interest-sensitive life insurance, the cost of the insurance is guaranteed. In industry parlance, this is the *mortality cost,* which means that certain numbers of people are expected to die at certain ages, so that's when the company will have to pay the insurance proceeds.

Universal life insurance also has a *guaranteed mortality rate.* However, if the premiums were based on that rate, that would result in a high cost. Instead, the policy premiums are based on the *current mortality rates.* So, if people continue to live longer, as has been the case, mortality rates will go down and insurance will cost less. If the trend reverses itself and people die sooner than expected, insurance costs will increase until they reach the guaranteed mortality rate.

A similar situation exists regarding cash values. There's a low guaranteed rate and a higher but variable current interest rate. What's more, that rate may fluctuate rapidly because the money that comes into universal life policies isn't blended with the insurance company's overall portfolio. Your cash value might earn 9 percent one year, 10.5 percent the next, 8 percent the year after that, etc.

Therefore, universal life has much weaker guarantees than interest-sensitive life insurance and much more exposure to variations in interest rates. On the other hand, universal life gives you much more flexibility— you can skip a premium or pay a lower one, if necessary, and still keep a policy in force. In addition, universal life generally is less expensive: you pay about 20 percent more for the guarantees of interest-sensitive life insurance.

Cash Values Don't Count

Which works best for wealth transfer, interest-sensitive life or universal life? If you're insuring a single life, we prefer universal life, especially as you grow older. Because the premiums are lower, you get more leverage. That is, every dollar that you transfer to a tax-free inheritance trust to buy life insurance will bring more money to your family in the future. In wealth-transfer strategies, you're not that interested in cash values, so universal life's unpredictable cash values won't be a drawback.

However, many wealth-transfer strategies today involve second-to-die policies, which we'll explain more fully in Chapter 20. For second-to-die policies, we usually mix permanent and term insurance. Since the term insurance provides the leverage (low premiums), we prefer to use interest-sensitive insurance for stability in the permanent insurance part of the strategy.

- Originally, permanent life insurance had no cash value. If you stopped paying premiums, you walked away with nothing.
- Government regulation forced insurance companies to provide cash values. Now if you cancel a policy, you can receive cash or paid-up life insurance.
- From the 1920s to the 1970s, permanent life insurance was mainly whole life, with guaranteed premiums, cash values and death benefits. Cash-value earnings were around 4 percent per year.
- The inflation and high interest rates of the 1970s made whole life insurance unattractive. Policyholders borrowed money from insurance policies and reinvested in other vehicles paying higher rates.
- In response, insurance companies made whole life policies interest-sensitive. Besides low guaranteed earnings on cash values, these policies offered higher current interest rates on cash-value buildup.
- Universal life was created as an alternative to whole life. There are fewer guarantees and a chance for greater cash values if interest rates stay high. Because universal life is more volatile, premiums are lower than whole life premiums.
- In wealth transfer, universal life is preferred for policies that cover one person's life because premiums are lower.
- Second-to-die policies usually combine interest-sensitive (whole life) insurance with lower cost term insurance.

You Bet Your Life

Earlier in this chapter, we described how whole life insurance has evolved into interest-sensitive life, with strong guarantees, and universal life, with few guarantees. There are, to be sure, important differences between these two types of life insurance, but there are also similarities. In both cases, the insurance company decides how your premium will be invested. And, as a rule, your cash value will grow relatively slowly. Interest-sensitive and universal life cash values will compound at a rate comparable to the return on high-quality bonds—ahead of inflation but not spectacular.

There's an axiom in investing: to earn high returns you have to take high risks. This may not always be strictly true, but it has proven to be the case for long time periods. For example, Ibbotson Associates, Chicago, has studied investments since 1926 with these results:

$1 invested and reinvested, over 64 years	
in	would grow to
Treasury bills	$ 9.67
Long-term government bonds	$ 17.30
Common stocks	$534.45

Bonds, which are riskier than cash equivalents, pay higher returns. But stocks, which are riskier than bonds, pay even greater returns.

Invest in Mutual Funds Without Paying Income Taxes

Can we apply this to life insurance? Yes, there is a type of life insurance that allows you to earn high cash values and high death benefits if you're willing to take some risks. This insurance is called *variable life,* because your results will vary according to investment performance.

Variable life was created in the mid-1970s, when disenchantment with whole-life insurance was growing. The Equitable Life Assurance

Society offered a policy in which premiums would be invested in common stocks, as chosen by Equitable. The cash value of the policy would be determined by the performance of the stocks.

Within a few years, variable policies were offering three choices. Policyholders could choose among stocks, bonds or a money-market fund. They could put all their premiums into one vehicle or they could allocate their premiums among the three choices in whatever proportion they chose. Within certain limits, they could move their money from one category to another. Again, the cash value of the policy would be determined by the success of their investment strategy.

By the mid-1980s, variable life had taken its present form. When you invest, you can choose among mutual funds, managed not by an insurance company but by professional fund managers, including "stars" such as Ken Heebner and Marty Zweig. Rather than just a stock fund and a bond fund, you can choose among growth stock funds and aggressive growth funds and growth-and-income funds and international funds and long-term bond funds and short-term bond funds and more, depending on the policy. Aside from these special mutual funds, you might be able to direct some of your premium into real estate or precious metals or zero-coupon bonds. Most variable life policies also include a *balanced account*, in which a professional strategist will make the allocation decisions.

Therefore, variable life insurance (and variable annuities) can be a tax-efficient way to invest in mutual funds. If you're like most mutual fund investors, you reinvest your dividends but you pay tax every year. With a variable life-insurance "wrapper," you can invest in similar mutual funds, under the same managers, and choose when you want to pay income taxes.

Where does the life insurance come in? With a variable life policy, you have a fixed premium, just like interest-sensitive life insurance. (Some variable life policies are modified endowment contracts, requiring only one payment, which we'll explain in Chapter 21.) That fixed premium buys you a guaranteed amount of life insurance no matter what.

If you invest well with your variable life premiums, your cash value and your death benefit will increase. If you invest poorly, your cash value will shrink, but you'll still have the minimum death benefit that was guaranteed.

Does it make sense to take the risks of variable life? Mathematically, yes. If you expect to hold on for an extended time period, say 20 years or more, you're likely to be better off buying variable life and putting all your premiums into a stock fund run by a first-rate manager. Over every long time period, stocks and stock funds have outperformed insurance company general accounts. That probably will be the case in the future, too.

But people don't live by math alone. Many just aren't willing to accept stock market risks in their life insurance: they remember October 1987 all too well. They'd rather take a reasonably certain 8 percent or 9 percent per year in universal or interest-sensitive life than shoot for 12 percent per year in variable life. In fact, most of the people who buy variable life choose the balanced accounts, which typically invest only 50 to 70 percent in stocks.

Keeping Control

How can variable life be used in wealth transfer? Consider the case of Valerie, a 69-year-old widow who is remarried to a younger husband. Valerie's father was a well-known banker and her estate now is around $10 million.

Valerie wants to provide for Seth, her handsome new husband, and she has made a $600,000 gift to him, exempt from gift and estate taxes (because they're married). That $600,000 is in a trust where the money will grow until Valerie's death. Because Valerie is in good health and comes from long-lived parents, she expects to live another 15 or 20 years or more. By that time, the $600,000 will have grown to a sizable amount, certainly enough to provide for Seth if he outlives her.

That still leaves the rest of her estate, which she plans to leave to her two children, along with an estate-tax obligation that could reach $5 million. So Valerie has set up a tax-free inheritance trust to purchase life insurance.

Now Valerie, who keeps up with tax and financial matters, is a firm believer that the $600,000 estate-tax exemption won't last forever. To reduce the federal budget deficit, she expects Congress will reduce that exemption to $300,000 or even less. Therefore, she has decided to use the full exemption while it's still available. So she has made a $600,000 gift to the tax-free inheritance trust, using up the tax exemption now, and naming her children as co-trustees. With that $600,000, at her age and health, the trustees should be able to purchase a $2.5 million paid-up insurance policy on Valerie's life.

Up to now, Valerie's story is similar to others we've recounted in this book. Valerie, however, does not want to give control of that $600,000 to an insurance company. She remembers that her family has made money in stocks over the years, and she fully expects stocks to be a good investment. Especially if she lives for another 20 years, as she anticipates, stocks probably will beat the bonds and mortgages that insurance companies tend to invest in.

Thus, she suggested to her children, rather forcefully, that they buy a variable life policy. The premiums will be invested in that policy's stock fund, directed by a first-rate portfolio manager.

If Valerie is right, and the stock fund performs well, her cash value will grow strongly over the years. But what good will this do, if the insurance is needed for wealth transfer? Tapping the cash value isn't likely, if Valerie so restricts the trustee's power.

However, in all types of permanent life insurance, including variable life, cash values may be used to buy additional paid-up insurance protection. Thus, over the years, a $2.5 million policy might grow to $3 million, even $4 million, depending upon investment performance. Valerie intends to keep the (unneeded) cash value low and buy as much extra insurance as possible. But even if the stock market crashes and never recovers, the life-insurance proceeds are guaranteed to be at least $2.5 million.

So far, there are no second-to-die variable-life insurance policies on the market. (We expect some will appear soon.) If you are looking for a single-life policy for wealth transfer, you can consider variable life if (1) you prefer to make the investment decisions, rather than trust an insurance company that might speculate in junk bonds or construction loans; and (2) you expect to live long enough to overcome market swings and benefit from long-term stock market performance.

That's especially true if you think your estate may grow over time. Let's say you buy $1 million worth of insurance at age 65 to cover your anticipated estate tax. Your assets grow and, when you're 75, you now figure you'll need $2 million worth of life insurance. At this point you're 10 years older and possibly in poorer health. You may not be able to buy the extra $1 million in life insurance, or the cost may be extremely high.

If you had started out with $1 million in variable life, and diverted as much cash value as possible to extra insurance coverage, you may have $1.5 million or $2 million worth of coverage from your original policy.

Another possibility: universal variable life. The variable life policies we've been describing have been offshoots of interest-sensitive life, with guaranteed premiums and death benefits. Universal variable, offered by some insurers, gives you all the investment options described above, along with fewer guarantees and lower premiums.

Piling on the Protection

There's another aspect of variable life that you might like: safety. Safety? But didn't we say that variable life allowed you to take higher risks in return for potentially greater rewards? That's true, but variable life insurance offers added protection against insurance company insolvency.

If you follow our insurance company guidelines (100+-year-old company, $1 billion+ in assets, top marks from ratings agencies), you're unlikely to run into trouble. Nevertheless, there are few certainties in this world, so an extra layer of protection can't hurt.

By law, all variable life accounts are *segregated accounts*. That means that they're separate from other corporate assets: the insurance company can't use them like a piggy bank. If the insurer suffers a financial disaster, the segregated accounts can't be attached by the insurance company's creditors.

Variable life insurance isn't for everyone. It's not for those who can't stand seeing cash value go down as well as up. If you want extra safety for your death benefit, control over your investments and long-term growth potential, variable life has a lot to offer. In the future, we predict, it will be used more and more in wealth-transfer strategies.

- Variable life is another variation of permanent life insurance.
- Policyholders direct how their premiums will be invested, choosing among stock funds, bonds funds, money-market funds, real estate, precious metals and other alternatives.
- If stock funds are chosen, long-term results may be superior because stocks historically have outperformed insurance companies' general investment accounts.
- The long-term growth in cash values, if realized, can be translated into higher death benefits, providing more wealth to transfer.
- Variable life accounts are not mixed in with an insurer's general fund and they can't be attached by creditors.
- So far, variable life second-to-die policies aren't available. Single-life policies should be considered for wealth transfer by those with a long time horizon, a desire for increasing death benefits and a preference for keeping control of investment decisions.

20

When Second Is Best

As we've mentioned earlier, the 1981 tax act drastically altered wealth-transfer planning. Perhaps the most significant change was the creation of the unlimited marital deduction. Now one spouse can transfer most or all of his or her wealth to the other spouse, during life or at death, without incurring a gift tax or an estate tax.

You can see what this means for most married couples. When the first spouse dies, little or no taxes will be due. Therefore, life insurance won't be necessary at that point to cover the tax bill.

The drawback is that all the wealth is now in the hands of the surviving spouse. Unless that spouse uses some of the strategies we've described (lifetime gifts, charitable trusts, private annuities), that wealth will be in his or her estate. In fact, that wealth may increase in the intervening years. So there may be a considerable estate-tax burden. That's when the life insurance will be needed: at the death of the second spouse.

Guessing Games

This presents a planning problem. How do you handle the life insurance so that it will be there when it's needed? Nick and Nora, for example, decide that they'll need $1 million in life insurance to cover estate taxes. So they set up two tax-free inheritance trusts, each to hold a $500,000 life-insurance policy: one on Nick's life and one on Nora's. Now, no matter which one dies first, there will be $1 million in the trusts at the second death. In fact, there might be more, because the proceeds received at the first death will grow in the interim.

This is a costly strategy. Nick and Nora have to pay to establish and maintain two trusts, pay two sales commissions, pay to administer two policies. Besides, there is always the chance that either Nick or Nora won't be insurable at a reasonable cost because of poor health.

As an alternative, Nick and Nora could choose to insure Nora, the younger, healthier spouse, for $1 million. Now there's only one trust, one commission, one policy. If Nick dies first, all will go as planned. If the unforeseen happens and Nora dies first, the tax-free inheritance trust receives the policy much earlier, so the proceeds will compound until Nick's death.

But there's another alternative. Nick and Nora can buy a policy that will pay only after they both die, no matter who dies first. As long as the older spouse (Nick) is not at death's door, the insurance company will charge you less for a policy that covers two lives than for a policy that covers only one life.

Why the lower cost? If you insure only Nora, the insurance company has some risk that Nora will be hit by a truck tomorrow or suffer an unpredicted heart attack. Your premium reflects that risk. But if you include Nick in the policy, too, then Nora could have that accident and the insurance company could still defer its payment until Nick dies. Thus, an insurance company stands to lose only if two people die prematurely.

The specific comparison will depend on the ages of the spouses involved and on their health (or lack of it). As a general rule, *second-to-die* policies cost about 20 percent less than policies that insure only the younger spouse.

Lower costs, as we've seen, mean more leverage. Suppose you transfer $200,000 to a tax-free inheritance trust to pay life-insurance premiums. That $200,000 might buy an $800,000 policy if you insure only the younger spouse; a second-to-die policy, bought with that same $200,000, might pay $1 million. That's an extra $200,000 in tax-free dollars for your children.

To see how second-to-die life insurance will work, consider Jim, aged 65, who's married to Jan, aged 60. Both are in good health. According to recent projections from a major insurer, this would be the cost of splitting $1 million worth of coverage:

$500,000 policy on Jim's life	$208,000
$500,000 policy on Jan's life	$145,000
Total cost	$353,000

This is an estimate, assuming total premiums paid over 10 years. Now suppose they want to insure only Jan for $1 million:

| $1 million policy on Jan's life | $290,000 |

This is again an estimate, assuming total premiums paid over 9 years.

A second-to-die policy from the same insurer, one that will pay off after both deaths, will cost much less:

| $1 million policy covering two lives | $164,000 |

Again an estimate, assuming total premiums paid over 11 years. To see how a second-to-die policy might work, see Table 20-1.

Don't Starve Your Donkey

Most married couples should use second-to-die policies (also called *joint-and-survivor* or *survivorship* policies) for wealth transfer. Second-to-die policies have become popular only in the last few years, so many agents aren't familiar with them. If you're interested, insist on working with a second-to-die specialist.

If you had to have your gallbladder removed, would you prefer a doctor who's already removed hundreds of gallbladders successfully, or one who has seen the operation once or twice and can call in a consultant if necessary? You'd want a specialist, of course. The same with second-to-die life insurance. But how can you tell who the pros are?

More likely than not, he or she will recommend a combination of term and permanent life insurance. If you use only permanent insurance, second-to-die will be very expensive. If you use only term, you risk that one spouse will live so long that the premiums eventually will become prohibitive. If that happens, and the premiums aren't paid, there will be no insurance to fund your wealth-transfer strategy.

What's the best mix? Keep in mind the story of the farmer who got tired of feeding expensive hay to his donkey. He decided to cut his costs by substituting sawdust for one-tenth of the hay. Everything seemed to be okay, so he cut his costs further by increasing sawdust to one-third of the donkey's feed.

There were no ill effects, so he increased the ratio to half hay, half sawdust. Shortly thereafter, the donkey died.

So it is in second-to-die life insurance. A little term insurance is good but too much term insurance can be a killer.

Refining the Ratio

Most people buy second-to-die policies when they're in their late 60s. At that age, they have a good idea of what their estate-tax obligation can be, and they can afford to transfer wealth into a tax-free inheritance trust. For people in this age range, the best combination usually works out to be 70 percent permanent insurance, 30 percent term insurance.

The term insurance holds down the costs in the initial years. The permanent insurance (usually interest sensitive or whole-life, for guaranteed premiums) generates a cash value. Over the years, the cash value in the permanent insurance builds up; as the term coverage becomes more expensive, less term is bought and the cash value is used to buy more permanent insurance.

Younger people may use more permanent insurance. It's more likely that they'll live long enough to enjoy the fruits of the cash-value buildup, which starts slowly because of the initial sales commissions. By increasing the permanent insurance—and the cash value—you increase the possibility that you'll be able to make the premium "vanish" after 10 years or so. Thus, you'll wind up with the coverage you want yet no more need to pay premiums.

Those who buy second-to-die policies while they're in their 70s, though, may want only 67 percent permanent insurance and 33 percent term insurance. They're less likely to be able to realize great benefits from cash-value buildup starting at that age, so they might as well cut their costs with more term insurance.

Table 20-1
Second-To-Die Policy Illustration
Husband Age 65; Wife Age 60

Policy Year	Annual Payment	Annual Dividend*	Total Cash Value*	Total Death Benefit*	IRR % on Death*
1	15,041	0	0	1,000,000	—
2	15,041	0	1,260	1,000,000	—
3	15,041	1,085	17,871	1,000,000	—
4	14,906	1,946	35,572	1,000,000	—
5	14,906	2,947	54,645	1,000,000	—
Sum @ 5:	74,935	5,978	54,645	1,000,000	
6	14,906	5,271	76,400	1,000,000	102.69
7	14,906	7,168	100,526	1,000,000	75.50
8	14,906	8,379	126,451	1,000,000	58.60
9	14,906	9,667	154,284	1,000,000	47.21
10	14,906	11,053	184,188	1,000,000	39.06
Sum @ 10:	149,465	47,516	184,188	1,000,000	39.06
11	14,906	13,118	216,864	1,000,000	32.99
12	†	14,735	235,708	1,000,000	28.54
13	†	16,450	255,601	1,000,000	25.06
14	†	18,263	276,483	1,000,000	22.28
15	†	20,202	298,299	1,000,000	20.02
Sum @ 15:	164,371	130,284	298,299	1,000,000	20.02
16	†	21,483	320,837	1,000,000	18.15
17	†	23,548	344,138	1,000,000	16.60
18	†	25,550	368,105	1,000,000	15.26
19	†	27,426	392,568	1,000,000	14.14
20	†	29,197	417,370	1,000,000	13.15
Sum @ 20:	164,371	257,488	417,370	1,000,000	13.15
21	†	30,548	441,811	1,000,000	12.28
22	†	32,004	465,833	1,000,000	11.52
23	†	33,369	489,068	1,000,000	10.85
24	†	34,629	511,069	1,000,000	10.25
25	†	35,791	531,453	1,000,000	9.72
Sum @ 25:	164,371	423,829	531,453	1,000,000	9.72

table 20-1, cont.

Policy Year	Annual Payment	Annual Dividend*	Total Cash Value*	Total Death Benefit*	IRR % on Death*
26	†	37,709	551,488	1,000,000	9.23
27	†	39,228	570,475	1,000,000	8.79
28	†	40,733	588,374	1,000,000	8.39
29	†	42,434	605,581	1,000,000	8.02
30	†	44,219	622,224	1,000,000	7.68
Sum @ 30:	164,371	628,152	622,224	1,000,000	7.68
31	†	46,186	638,514	1,000,000	7.38
32	†	48,293	654,561	1,000,000	7.09
33	†	50,547	670,660	1,000,000	6.82
34	†	52,493	687,161	1,000,000	6.58
35	†	53,291	704,607	1,000,000	6.35
Sum @ 35:	164,371	878,962	704,607	1,000,000	6.35
36	†	53,291	699,204	1,000,000	6.14
37	†	59,220	717,212	1,000,000	5.94
38	†	65,142	736,181	1,000,000	5.75
39	†	74,445	756,300	1,000,000	5.57
Policy year 30	†	44,219	622,224	1,000,000	7.68

NOTES:

This table is an illustration only. The figures can change from company to company and as interest rates rise and fall.

The abbreviated payment alternative uses dividend values to limit the number of payments made in cash. Results are not guaranteed.

* Not guaranteed.

† Based on the current dividend scale, which is not guaranteed, no out-of-pocket cash outlay is required. Premiums are assumed to be paid by application of dividend credits. A reduction in the current scale could require you to make additional out-of-pocket cash outlays in one or more of these years.

Sometimes one of the two spouses has a health problem. Such a problem may not be serious enough to make insurance impossible to obtain, but it does shorten their life expectancy and thus increase premium costs. In this kind of situation, you may have to go to a 50–50 ratio between permanent and term insurance to keep costs affordable.

Ask about Unhappy Endings

Besides the right mix, what should you look for in a second-to-die policy? A solid insurance company, of course. The criteria we set out in Chapter 18 should be your guidelines.

You also need to be careful with the policy illustrations you get from your agent. As we'll explain later, every time you shop for permanent life insurance, your agent will show you a computerized printout based on information from the insurance company. This printout "illustrates" the premiums you'll have to pay, the cash value you'll likely build up and the death benefits your family can expect to collect.

But some companies play games with premiums. For a second-to-die policy, for example, an illustration might show both spouses living to age 95, certainly an unlikely possibility. In those circumstances, premiums are projected to stay low.

The policy may have a trap that's not disclosed. After the first death, the policy may be repriced as a single-life policy covering the surviving spouse. Premiums will increase dramatically, which may make it much harder to keep the policy in force.

Not all second-to-die policies are structured like this. Just to make sure, ask your agent for an illustration showing what happens if both spouses live to their life expectancies. Also, ask for worst-case scenarios, in which one spouse dies soon and the other lives for many years, paying premiums to keep the policy in force.

Second-To-Die for Smaller Estates

Although second-to-die life insurance is designed primarily to help pay estate tax, it can be used even if no estate-tax obligation is expected. For example, these policies can enable you to enjoy a carefree retirement and still be certain you'll leave a substantial amount to your children.

Peter and Paula are 65 and 62, respectively, with two grown children. They're retired, with about $1 million in total assets. While they're still in good health, they'd like to travel, dine at fine restaurants and generally enjoy life.

Peter and Paula also realize that their good health may not last forever. At some point, one or both of them may become too ill to live independently. They don't want to burden their children—who have three children of their own already, with more likely to come—by moving in with them. Instead, they're prepared to live in a nursing home if it's a good one, but they know that good nursing homes are expensive.

Between good living and not-so-good living, Peter and Paula fear that they'll go through their entire $1 million in assets. They'd also like to know that they were leaving behind $1 million, $500,000 to each child.

So they met with an experienced life-insurance agent and established a tax-free inheritance trust, naming their two children as co-trustees. The agent showed them an illustration from a life-insurance company rated AAA by Standard & Poor's: according to the illustration, paying a $16,500 premium each year for 10 years will pay for a $1 million life-insurance policy, payable after they both die. (If interest rates go up or down, premiums will have to be paid for fewer or more years, respectively.)

Now Peter and Paula give $16,500 to the trust each year to cover the insurance premiums. After that $16,500, they can spend whatever they want. If they eat into their $1 million, they're not concerned. They know that, as long as they maintain those $16,500 gifts for about 10 years, there will be $1 million for their children tax-free.

Because their total assets add up to $1 million and are likely to shrink rather than grow over the years, Peter and Paula probably won't leave a taxable estate after the second death. Therefore, their children don't have to keep the policy intact for that purpose.

Instead, as co-trustees, they can borrow against the policy's cash value if they need the money before Peter and Paula die. Policy loans will be tax-free, although excess borrowing can jeopardize the policy and whatever they borrow, plus interest, will be deducted from the insurance proceeds they'll eventually receive.

In sum, Peter and Paula have decided to pay $165,000 over 10 years for peace of mind. They can enjoy their retirement without worrying about squandering their children's inheritance. Best of all, they've merely transferred their wealth to the children, not spent it. If their children need emergency funds, the policy's cash value will be available.

- Wealth-transfer strategies usually call for a couple to defer estate taxes until both spouses have died.
- Many families rely upon life insurance to cover their estate-tax obligations.
- Second-to-die life-insurance policies are designed primarily for wealth transfer because they assure you that the money will be available at the right time. Such policies pay off after both spouses die.
- Because two lives are covered, premiums are considerably less than they are for a similar policy covering only one life.
- Second-to-die policies should mix permanent and term insurance, generally in a 70 to 30 ratio. The younger you are and the better your health, the more permanent insurance you should include in the mix.
- When you shop for second-to-die insurance, ask to see illustrations covering a range of possible scenarios.
- Even if you don't anticipate an estate-tax obligation, second-to-die life insurance may be appropriate. Such a policy, for example, may enable you to enjoy your retirement fully yet leave sizable funds to your children.

21 ... And Congress Created MECs

Earlier, we mentioned the three tax advantages offered by permanent life insurance: no income tax on the death benefit, tax-free buildup of the premiums invested and tax-free borrowing against the cash value. In the mid-1980s, some savvy promoters put together a product designed specifically to take advantage of these tax breaks: single-premium life insurance.

As the name suggests, you could buy a paid-up life insurance policy with one (single) premium. Typically, investments were $25,000, $50,000 and more. As little as possible went into the purchase of life insurance while as much as possible went into the cash value. Thus cash values would grow rapidly.

Single-premium life insurance was either whole life or variable life. With single-premium whole life, your single premium would earn interest somewhere around the going CD rate. Each year, the rate would be changed to reflect whether interest rates were higher or lower than a year earlier.

Suppose you put $50,000 into a single-premium whole life policy. If the interest rate averaged 8 percent, your cash value would be about $100,000 after nine years. Inside a life insurance policy, there would be no tax on the buildup. If you needed the money, you could take tax-free policy loans. (Insurance companies generally let you borrow at the same rate your cash value was earning, or a point higher, resulting in a no-cost or low-cost loan.) If you never needed the money, your beneficiaries eventually would receive the death benefit. In this entire process, no income tax ever need be paid. (If, on the other hand, you just put your money into CDs, you'd owe income tax each year, even if you kept rolling over the balance.)

Single-premium variable life worked the same way. However, just like the variable life insurance described in Chapter 19, you had many investment options. You could put your $50,000 into a stock fund, for example, and hope it would grow over the years sheltered from income taxes. If you needed the cash value, you could take tax-free policy loans. Your cash value might go up or down, but you had a guaranteed death benefit.

If this sounded too good to be true, it was. Congress changed the law in 1988. What changes were made?

First, Congress redefined life insurance. A life insurance policy entitled to all the tax benefits of life insurance generally must schedule premium payments over at least seven years. (It's possible to shorten this to about five years with a "vanishing premium" strategy, if assumed levels of interest or dividends are achieved.) If a policy meets this *seven-pay test,* all the tax benefits apply.

If a policy is paid up in a shorter time period, it's usually a *modified endowment contract,* abbreviated MEC and pronounced "meck." Single-premium life, of course, is now a MEC. (Single-premium policies sold before the law was changed generally continue to be treated as true life insurance.)

What difference is there between a MEC and life insurance? Just one: withdrawals are LIFO (last in, first out) taxed rather than FIFO (first in, first out) tax. The result is that you can't take tax-free loans from a MEC.

If you borrow from a MEC, or take any other kind of withdrawal, the investment income will be taxed along with all your other income. Suppose you invest $50,000 in a MEC and the cash value grows to $75,000 in five years. If you want to take distributions from the MEC, the first $25,000 will be subject to income tax. After that $25,000, further withdrawals will be tax-free returns of your own money.

In addition, there's a 10 percent penalty tax for any withdrawals or policy loans before the policy owner turns age 59½. (The MEC distribution rules are similar to those that apply to withdrawals from a deferred annuity, which we covered in Chapter 12.)

Otherwise, MECs are treated the same as life insurance. The cash value still builds up tax-free, and there are death benefits that go to your beneficiaries free of income tax.

Therefore, MECs still are being sold, as whole life or variable. A whole-life MEC is similar to investing in a series of CDs, except that you decide when (or if) you'll pay the income tax. A variable MEC is like investing in mutual funds and deciding when (or if) you'll pay the income tax.

It is true that you'll probably earn less with a MEC than you would with, say, corporate bonds or mutual funds held outside of a MEC. A stock fund on which you'd earn 10 percent per year outside of a MEC might pay you 8 percent inside a MEC, because of all the costs. In return for those costs, you get life insurance protection for your family.

If you're in your late 50s, for example, a $50,000 single premium might buy you a $120,000 life insurance policy. Over the years, as your cash value increases, your death benefit will increase, too: it has to, under the tax laws governing life insurance.

Savings Plus Protection

When might a MEC be used in wealth transfer? Take the case of Ray and Stephanie, who would like to provide for their three grandchildren. They give $20,000 to each one, using their annual gift-tax exemptions. The gifts are used to buy three MECs, each with a $20,000 single premium. In each case, the insured individual is Charles, the son of Ray and Stephanie and the father of the three grandchildren. At Charles's age, each MEC originally provides $60,000 worth of life insurance coverage.

Assume that each MEC earns 8 percent per year. After 18 years, there will be about $80,000 in each one, thanks to tax-free compounding. The grandchildren might want to take low-cost policy loans then, perhaps for a down payment on a house. They'll pay tax on the withdrawals, but they can figure out how much they'd net after tax, and take out a loan to meet their needs.

All the while, the grandchildren have life insurance protection in case their father dies. That protection starts at $60,000 and will grow to $80,000, $100,000, etc., as long as the cash value keeps growing.

Besides reducing their taxable estate and providing for their grandchildren, Ray and Stephanie like the MEC for other reasons too. They're extremely privacy-oriented. They like the fact that no gift-tax return need be filed as long as each one makes a $10,000 gift, rather than a $20,000 joint gift. They like the fact that no 1099 income is reported to the IRS as MEC cash value grows. And they like the fact that no probate will be involved when Charles dies and the proceeds pass to their grandchildren.

In addition, Ray and Stephanie are concerned about the safety of life insurers. So they're putting their money into variable MECs, not only to shoot for greater long-term growth but also because each fund is a separate custodial trust, as we explained in Chapter 19, on variable life insurance. Because their money isn't commingled with an insurance company's general account, they feel it's safer, and they can pay less attention to how the ratings agencies view the insurance company.

Creditor-Proof

Another MEC buyer is Brad, a successful Midwestern attorney. His main concern is that he'll be sued, he'll be wiped out by a huge award for damages and he won't be able to pass anything on to his children and grandchildren. He's also apprehensive that the $600,000 gift- and estate-tax exemption will be scaled back.

Therefore, Brad and his wife Anne have used up $1 million worth of their $1.2 million gift-tax allowance to establish an irrevocable trust and purchase a MEC that the trust will hold. He has chosen a variable MEC and designed an asset-allocation strategy: several top fund managers will invest his $1 million in a combination of stocks, bonds, real estate and natural resources.

If Brad dies within the next few years, his children will receive almost $2 million in life-insurance proceeds. If he lives longer and his cash value continues to grow, his cash value may increase to $3 million or $4 million in 10 or 15 years, with a simultaneous increase in death benefits. Thanks to the required *corridor* (gap between the cash value and the death benefit) under the Internal Revenue Code, the death benefit may reach $4 million or even $5 million.

Because Brad and Anne's $1 million goes into an irrevocable trust and then into a MEC, there's a double layer of protection against creditors. They have removed $1 million from their taxable estate as well as from potential lawsuits. Their children eventually will receive $2 million in tax-free life-insurance proceeds, and perhaps much more. The children are the trustees, so they can tap the MEC's cash value in case of an emergency. (Brad, who still works full-time, sees no need for current income; in case of his death, Anne is protected by his retirement plan.)

- A modified endowment contract (MEC) is a life-insurance policy that is paid up after a single premium or after a few premiums.
- MECs are similar to permanent life-insurance policies except that they don't offer tax-free loans against cash value. Instead, if you borrow or withdraw from a MEC, the proceeds are subject to income tax, up to the amount of investment income that has built up. There's also a 10 percent penalty tax for loans or withdrawals before the policy owner turns age 59½.
- MEC distribution rules are the same as the rules on distributions from deferred annuities.
- If you don't need extra income, a MEC can be an excellent vehicle to provide income or insurance protection for children or grandchildren.
- MECs can also be used to protect assets from potential lawsuits, especially if held in an irrevocable trust.

MECs: "Turbo-Charged Annuities"

Why buy a MEC? Why not buy real life insurance and get the ability to take tax-free policy loans?

Some people like the idea of paying one premium for a paid-up policy. They don't want to have the ongoing obligation for annual premiums. In addition, there's more cash-value growth with a MEC. If you pay $50,000 in year one, everything starts to earn tax-deferred income. If you stretch out that $50,000 premium over five years or seven years, you'll have less money working for you tax-deferred.

There's a way to get the MEC advantages (single payment, immediate growth) and still have access to tax-free loans. How? By using a MEC hybrid.

Suppose you have $50,000 you want to put into a MEC. Instead, you choose a life-insurance policy that qualifies under the "seven-pay" test, requiring $10,000 annual payments for approximately five years. So you make a $10,000 premium payment.

What about the other $40,000? You can put that into an *immediate annuity* (see Chapter 12), selecting a total payout over four years. So right away your entire $50,000 is earning income.

The immediate annuity will spin off $10,000 each year, plus investment income (which will be subject to income tax). Those distributions can be directed into the life insurance policy. By the end of four years, your immediate annuity will be fully liquidated and you'll have "vanished" the premium on your life insurance policy. You'll have an insurance policy on which the premiums are paid, and you'll be entitled to tax-free policy loans and tax-favored withdrawals.

Apples to Apples

Comparing MECs to life insurance really isn't appropriate. Life insurance, as we've seen, is intended to protect your family or cover your estate-tax burden. A MEC, on the other hand, is primarily an investment vehicle. As such, it's more properly compared to deferred annuities, which have been very popular.

As you'll recall, a deferred annuity is a contract with an insurance company. You pay premiums, the money compounds without current income tax and you eventually pay taxes when you take your money out. Deferred annuities are used mainly to provide extra retirement income.

MECs resemble single-premium deferred annuities. There is the same tax-free compounding of investment income, the same tax rules on withdrawals. The difference: MECs provide a death benefit. Let's say that you pay $50,000 for a MEC and $50,000 for an SPDA, then die 10 years later:

	Single-Premium Deferred Annuity	Modified Endow- ment Contract
Single premium	$50,000	$50,000
Ten-year buildup	$68,000	$58,000
Investment value	$118,000	$108,000
Death benefit	$118,000	$150,000*

*May be more or less, depending upon age, sex and health.

You may have noticed that the annuity has greater buildup than the MEC. That's because an insurance policy has mortality expenses that increase costs. Let's say you invest in a no-load mutual fund for which the total return is 11 percent per year. After paying 1 percent to the fund manager, you'd net 10 percent per year.

That same fund, with the same performance, would return around 9 percent in a deferred annuity because of the added expense of administering the contract. And that same fund inside a variable-life insurance policy or variable MEC would return 8 percent, because of the added cost of the life-insurance benefit.

In our table, we've assumed a 9 percent annual return for the SPDA and 8 percent for the MEC. Over 10 years, the SPDA is ahead by $10,000 on a $50,000 investment. However, if you die then, your beneficiary would receive only the investment value. With a MEC, there's a guaranteed death benefit, one that has to be considerably larger than the cash value, by law.

The Mega-Tax Break Most Attorneys Miss

MECs have another advantage over SPDAs, one that's not recognized by many financial professionals, including attorneys. No matter what you do, you can't escape the income tax in a deferred annuity. If you take money out while you're alive, part of each payment will be taxable income. If you hold onto a deferred annuity until you die, there's no step up in cost basis for tax purposes. Your beneficiary will have to pay the income taxes.

In our example, the SPDA beneficiary receives $118,000, but $68,000 of that is investment income—taxable income. Assuming a 35 percent tax rate, $24,000 would go toward income tax. That would leave only $94,000.

On the other hand, the MEC gets a full step up, just like any life insurance policy. If the death benefit is $150,000 at the time of death, your beneficiaries would get that money with no reduction for income tax.

What are the implications? Say you're considering a single-premium deferred annuity to increase your retirement income. If you're in good health (so that you're insurable) and if you have a spouse, children or others you care about, look into a MEC instead: MECs have been called "turbo-charged annuities."

You'll get the same tax-deferred buildup, albeit a bit slower. If you need the extra income in retirement, you can borrow from your MEC and pay income taxes. If you don't need it, or need relatively little MEC money, you'll pass on a nice bundle to your beneficiaries free of income tax.

Yours or Theirs?

If you do invest in a MEC, you have a difficult decision to make. You can hold a MEC in your own name for access to the cash value. That can provide extra retirement income. If you do, however, your MEC will be included in your estate and be subject to estate tax.

You can set up a tax-free inheritance trust to hold your MEC and remove it from your taxable estate. These trusts, though, are irrevocable, and you can't serve as trustee. Thus, you generally lose access to your cash value. Now, it's the trustees—probably your children—who can borrow against the cash value.

Which way should you go? As long as there's any chance you'll need the income, hold the MEC in your own name. Don't stunt your retirement lifestyle because you're worried about estate tax. If you reach the point where you're sure you won't need the money, transfer your MEC to a tax-free inheritance trust, giving up all your rights to the MEC. As long as you live for another three years, the MEC proceeds will escape estate tax as well as income tax.

- While life insurance is designed for family protection, MECs appeal to people who are investment-oriented.
- Investors may prefer MECs because they require only a single payment and there's full tax-deferred growth from the beginning.
- "Hybrid" MECs, which also use immediate annuities, can give you MEC-type benefits as well as tax-free policy loans.
- MECs really should be compared to deferred annuities rather than to life insurance.
- Deferred annuities have slightly greater investment buildup, but MECs have a greater death benefit.
- MEC death benefits have a full step up in basis, meaning your beneficiaries won't have to pay income taxes. There's no avoiding income tax with a deferred annuity.
- If you're in good health and have someone you care about, a MEC may be a better choice than a deferred annuity.

22 Don't Believe Everything You Read

Whenever you're shopping for a permanent life insurance policy, your agent likely will supply you with an impressive-looking computer printout. This "policy illustration" will contain columns of figures showing the premiums you'll pay, the cash value you'll build up and the proceeds your beneficiaries will receive. These figures certainly will seem precise, forecasting 20 or 30 or 50 years of results down to the last dollar.

These illustrations are mainly projections, not guarantees. The farther out you go, the less likely it is that these projections will be realized and the numbers in the illustration will come to pass.

Illustrations have their uses. You can get a rough idea of how permanent life insurance will work. That's why it's so upsetting that some life-insurance companies use illustrations as a sales tool. They make unrealistic assumptions to make their policies look better than those of competitors. In general, it's the weaker life insurers who inflate sales illustrations the most. That's how they compete against insurers with more financial strength.

For example, suppose low-rated Company A projects it will increase your cash value at 10 percent while top-rated Company B projects 8 percent growth in cash value. Over the years, Company A's policy will "illustrate" much better than Company B's. You might think you can pay a lower premium to get a certain level of insurance protection. (See Table 22-1.)

In reality, there is no guarantee that Company A will outperform Company B. In fact, to make its 10 percent projection, Company A may invest in riskier vehicles—junk bonds, construction loans—and may wind up with sub-par results.

Table 22-1
How Assumptions Affect Cash Value Projections

Face Value: $100,000.00
Male age 45

End of Yr	Att Age	Annual Outlay	8.00% Current Values		6.00% Assumed Values		4.50% Guaranteed Values	
			Cash Value	Death Benefit	Cash Value	Death Benefit	Cash Value	Death Benefit
1	46	5,967.57	221	500,000	221	500,000	221	500,000
2	47	5,967.57	4,843	500,000	4,742	500,000	4,181	500,000
3	48	5,967.57	9,665	500,000	9,366	500,000	8,214	500,000
4	49	5,967.57	14,707	500,000	14,102	500,000	12,265	500,000
5	50	5,967.57	19,991	500,000	18,960	500,000	16,339	500,000
Cumulative:		29,837.85						
6	51	5,967.57	26,488	500,000	24,894	500,000	20,439	500,000
7	52	5,967.57	33,404	500,000	31,080	500,000	24,512	500,000
8	53	5,967.57	40,833	500,000	37,597	500,000	28,560	500,000
9	54	5,967.57	48,820	500,000	44,465	500,000	32,529	500,000
10	55	5,967.57	57,359	500,000	51,654	500,000	36,419	500,000
Cumulative:		59,675.70						
11	56	5,967.57	66,444	500,000	59,133	500,000	40,176	500,000
12	57	5,967.57	76,181	500,000	66,979	500,000	43,740	500,000
13	58	5,967.57	86,578	500,000	75,166	500,000	47,109	500,000
14	59	5,967.57	97,698	500,000	83,723	500,000	50,221	500,000
15	60	5,967.57	109,562	500,000	92,630	500,000	53,015	500,000
Cumulative:		89,513.55						
16	61	5,967.57	122,244	500,000	101,917	500,000	55,478	500,000
17	62	5,967.57	135,782	500,000	111,571	500,000	57,487	500,000
18	63	5,967.57	150,310	500,000	121,676	500,000	58,914	500,000
19	64	5,967.57	165,844	500,000	132,178	500,000	59,673	500,000
20	65	5,967.57	182,495	500,000	143,122	500,000	59,616	500,000
Cumulative:		119,351.40						

NOTE: This table is an illustration only. The figures can change from company to company and as interest rates rise and fall. In this example, you pay almost $120,000 over 20 years for a $500,000 policy. Your cash value is over $180,000 with an 8% return—less than $60,000 with a 4.5% return.

There are other games insurance companies can play with illustrations. For instance, they can change *mortality charges*. That is, they can assume that people will live longer and longer, delaying the time until the companies will have to pay death benefits. That has been the case in the past, but will it continue, especially if the AIDS epidemic isn't checked?

Some companies pump up projections of cash values and death benefits by using *persistency bonuses*. That is, these insurers assume that many policyholders will allow their policies to lapse. They'll leave before they can enjoy much buildup of cash value; they may even pay surrender charges for early withdrawals. That means more will be left for the policyholders who stick around.

Therefore, some illustrations show a cash-value bonus after the 10th year, perhaps, or after the 20th year. Long-term results look excellent. But if you're one of the policyholders who surrender their policies early, you'll never collect that persistency bonus.

Further, suppose the persistency bonus is so enticing that most policyholders hold onto their policies. The bonus pool will be smaller and it will have to be spread among more recipients, so each bonus will be skimpier than projected.

Read Between the Lines

How can you win the policy illustration game? First, make sure you choose life insurers who meet the criteria we described in Chapter 18: over 100 years old, over $1 billion in assets, top ratings from the various agencies. That's the single most important step you can take to avoid being victimized. Second, pick a competent, caring agent.

When evaluating illustrations, you need to know the assumptions on which they're based. These assumptions are not always spelled out on the computerized printout. What's the rate at which cash value is expected to grow? Is the mortality expense based on current experience or on a projection of longer life expectancies? Is insurance company overhead expected to decrease? Is there a persistency bonus?

Once you know what the assumptions are, you can judge to see if they're reasonable. If not, ask to have the illustration rerun using more conservative assumptions.

For example, you can "split the difference" between current and guaranteed interest rates. Suppose the current rate (the assumed long-term growth rate) is 8 percent while the guaranteed rate is 5 percent. Ask your agent for a run at 6.5 percent, to see what kind of a premium you'd need to pay to keep your insurance in force in case interest rates drop sharply. (This exercise is particularly useful for universal life policies, which don't offer strong guarantees.)

Using a 6.5 percent interest rate rather than an 8 percent interest rate may mean that you pay higher premiums up front. But you won't have to increase your premiums unless rates drop below 6.5 percent. And if rates stay at 8 percent, you'll have a faster buildup of cash value, which may enable you to cease paying premiums earlier than expected.

The next step is to ask your agent for an insurer's *net investment yield* in the past few years. This number is readily available from A.M. Best Co. Although Best has been criticized for its ratings in recent years, it still publishes excellent statistics on the insurance industry. (If your agent isn't capable of using the A.M. Best statistics, find another agent.)

Then compare the company's net investment yield with the median cash-value return you have determined. For example:

Company B	
Current (assumed) rate of cash-value growth	8%
Guaranteed rate of cash-value growth	5%
Median rate (split the difference)	6.5%
Company B's recent net investment yield	8.5%
Comfort level	2%

Thus, it seems likely that Company B will deliver the conservative 6.5 percent you're using for your projections. It may even deliver the 8 percent it's assuming. Now, let's look at Company A, whose initial projections look much better:

Company A	
Current (assumed) rate of cash-value growth	10%
Guaranteed rate of cash-value growth	5%
Median rate	7.5%
Company A's recent net investment yield	8.5%
Comfort level	1%

Now you can see that there is virtually nothing to show that Company A can generate 10 percent investment income, its "current" illustration rate. You're better off going with conservative, higher-rated Company B and making a modest assumption of 6.5 percent growth in cash value.

The Past Is Not Always Father of the Future

There's a sidelight to this issue. Many companies will point to their long-term performance record as an indicator of their investment skill. They might say, "So-and-so bought a policy in 1968, expecting to pay $1,000 per year indefinitely. Instead, cash value built up so well that premiums were all paid up by 1984, and so-and-so now receives tax-free refunds from policy dividends."

Although there may be exaggerations, by and large such stories are true. Back in the 1960s, permanent life policies assumed low interest rates. (Those were the days of the 6 percent home mortgage.) In the 1970s and 1980s, interest rates were much higher than originally projected. Cash values built up much faster than expected, to the benefit of policyholders. This didn't reflect any great investment skill by insurance companies.

Nor do these results tell you what the insurers will do in the future. Of all the life insurance now in place, about 90 percent has been bought in the past 10 years. Thus, insurers have to invest much larger sums than they did in the 1960s, and they have to live up to projections of 8 percent or 9 percent, rather than the 4 percent or 5 percent they were projecting in the 1960s. Long-term past performance has nothing at all to do with future performance; you're better off focusing on results in the last few years as well as a company's overall financial strength.

What Illustrations Mean for Wealth Transfer

In general, beware of policies showing persistency bonuses for wealth transfer. Such policies often are back-loaded: you get less cash value now and more later. For wealth transfer, though, you want more cash value up front to pay for increased insurance coverage. In most wealth-transfer situations, you're not interested in a large pool of cash value 20 or 30 years in the future.

What else should you look for in wealth-transfer policy illustrations? Ask what happens to a second-to-die policy in case of a divorce. What if there's a major change in tax law? (Perhaps the unlimited marital deduction will be restricted.) Can the policy be split into two single-life policies? Quality second-to-die policies will have *escape clauses* for such events.

Some second-to-die policies offer an added bonus, often at no charge. Suppose a question of policy ownership arises if both spouses die within three years of purchasing the policy, and the proceeds are included in the estate of the second spouse to die after an IRS challenge. Some policies will pay twice the face value, or more, making up for the increased estate taxes. (If you follow our advice on handling policy applications, this is unlikely to happen, but it's a nice feature to have, especially if there's no extra premium to pay for it.)

Be sure that illustrations are run out to at least age 95 with one spouse surviving to see what happens. In some policies, usually universal life with a vanishing premium, the cash value will be gone by then. Your policy will lapse unless you pay more premiums. (Interest-sensitive or whole-life policies, on the other hand, will call for extra premiums if there's a danger of a lapse.)

As a final test, ask your agent for the *internal rate of return* on life-insurance death benefits, whether you're using a single-life policy or a second-to-die policy. That is, you and your spouse may be paying $165,000 in premiums over the next 10 years for a $1 million policy. Suppose you each die at your life expectancies. What return would you have to get from a bank on those ten $16,500 premiums to get $1 million then? Software programs are widely available, so your agent should be able to calculate this time-weighted return, called the internal rate of return. Obviously, you'd rather buy a policy with a 10 percent IRR than an 8 percent IRR, if the 10 percent policy passes all our other tests.

Policy Illustrations Shouldn't Be Risk-Free

There's another way in which policy illustrations can deceive. Whenever an illustration has no *risk rating,* it's a waste of time to pay attention to it.

What's a risk rating? When you apply for life insurance, insurance companies will put you through their *underwriting* process. They'll select applicants they wish to insure and decide how risky each one is. The main criteria in the underwriting process are the applicants' health histories.

Typically, insurance companies have a *standard* risk category for people who are in normal physical condition. People in exceptionally good health (usually nonsmokers) are *preferred* risks. People in sub-par health are graded down to *Table 16,* the riskiest condition. The further down the scale you are, the higher your premiums will be. Therefore, an illustration that's based on a standard risk will be meaningless if you're *Table 5* or *Table 6.*

Some companies grade A, B, C, etc. For example, a 45-year-old male who wants $500,000 worth of life insurance might have to pay less than $7,000 per year if he's rated B (good health). He might have to pay nearly $8,000 if he's rated D (not so good) and over $8,500 per year if he's rated F (not great).

The grading process sounds extremely precise, but that's not really the case. Insurance companies vary widely in their risk ratings, even for the same people!

Recently, for example, a married couple in their early 70s asked a life insurance agent for quotes on a second-to-die policy. The agent applied to three companies. Company A rated the wife a standard risk while the husband was a Table 4. Company B came in with the reverse rating: standard risk for the husband but Table 4 for the wife.

This distinction is more than trivial. For a $1 million policy, Company A quoted a $25,000 annual premium while Company B quoted a $30,000 premium. That's a difference of $50,000 over 10 years.

What about Company C? A fact of life that insurance companies are reluctant to discuss is that risk ratings may be negotiable, if an agent knows the business well. In this example, the agent approached Company C and offered to place a policy there if the wife could be rated standard and the husband rated Table 2. The insurer agreed and the policy was written at an even lower rate.

Dip a Toe Before Taking the Plunge

Therefore, don't put absolute faith in insurance policy illustrations. And don't put any faith at all in illustrations until the company has assigned a risk rating to you (and to your spouse, on a second-to-die policy).

A problem can arise when someone in doubtful health wants to implement a wealth-transfer strategy. As we've mentioned, if you're going to use life insurance, you should hold the policy in an irrevocable trust to avoid estate tax and shield the policy from creditors. To make sure the policy belongs to the trust and not to you, the trust should be established beforehand and the trustee (not you or your spouse) should make the policy application.

But irrevocable trusts cost money—perhaps a couple of thousand dollars—to set up. Most people don't want to go to the expense of setting up the trust only to find out later that they can't get insurance or that their risk rating is so high that the cost of insurance would be prohibitive.

If you have questions about your health, what can you do? There's no easy answer, but some attorneys have been working with "mini-trusts" or even oral agreements. The gist is that you (the trust creator) agree with a selected trustee (probably an adult child or a trusted adviser) to establish an irrevocable trust. This agreement is recorded and dated. However, no extensive drafting is done, so that the costs are minimal to this point.

Then, your grown child, acting as trustee, applies for an insurance policy on your life to be owned by the trust. Insurers go through their medical reviews. If you're found to be insurable at a reasonable cost, a detailed trust is drafted. If you flunk the physical, you may decide to abandon the trust. (Or you can go ahead with the trust, funding it with other types of investments. The decision is yours.)

This approach may work, but it has yet to be ruled upon by the IRS or the courts. So be sure you're working with an experienced estate-planning attorney.

Another approach is to have your son or daughter apply for the policy on your life, or the lives of you and your spouse. After the physical exam and the medical review, your son or daughter can cancel the application. Then, if you have discovered that insurance will be available at a reasonable cost, you can create a trust to make a new application.

- Illustrations of permanent life policies purport to show how cash values and death benefits will build up if you pay certain premiums.
- Policy illustrations really are projections, not guarantees.
- Some companies make unreasonable assumptions to make their illustrations look better. For example, they may assume extremely high investment income.
- Be sure you know the assumptions on which policy illustrations are based.
- Here's a simple strategy for picking a wealth-transfer policy:
  - □ Stick with large, experienced, well-rated insurance companies.
  - □ Assume cash value will grow at a rate midway between the current rate and the guaranteed rate.
  - □ Be sure that the company's recent net investment yield comfortably exceeds the median rate from Step 2.
  - □ Of all the companies still in the running after Steps 1 through 3, pick the one with the highest internal rate of return on death benefits.
- Insurance companies rate the people they insure according to their health. The better your health, the lower the premium. Policy illustrations are worthless unless they consider your risk rating.

- You may get better risk ratings by shopping around among insurance companies.
- You may want to find out your risk rating, and your likely cost, before going to the expense of creating an irrevocable life insurance trust. Some low-cost techniques may be available.

Afterword:
The Winning Team Wins

If you think wealth transfer can be a complicated process, you're right. To make sure all your wealth stays in your family, rather than see it shrink by hundreds of thousands of dollars, you'll need to devote some time and effort.

Fortunately, you don't have to do it yourself. You don't have to become an expert on the Internal Revenue Code or trusts or life insurance or money management. Instead, you can assemble a team of professionals to implement your wealth-transfer plan. The better your team, the smoother your wealth transfer will be.

Then why bother learning about wealth transfer at all? Why not just hire an attorney and an accountant and let them do it? Because you're the one who has to make the ultimate decisions. An attorney might draw up a charitable remainder trust, for example, but you're the one who has to decide whether it makes sense for you.

Similarly, the more you know about wealth transfer, the better the team you can put together. There are plenty of people out there in all fields calling themselves "experts," who are in fact not very knowledgeable. When you know how wealth transfer is supposed to work, you can ask the right questions and select the right professionals, avoiding costly mistakes for yourself and your family.

The Estate-Planning Attorney: The Key Player

Of all the people you'll need on your team, the estate-planning attorney is the most important. He or she will draw up any trusts you'll need; after your death, the attorney will work with your family to settle your estate. Picking the wrong attorney can wreck a wealth-transfer plan.

How can you select the right attorney? Ideally, you'll want a lawyer who's also a CPA, who has a master's degree in tax law and who specializes in trusts and estates. Unfortunately, such attorneys are hard to find.

Being more realistic, your family lawyer is the logical one to start with, or the lawyer who handles your company's legal matters. At least he or she will be familiar with your family and your affairs.

Should your lawyer handle your estate? It helps if he or she is your own age or (preferably) younger. You don't want someone who's ready to retire and won't be around to settle your estate.

Youth isn't the only criterion, though. You need to find out how knowledgeable the attorney is about wealth transfer. You should ask "How many irrevocable life insurance trusts have you done?" If the answer is "None" or "Just a few," that's a red flag.

Suppose the lawyer says "I don't believe in life insurance trusts." Does that mean he'd rather spend time helping your family liquidate half your estate to pay taxes, and bill you by the hour?

Besides life insurance, there are other questions to ask. How do you feel about living trusts? Are you familiar with the "shrinking trust" strategy? Do you have experience with charitable remainder trusts? private foundations? family limited partnerships? wealth trusts?

As you can see, if you're armed with knowledge about wealth transfer, you can interview the attorney rather than have the attorney interview you. You want a wealth-transfer attorney who has kept up with the field. The principle is similar to looking for a doctor: you want one whose practice is state-of-the-art, not one who is limited to what he learned in medical school 20 years ago.

Choosing an estate-planning attorney is like hiring any other professional, or even like hiring an employee. You need a qualifying interview first to see if an attorney is skilled and if you two get along. After all, you'll be confiding all your personal and financial secrets to this lawyer.

Bringing In a Power Hitter

In some situations, you'll want to work with your own lawyer whom you know and trust, but who is not an estate-planning expert. If so, you might ask if he or she is willing to work with a specialist. This effectively puts two lawyers on your team: a pro who spends a lot of time drafting trusts, foundations, partnerships, etc., and your own local attorney, who'll work with your family. This can be a powerful combination.

If your local attorney is willing to work with a wealth-transfer specialist, how do you find one? Start by asking the local attorney. If he or she is with a sizable law firm, there may be an estate-planning specialist right down the hall. Or your lawyer may know, personally or by reputation, a highly regarded estate-planning attorney with another firm.

Your local lawyer may not know of a wealth-transfer pro. In that case, it's up to you to find one. Your CPA, for example, may have a suggestion (major accounting firms have their own specialists in trusts and estates). If you intend to provide for your alma mater or some other public charity, that organization may be able to refer you to an estate-planning attorney. Other possible sources for referrals include the bank that you use and nearby law schools.

Life insurance professionals may help you too. If you're working with a competent agent, he or she may refer you to an attorney with the right skills. In addition, the advanced underwriting departments of major life-insurance companies often have experienced estate-planning attorneys on staff or on retainer.

If you tap the people in your network, you should be able to find an experienced estate-planning attorney. But just because someone has been introduced to you as an expert, don't take him or her at face value. You'll still need to interview even the most highly recommended professionals. Be sure to ask the questions we posed at the beginning of this chapter to find out how knowledgeable a lawyer really is.

Top-Notch Teammates

Once your estate attorney is in place, the rest of the team can be assembled. You'll need an accountant, for example. The CPA who prepares your tax return or your business return probably will be suitable. The main role of your accountant is to help you value your assets and figure out your estate-tax liability. He or she should be able to tell you how much your family will owe if you die today and project your estate-tax liability in 10 or 20 years.

Should a financial planner be on the team? If you have been working with a planner, one that you trust, by all means include your planner. He or she may be able to direct the team, help you find a good attorney, etc. But don't hire a planner solely for wealth transfer if you wouldn't use one otherwise.

Another professional you might need is a money manager. Suppose you set up a charitable remainder trust and donate raw land that has appreciated in value. The trust can sell the land without incurring a capital-gains tax. But now the trust has cash, perhaps a considerable amount of cash. For your wealth-transfer strategy to work well, that cash must be invested well.

For these and similar situations you may want a professional money manager. Your broker or financial planner may recommend someone. You'll want to check on the money manager's long-term track record, of course. But you'll also want to sit down with the manager to see if you're comfortable with his or her philosophy and make sure he or she is aware of your goals. If you have a charitable remainder trust that's obliged to pay annual income, for example, you don't want a money manager whose specialty is low-yielding emerging growth stocks.

If you've had success managing your own investment portfolio, you might manage trust assets while you're alive (assuming you're the trustee). If, however, the trust will continue with assets to manage after your death, you should pick a pro to manage the money then.

When you pick a money manager, you probably can do better than to select the trust department at your local bank. Bank trust departments usually don't employ top professionals—the best performers leave banks to set up their own money-management firms—so they tend to be too conservative. Some banks, for example, have invested mainly in long-term bonds, which historically have not kept up with stocks or inflation, after taxes.

Finding a Life-Insurance Agent Who'll Go to Bat for You

If you decide that you'll need life insurance to fund your wealth-transfer strategies, you'll need an insurance agent on your team. To choose an agent, exercise the same care as in choosing an estate-planning attorney. There's no apprentice system in the insurance industry, so it takes work to discover who is a real professional and who is a polished longtime novice.

If you're married, be sure to ask any prospective agent if he or she has worked extensively with second-to-die life insurance. That may be the most effective tool in wealth transfer the insurance industry offers today.

Ask about the agent's day-to-day operating procedures. Some experienced agents will *triple submit*—they'll routinely ask for offers from three different companies. Agents who work with only one company may not be providing the best service for their clients.

Why is this important? Because insurance underwriting (see Chapter 22) is more art than science. If you apply to three companies, you'll get three medical exams and three evaluations. Often there will be significant differences in the premiums different companies will charge for the same amount of insurance coverage.

A savvy agent not only will submit to three companies, he or she will tell the companies they have competition. The idea is to play one against the other to get better offers. If two offers for a $1 million policy, for example, are reasonably close, a good agent will buy a $500,000 policy from both companies.

Why do that? Because now the agent has relations with two insurance companies, not just one. Over the course of a year, that agent may give business to as many as 10 different life insurers. When the agent triple submits, these 10 companies will be among the ones that provide offers. If the agent never gave any business to a life insurer, that insurer would soon stop providing offers. A good agent keeps all the avenues open for his or her clients.

A good life-insurance agent handles the little details you might not even know about. For example, whenever you apply for life insurance, you'll have to take a physical exam. The insurance company also will ask for an *attending physician's* (AP) *statement*. That is, it will require a report from your family physician to get a good picture of your overall health.

Some professional agents will write for an AP statement before asking for offers. The AP statement can help the agent preselect certain insurers. These agents know which insurance companies are the best prospects if a client has a heart condition, for example, or the best for clients who have had cancer operations. If the agent finds out that you're a superman from your medical records, he or she may know which companies are best for preferred risks. Then the agent will copy the AP statement and send the copies to the chosen insurance companies.

Little things like getting AP statements first can steer you to the right insurers and speed the entire process. Also, your physician will appreciate getting one request, rather than three, for AP statements.

Note that we said that a good insurance agent will get three *offers,* not three quotes. Any agent can get quotes from insurers by simply tapping a computerized data base. Those quotes assume the applicant is a standard health risk; they're not binding on the insurance company.

An offer from an insurance company comes only after the applicant has been examined and his or her medical history has been reviewed. These offers, therefore, are 100 percent binding on the insurance company. Today, there can be wide variations from one insurer to another, so it really pays to triple submit and get three binding offers.

Is this extra work and extra expense for an insurance agent? Definitely. But if you find an agent who'll hustle for you, you're likely to have a player worth putting on your wealth-transfer team.

Don't Lose the Numbers Game

A few more words on the professionals who'll serve on your wealth-transfer team. These professionals may be great guys or gals, but they all need to be paid. You don't want to be penny-wise and pound-foolish, looking for cut-priced expertise. But you also can't assume that a professional is the best just because he or she is the most expensive.

Don't be shy. Before you add anyone to your wealth-transfer team, ask, "How are you compensated?" Will it be on a retainer basis, per hour or per piece of work (i.e., so much to prepare a trust)? Money managers typically get 1 percent or 2 percent of assets under management. Get agreements in writing, especially from your estate-planning attorney. If you know the rules from the start, you can avoid unpleasant surprises later on.

Chances are, you'll be able to tell if a fee seems out of line. If you're used to paying $100 per hour for legal work in your area, you don't need to pay $250 per hour to an estate-planning attorney. If you're not sure, check with friends and associates for an idea of the going rates.

Your life insurance agent will be paid a commission if you buy life insurance from him or her. The same may be true of a financial planner, for an insurance product or a mutual fund. Just be sure that all commissions are disclosed and reasonable—why is he or she putting you into a mutual fund with an 8.5 percent load when there are similar no-load or low-load funds?

Besides compensation, you want to know if a professional has ability and integrity. How can you find out? Ask for references and check them. Particularly ask for clients with long-standing relationships, because you want to be sure that your professionals will be around for the long haul, serving you and your family.

Amateurs Can Play, Too

Your wealth-transfer team has a couple of slots that needn't be filled by professionals. You'll certainly need an executor, now sometimes called a *personal representative.* Your executor will be the one responsible for handling your estate after your death.

Usually, your spouse or a grown child can act as executor. The position doesn't require any technical expertise, just common sense and the ability to handle paperwork. Experts—accountants, attorneys, appraisers—can be hired, if needed. So if you have a family member with a sense of responsibility, he or she likely will make a good executor.

What if nobody seems qualified? Say your spouse gets flustered while filling out forms and both of your grown children live thousands of miles away. A personal friend or business partner might serve as an executor; as a last resort, choose an accountant or bank executive who's familiar with your affairs.

You also will have to name trustees if you're setting up trusts that will continue after your death. An irrevocable life-insurance trust, for example. Someone will have to collect the insurance proceeds, inject liquidity into the estate, dispose of trust assets, etc.

Again, a responsible family member, especially a grown child, can serve as trustee. If expert advice is needed—a money manager, for example—the trustee can hire the appropriate person. In case there's no one in your family who can serve as trustee, or if your trust is particularly complex, you might turn to your local bank's trust department. However, be certain that you specify that the bank administer the trust rather than manage money; you'll want a top-rated investment adviser for the money management.

Don't forget to name successor executors and trustees in case your first choices die or run into personal difficulties.

Should your wealth-transfer team be a real team? Should it hold regular meetings? That's not practical in most cases. The different players should, however, know who else is on the team and how to get hold of each other.

Some team players especially need to know each other. Your executor, for example, should know the attorney who'll be handling your estate and how the attorney will be compensated. If you have a trustee who'll have money to manage, you may want to decide beforehand that you and your trustee agree on which investment adviser will be selected, if desired. Your team can win the wealth game only if everyone knows what position they'll be playing and how you want them to play.

- Finding a knowledgeable estate-planning attorney is the key to a successful wealth-transfer plan.
- You'll probably need to work with an accountant, too, and perhaps a life-insurance agent, a financial planner and a money manager.
- Other team members, your executor and trustees, can be responsible family members, especially grown children.
- When selecting an estate-planning attorney, ask questions to see if he or she is familiar with sophisticated wealth-transfer strategies.
- If you'd like to work with your family's or company's lawyer, but he or she is not an expert in wealth transfer, you may have your lawyer team up with a pro who specializes in trusts and estates.
- If life insurance is in your wealth-transfer plan, a competent agent is another necessity. Find out how he or she goes about providing service to clients.

- Find out how professionals will be compensated right from the start to avoid misunderstandings later on. Get agreements in writing.
- Check references before hiring professionals.
- Make sure all the members of your team know each other, and what each is supposed to do.

THE WEALTH-TRANSFER NUMBERS GAME

Asset Inventory Worksheet

Making a complete inventory of your assets is the first step in preparing a wealth-transfer plan. The worksheet below shows you how to organize your inventory for easy reference.

Assets	In Your Name	In Your Spouse's Name	In Joint Names
Your home (current market value)	$_____	_____	_____
Other real estate	_____	_____	_____
Bank accounts (checking and savings	_____	_____	_____
Other cash accounts (money-market funds, savings bonds, brokerage cash accounts, etc.)	_____	_____	_____
Stocks, bonds and mutual funds	_____	_____	_____
Life insurance (face value)	_____	_____	_____
Business interests	_____	_____	_____
Retirement plan accounts • IRA	_____	_____	_____
• Pension	_____	_____	_____
• Other (401k, profit-sharing plan, etc.)	_____	_____	_____
Personal property (replacement value of jewelry, autos, household furnishings, etc.)	_____	_____	_____
Annuities, trusts or other assets	_____	_____	_____
Collectibles (market value of fine art, precious metals, etc.)	_____	_____	_____
Total Assets:	$_____	$_____	$_____

Liabilities

	In Your Name	In Your Spouse's Name	In Joint Names
Mortgages	_____	_____	_____
Life insurance loans	_____	_____	_____
Other loans or debts	_____	_____	_____
Total Liabilities:	$_____	$_____	$_____
Net Estate (assets less liabilities)	$_____	$_____	$_____

Unified Federal Gift and Estate Tax

To determine your federal tax obligation, subtract the unified credit from the tax in the third column. On a $1 million estate, for example, the tax would be $345,800 − $192,800 = $153,000.

Gift and Estate Tax Credit		
Time of Death or Gift	Unified Credit	Tax-Sheltered Estate
After 1986	$192,800	$600,000

Taxable Gift or Estate		Tentative Tax	
Column 1 FROM	TO	Tax on Column 1	Rate on Excess (%)
$ 0	$ 10,000	$ 0	18
10,001	20,000	1,800	20
20,001	40,000	3,800	22
40,001	60,000	8,200	24
60,001	80,000	13,000	26
80,001	100,000	18,200	28
100,001	150,000	23,800	30
150,001	250,000	38,000	32
250,001	500,000	70,800	34
500,001	750,000	155,800	37
750,001	1,000,000	248,300	39
1,000,001	**1,250,000**	**345,800**	**39**
1,250,001	1,500,000	448,300	43
1,500,001	2,000,000	555,800	45
2,000,001	**2,500,000**	**780,800**	**49**
2,500,001	3,000,000	1,025,800	53
3,000,001	**10,000,000**	**1,290,800**	**55**
10,000,001	20,000,000		60
20,000,000+			55

State Tax Scoreboard

Nine states that tax your estate **and** your heirs—with no spousal exemption on the death of the first spouse:

Connecticut	Louisiana	Montana
Delaware	Maryland	Pennsylvania
Idaho	Michigan	Tennessee

Ten states that tax your estate **and** your heirs—but with a spousal exemption on the death of the first spouse:

Indiana	Nebraska	North Carolina
Iowa	New Hampshire	South Dakota
Kansas	New Jersey	Wisconsin
Kentucky		

Nine states that collect estate taxes that may exceed the federal credit:

Maine	New York	Oregon
Massachusetts	Ohio	Rhode Island
Mississippi	Oklahoma	South Carolina

Twenty-two states that claim a dollar-for-dollar offset against federal estate taxes (You pay no extra estate tax, but these states claim a share of what your heirs send the IRS):

Alabama	Hawaii	Texas
Alaska	Illinois	Utah
Arizona	Minnesota	Vermont
Arkansas	Missouri	Virginia
California	Nevada (no tax)	Washington
Colorado	New Mexico	West Virginia
Florida	North Dakota	Wyoming
Georgia		

NOTE: If you own property in more than one state, you could be subject to multiple state jurisdictions.

Table A-4
Using Life Insurance for Wealth Transfer

Do Nothing   **12.5:1 Leverage**
                              Spouses Aged 50 and 52

Estate Tax Due: $1 million   **Estate Tax Due:** $1 million

You need: $1 million at death   **You need:** $80,000 gifted to irre-
of second spouse.   vocable life-insurance trust. See
                                     chart below.

Year	Annual Premium	Death Benefit
1	$8,000	$1,000,000
2	$8,000	$1,000,000
3	$8,000	$1,000,000
4	$8,000	$1,000,000
5	$8,000	$1,000,000
6	$8,000	$1,000,000
7	$8,000	$1,000,000
8	$8,000	$1,000,000
9	$8,000	$1,000,000
10	$8,000	$1,000,000
Total Paid	$80,000	

After ten years, the cash value is likely to exceed the premiums paid. The cash value will keep growing until age 95, when it will equal the face value of the policy.

table A-4, cont.

7.5:1 Leverage
Spouses Aged 60 and 62

Estate Tax Due: $1 million

You need: $135,000 gifted to irrevocable life-insurance trust.

Annual Premium	Death Benefit
$13,500	$1,000,000
$13,500	$1,000,000
$13,500	$1,000,000
$13,500	$1,000,000
$13,500	$1,000,000
$13,500	$1,000,000
$13,500	$1,000,000
$13,500	$1,000,000
$13,500	$1,000,000
$13,500	$1,000,000
$135,000	

4.5:1 Leverage
Spouses Aged 68 and 70

Estate Tax Due: $1 million

You need: $225,000 gifted to irrevocable life-insurance trust.

Annual Premium	Death Benefit
$22,500	$1,000,000
$22,500	$1,000,000
$22,500	$1,000,000
$22,500	$1,000,000
$22,500	$1,000,000
$22,500	$1,000,000
$22,500	$1,000,000
$22,500	$1,000,000
$22,500	$1,000,000
$22,500	$1,000,000
$225,000	

NOTES:
- The examples show the advantages (12.5:1, 7.5:1, and 4.5:1) of the insurance-trust method over doing nothing at three ages.
- Estimated annual premiums and 10-year vanish point assume a certain current interest rate. A lower rate continues premiums longer; if rates rise, premiums could end sooner.
- Premium and death-benefit illustrations on these pages are based on a composite of contracts with two major $10 billion insurance companies rated A+ by A.M. Best. To be conservative, split insurance coverage between two or three top insurance companies.

B

A TAX-FREE INHERITANCE TRUST— PLUS HOW A CHARITABLE REMAINDER TRUST WORKS

STEVEN A. SCIARRETTA
PROFESSIONAL ASSOCIATION

ATTORNEY AT LAW

LL.M IN TAXATION
TAXATION AND BUSINESS PLANNING
ESTATE PLANNING AND ADMINISTRATION

ONE BOCA PLACE
2255 GLADES ROAD, SUITE 405 EAST
BOCA RATON, FLORIDA 33431

TELEPHONE: (407) 241-6600
TOLL FREE: 1-800-545-8454
FAX: (407) 241-6617

May 1, 1991

Mr. and Mrs. Andrew D. Westhem

Re <u>Irrevocable Trust</u>

Dear Andrew and Emily:

We drafted a WEALTH TRUST for you. Your children, DAVID WESTHEM and LISA WESTHEM are named as the initial Trustees of the Trust Agreement.

Normally, a Federal Gift Tax Return (form 709) must be filed when a gift is made to an individual. An exception exists for gifts not in excess of $10,000 made to any individual. This exclusion exists only for gifts of present interests in property. Because a gift to an Irrevocable Trust is generally not a gift of a <u>present</u> interest, but is a gift of an interest to be received in the <u>future</u>, the $10,000 exclusion does not normally apply.

In order to obtain the $10,000 exclusion, we included in your Irrevocable Trust the right for each of the beneficiaries of the Trust to withdraw his or her prorata share of the annual gifts to the Trust, up to a maximum of $10,000, with certain limitations. Please be advised however, that gifts in excess of $5,000 per donor per beneficiary may create adverse tax implications for the beneficiary, if said beneficiary should decline to exercise his or her annual right to withdraw these sums. Therefore, if sums aggregating in excess of $5,000 are needed in order to provide for required trust expenditures, it may be necessary for someone other than you to make additions to this trust.

In order to document your intent to make a present gift to the beneficiaries of the Trust, we have drafted a letter from you to the Trustee, indicating that gifts made to the Trust should be subject to the withdrawal right contained in the Trust Agreement.

Similarly, the Trustee should communicate to each of the beneficiaries their right to make the withdrawal. Therefore, in order to document this communication, we have drafted a sample letter that the Trustee can use to communicate to each beneficiary their withdrawal right. If the beneficiary is a minor, the letter should be addressed to the parent or guardian of the child, on behalf of the child. When any child reaches the age of eighteen, his or her letter should be sent directly to that child. The letters should also be adjusted for births and deaths.

While the tax laws provide that each contributor will be exempt from gift taxation for contributions to each beneficiary through the trust not in excess of $10,000, as noted previously, a similar provision does not exist as regards the Federal Generation Skipping Tax. Therefore, in order to exempt from the Federal Generation Skipping Tax the amounts contributed to this trust on behalf of your grandchildren, it will be necessary for each contributor to elect to allocate to their contribution an amount of their Generation Skipping Tax exemption available pursuant to Section 2631 of the Internal Revenue Code of 1986, and as amended, equal to the amount of contribution made. Such allocation is made coincidentally on form 709 as noted previously. Therefore, you must be certain that a Federal Generation Skipping Tax return is filed for each year in which contributions are made to this trust. Please be sure to communicate the necessity of filing this return to your tax preparer.

It will also be necessary for the Trust to have its own federal identification number. We, therefore, have provided that number; it is fed tax #65-123456789. This number should be used by the Trustee in opening a bank account in the name of the Trust. The bank account must be opened and all payments for premiums should be made with checks drawn on this account. The money for premium payments should be deposited by the Trustee into this separate trust account at least thirty (30) days prior to the premium due date, so that the beneficiaries will have an opportunity to exercise their withdrawal rights.

If you should have any questions, please do not hesitate to contact me.

Sincerely,

STEVEN A. SCIARRETTA

SAS/sms

STEVEN A. SCIARRETTA, P.A.

STEVEN A. SCIARRETTA
PROFESSIONAL ASSOCIATION

ATTORNEY AT LAW

LL.M. IN TAXATION
TAXATION AND BUSINESS PLANNING
ESTATE PLANNING AND ADMINISTRATION

ONE BOCA PLACE
2255 GLADES ROAD, SUITE 405 EAST
BOCA RATON, FLORIDA 33431

TELEPHONE: (407) 241-6600
TOLL FREE: 1-800-545-8454
FAX: (407) 241-6617

TO: DAVID WESTHEM and LISA WESTHEM, TRUSTEES OF THE ANDREW D.
        WESTHEM AND EMILY WESTHEM IRREVOCABLE WEALTH TRUST DATED
        MAY 1, 1991

DATE: MAY 1, 1991

RE: ANDREW D. WESTHEM AND EMILY WESTHEM IRREVOCABLE WEALTH
        TRUST DATED MAY 1, 1991

The following Memorandum is designed to assist you, as the Trustee of the ANDREW D. WESTHEM AND EMILY WESTHEM IRREVOCABLE WEALTH TRUST DATED MAY 1, 1991 in implementing the terms thereof.

It is important for you, as the Trustee, to keep in mind that adherence to the deadlines outlined below is critical; failure to meet a deadline could result in the cancellation of an insurance policy or the loss of very significant tax benefits.

Any questions you may have in connection with the implementation of the terms of the ANDREW D. WESTHEM AND EMILY WESTHEM IRREVOCABLE WEALTH TRUST DATED MAY 1, 1991 should be directed to Steven A. Sciarretta, Esquire, 2255 Glades Road, Suite 405 East, Boca Raton, Florida, 334341, (800) 545-8454.

Questions regarding the insurance policies comprising the corpus of the ANDREW D. WESTHEM AND EMILY WESTHEM IRREVOCABLE WEALTH TRUST DATED MAY 1, 1991 should be directed to Mr. Andrew Westhem, Wealth Transfer Planning,Inc. 1925 Century Park East, Suite 2350, Los Angeles, California, 90067, (800) 423-4891

The Federal tax identification number of this trust is 65-123456789.

ASSETS

The trust consists of the following assets:

        second-to-die policy number LB3-45678.   Insured

        second-to-die policy number 1-888000-X6.   Insured
through

through   second-to-die policy number 045AXL27.   Insured

through   second-to-die policy number ABX-00000078.   Insured

through   second-to-die policy number 9-100028-405.   Insured

PAYMENT OF PREMIUMS

No later than May 15th of each year, the trustee should write to the Settlor inquiring as to whether the Settlor will be making a contribution to the trust. If the Settlor is so inclined, the Settlor may consider providing a contribution by check, payable to the trustee, which may be in an amount sufficient to satisfy the year's premium requirement.

In conjunction with the check, the Settlor should provide a letter to the trustee which directs the trustee to inform each beneficiary as to the beneficiary's withdrawal rights onder the Trust. A draft version of such a letter is attached hereto.

Upon receipt of any contribution to the trust, you, as the trustee, MUST notify each beneficiary as to his or her withdrawal rights. Such rights are enumerated in Article V of the Trust. A draft version of a letter sufficient to provide such notice is attached hereto.

This contribution, if in cash, should be held by you, as trustee, in a separate bank account in the name of the ANDREW D. WESTHEM AND EMILY WESTHEM IRREVOCABLE WEALTH TRUST DATED MAY 1, 1991. This account should bear the federal tax identification number as listed above.

If the contribution is in a form other than cash, you as the trustee should see to it that the gifted asset is properly titled in the name of the ANDREW D. WESTHEM AND EMILY WESTHEM IRREVOCABLE WEALTH TRUST DATED MAY 1, 1991.

In the event that any beneficiary should elect to exercise his or her right of withdrawal, then, you shall pay to the beneficiary the pro rata portion of the contribution to which the beneficiary is entitled.

As and when the withdrawal period has ended, or sooner if all beneficiary's have waived their rights of withdrawal, you, as trustee, may pay the outstanding insurance premium. Insurance premiums are due no later than July 1st.

STEVEN A. SCIARRETTA, P.A.

TAX RETURNS

The ANDREW D. WESTHEM AND EMILY WESTHEM IRREVOCABLE WEALTH TRUST DATED MAY 1, 1991 will be calendar year taxpayer and will be required to file its' annual federal income tax return by April 15, each year, if a return is necessary. You will need to speak with a qualified tax return preparer in order to determine if a return must be filed. Please be certain to provide the tax return preparer with all pertinent information as regards the trust.

STEVEN A. SCIARRETTA, P.A.

<u>**ANDREW D. WESTHEM**</u>
<u>**AND**</u>
<u>**EMILY WESTHEM**</u>
<u>**IRREVOCABLE WEALTH TRUST**</u>
<u>**DATED MAY 1, 1991**</u>

<u>INDEX TO PROVISIONS</u>

SUCCESSION OF TRUSTEES:
Including Provisions whereby each child
of Settlor and the Eldest child of each
child of Settlor may choose to act as a
Co-Trustee   Page 1

FUNDING:
Including provisions whereby property
may be added to THE WEALTH TRUST   Page 2

IRREVOCABILITY: Page 2

BENEFICIARIES:
Including provisions whereby after-born
grandchildren may be provided for   Page 2

ADMINISTRATION AND DISTRIBUTION
OF TRUST DURING LIFETIME OF SETTLOR:
For the benefit of the beneficiaries in the
event property other than life insurance
policies are contributed to the Trust   Page 2

ADMINISRATION AND DISTRIBUTION
OF TRUST AT DEATH OF SETTLOR:
Including the ability for the Trustee to
provide for children and grandchildren upon
the death of Settlor. The provisions herein
contained also include Dynasty Powers
whereby the Trustee is specifically empowered
to make distributions to purchase insurance
to perpetuate the Trust fund   Page 4

PROCEDURES FOR RESIGNATION OF TRUSTEES,
REMOVAL OF TRUSTEES AND APPOINTMENT OF
SUCCESSOR TRUSTEES:
Including the ability to appoint a
corporate Trustee, should one be
necessary in the future.   Page 8

TRUSTEE'S POWERS, RIGHTS AND DUTIES:
With specific emphasis added to empower
the Trustee to purchase and hold
residential real property. Additionally,

provisions are provided to enable the
Trustee to purchase property belonging
to the estate of the Settlor in order
to provide liquidity to the Settlor's
estate

Page 9

RIGHTS AND DUTIES OF TRUSTEES
BETWEEN THEMSELVES:
Including limitations whereby a Trustee
shall not make a discretionary distribution
to himself

Page 14

INSURANCE BENEFITS:
Specifically directing the Trustee to
immediately make diligent effort to
collect all death benefits payable to
the Trust

Page 15

GENERAL PROVISIONS:
With provision specifically exempting
the income and principal of this Trust
from each beneficiary's creditors,
including those arising through divorce
or other legal actions

Page 15

DEFINITIONS:

Page 16

GOVERNING LAW:

Page 17

EXECUTION PROVISIONS:

Page 17

ANDREW D. WESTHEM
and
EMILY WESTHEM
IRREVOCABLE WEALTH TRUST
DATED MAY 1, 1991

    THIS AGREEMENT of Trust is made by and between ANDREW D.
WESTHEM and EMILY WESTHEM, residents of the County of Los Angeles, State
of California, hereinafter collectively referred to as "Settlor", and
DAVID WESTHEM and LISA WESTHEM, hereinafter collectively referred to as
"Trustee", for the benefit of those persons designated in this
Agreement.

ARTICLE I
SUCCESSION OF TRUSTEES

    Section 1   DAVID WESTHEM and LISA WESTHEM, children of the
Settlor, shall be Trustee of all the trusts under this Agreement.
However, when any child of Settlor is acting as a Co-Trustee hereunder,
and said child may be entitled to a discretionary distribution under any
provisions of this instrument, then, said child shall not participate in
any determinations relating to such distribution, in accordance with the
provisions of Article IX hereunder.

    Section 2   If at any time either DAVID WESTHEM or LISA
WESTHEM should be unable or unwilling to continue to act as Trustee
hereunder, then, U.S. TRUST COMPANY, shall act along with the one of
them then remaining, as Successor Trustee of all the Trusts under this
Agreement.

    Section 3   If neither DAVID WESTHEM nor LISA WESTHEM should
be able or willing to act as Successor Trustee, then, U.S. TRUST COMPANY
shall act as sole Successor Trustee of all Trusts under this Agreement.

    Section 4   At any time after the death of the surviving
Settlor, the eldest living child of each child of Settlor then so
choosing, who has attained the age of twenty-five (25) years, shall have
the right to elect to act as a Co-Trustee along with any then acting
Trustee. However, if said grandchild may be entitled to a discretionary
distribution under any provisions of this instrument while said
grandchild is acting as a Co-Trustee, said grandchild shall not
participate in any determinations relating to such distribution.

    Section 5   When the term Trustee is used without other
words of description, it shall refer to any Trustee or to all Trustees
acting at the time the term is applied. Notwithstanding the foregoing
however, in the event there shall be more than one Trustee acting at any
time, then, any and all acts of the Trustee shall occur only upon a
majority vote of the Trustees then acting.

ARTICLE II
FUNDING

Property which is acceptable to the Trustee may be transferred to the Trustee by the Settlor or by others. Such transfers may be accomplished at any time by any instrument, including a LAST WILL AND TESTAMENT, REVOCABLE LIVING TRUST or other like document.

ARTICLE III
IRREVOCABILITY

This Agreement of Trust is irrevocable and may not be amended. The Settlor, under no circumstances, shall be entitled to exercise any control over any of the trusts under this Agreement in any manner.

ARTICLE IV
BENEFICIARIES

The beneficiaries of this trust for purposes of the withdrawal and remainder provisions hereinafter set forth are DAVID WESTHEM and LISA WESTHEM, children of the Settlor, and the living children of DAVID WESTHEM, and the living children of LISA WESTHEM (the grandchildren of Settlor). Any child born to or legally adopted by either DAVID WESTHEM or LISA WESTHEM, subsequent to the date of this trust shall also be deemed a beneficiary for purposes of the withdrawal and remainder provisions. The rights of any such beneficiary who shall have predeceased either Settlor shall pass to the lineal descendants of the deceased beneficiary pursuant to Articles V and VI hereunder.

ARTICLE V
ADMINISTRATION AND DISTRIBUTION
OF TRUST DURING LIFETIME OF SETTLOR

Section 1   Provided there are assets in the trust other than life insurance contracts, the Trustee may, until the death of the surviving Settlor and after paying the necessary expenses of the management and preservation of the trust estate, in the Trustee's sole reasonable discretion; (i) distribute to or for the benefit of the beneficiaries or accumulate for their benefit, all or any part of the income of the trust created hereunder; and (ii) distribute to or for the benefit of the beneficiaries all or any amount of the principal of the trust created hereunder as the Trustee deems appropriate for the health and support of the beneficiaries without regard to other resources available to the beneficiaries. Any income so accumulated shall be held and distributed on termination in accordance with Article VI hereof.

Section 2   Following each contribution to this trust, for
which contribution the contributor availed himself or herself of the
Gift Tax exclusion available to the contributor pursuant to Section
2503(b) of the Internal Revenue Code of 1986, and as amended, then,
notwithstanding any other provision of this Agreement, each beneficiary
shall have the absolute right, at all times during the one (1) month
period commencing on the date of receipt of written notice to said
beneficiary of the contribution, to withdraw from the contribution thus
made to such trust, in cash or royalty, as determined by the Trustee, an
amount equal to the lesser of: the beneficiary's pro rata share of the
entire contribution to the trust; or a portion of the contribution
having a fair market value equal to the amount specified for the gift
tax exclusion in Internal Revenue Code Section 2503(b), as from time to
time amended.   Said rights of withdrawal shall be subject to the
following terms and conditions:

(a) As set forth above, the amount subject to a
beneficiary's right of withdrawal in any calendar year shall not exceed
the amount provided as the "exclusion" by Section 2503(b) of the
Internal Revenue Code of 1986, as now or hereafter amended. Should the
amount of any beneficiary's right of withdrawal exceed the amount
provided for under Section 2514(e) of the Internal Revenue Code, as now
or hereafter amended, and should the beneficiary decline to exercise
such right of withdrawal, then the amounts represented by such right or
rights of withdrawal shall be cumulative to the beneficiary.   All
cumulative withdrawal rights shall remain available to the beneficiary
until the earlier of: the expiration of the trust as provided for in
Article VI hereunder; or upon the death of the beneficiary.

(b) Each such right of withdrawal shall be exercised only
by a written instrument executed by the beneficiary possessing such
right, delivered to the Trustee during the one (1) month period
commencing on the date of receipt of written notice by said beneficiary
of the contribution to the trust. If, in the opinion of the Trustee, a
beneficiary is under a disability of any nature, the Trustee, in the
exercise of its sole discretion, may require that the right of
withdrawal be exercised by written instrument executed by the legal
guardian of the beneficiary, however, in no event shall the Settlor
exercise such right of withdrawal on behalf of any beneficiary.

(c) The Trustee shall at all times, if amounts
represented by rights of withdrawal are still outstanding, retain
sufficient transferable assets from the contribution to the trust in
order to satisfy amounts representing all rights of withdrawals from all
beneficiaries which may then be outstanding.   Each beneficiary shall
have the right to compel the Trustee to convert whatever trust corpus
may be necessary into transferable form in order to enable each such
beneficiary to secure the benefits of the exercise of his or her right
of withdrawal.

(d)   In the event that the death of any beneficiary occurs prior to the termination of this trust, then, the amount of property represented by the accumulated rights of withdrawal of said beneficiary (and credited to said beneficiary's account) shall be paid to those issue of said beneficiary as said beneficiary may appoint by said beneficiary's Last Will and Testament.   In default of the exercise of such special power of appointment, said property shall be paid in equal shares to said beneficiary's surviving issue, per stirpes, or if none, said property shall be distributed free of trust to those persons who would have taken the beneficiary's personal estate if the beneficiary had then died intestate, domiciled in Nevada, under the laws of California which then obtain, the shares and proportions of taking to be determined by said laws, or if no such persons are then living, then to those persons who would have taken the beneficiary's spouse's personal estate if the beneficiary's spouse had then died intestate, domiciled in California, under the laws of California which then obtain, the shares and proportions of taking to be determined by said laws.

ARTICLE VI
ADMINISTRATION AND DISTRIBUTION
OF TRUST AT DEATH OF SETTLOR AND DYNASTY PROVISIONS

Section 1   Upon the death of the surviving Settlor, the Trustee shall distribute to or for the benefit of the beneficiaries pursuant to Article IV, so much of the income and/or principal of this Trust, in such equal or unequal shares and proportions, as the Trustee, in its sole, reasonable discretion, may determine is required for their health, support, maintenance and education.   The Trustee may also grant unto the beneficiaries pursuant to Article IV, the right to occupy any and all real property comprising a portion of the Trust corpus.   Any undistributed income shall be periodically added to principal. Distributions from this Trust shall be made first from current income, then from income previously earned but undistributed, and then from principal.

DYNASTY PROVISIONS

Section 2   The Trustee is hereby specifically empowered, only after obtaining the acquiescence of any beneficiary or beneficiaries hereunder so electing, to distribute funds for the payment of any premium due on any policy of insurance, which policy insures the life of any beneficiary of this Trust.   Such distribution may be made only to a Trust or other like instrument, the corpus of which, will not be included as a part of the gross estate (as such term is defined in Section 2031 of the Internal Revenue Code of 1986, and as amended) of the insured beneficiary.   Any such distribution from the income or principal of this Trust, which distribution is applied towards the payment of premiums due on any policy of insurance which insures the life of any beneficiary hereunder, shall be deemed a transfer without

4

consideration on the part of the beneficiary or beneficiaries hereunder acquiescing to said distribution to the ultimate beneficiary or beneficiaries of said policy of life insurance. Notwithstanding the foregoing, however, the Trustee is authorized to make such distributions only if such distributions are not deemed to be a distribution of a "future interest", unless the beneficiary or beneficiaries hereunder acquiescing to said distribution shall authorize the Trustee, in writing, to make a distribution that will be deemed a "future interest".

<u>Section 3</u>
(a) Upon the death of any grandchild of Settlor who is a beneficiary under this trust, said grandchild shall appoint by his or her Last Will and Testament, an amount of the then remaining trust corpus (including a ratable amount of the accumulated but undistributed income), which amount shall be determined by multiplying the amount of then remaining trust corpus (including a ratable amount of the accumulated but undistributed income) by a fraction, the numerator of which is one (1), and the denominator of which shall be equal to one (1) PLUS the number of grandchildren of Settlor then living, who are beneficiaries of this trust. The appointing grandchild of Settlor shall make specific reference to this power of appointment. The power of appointment granted hereunder shall be a General, rather than a Specific, Power of Appointment. The Trustee may rely on any Will purporting to be the Last Will and Testament of the beneficiary, if such a Last Will and Testament is admitted to Probate in any jurisdiction of the United States and the Trustee receives written notice in a form and manner satisfactory to it of the admission to Probate of such Last Will and Testament within six (6) months following the death of the beneficiary. If the Trustee does not receive such written notice within the six (6) month period of such a Last Will and Testament having been admitted to Probate, it may make distribution pursuant to the applicable sections of this Article. If the Trustee receives such written notice, the Trustee shall not be required to make any distributions to any persons taking under the Last Will and Testament of the beneficiary until the Trustee determines to its satisfaction the validity of the purported Last Will and Testament of the beneficiary and the final effectiveness of the exercise of the power of appointment. The Trustee shall not be required to make any distributions so long as the Trustee is in doubt whether there has been an effective exercise of the power of appointment. The Trustee shall be under no liability to any person for any delays in making distribution.

(b) In the event that the deceased grandchild of Settlor has failed to exercise the power of appointment granted to such beneficiary pursuant to subsection (a) above, then, the Trustee shall divide the share determined in Section 3(a) above, into separate, equal shares, per stirpes, one share for each living child of the deceased grandchild of Settlor and one share for each deceased child of the deceased grandchild of Settlor with then living issue. Each share so set aside for the issue of a deceased child shall be further divided into sub-portions by allocation, per stirpes, among the then surviving issue of said deceased child (whom said issue represent) said deceased child to be the stock. Each share and each sub-portion shall constitute a Separate Trust to be held, administered and distributed as hereinafter set forth. To facilitate identification, Trustee shall designate each share and sub-portion with the name of the beneficiary for whom it was set aside.

(1) Until the beneficiary of a Separate Trust attains the age of twenty-one (21) years, Trustee, in its sole discretion, shall pay to such beneficiary, or expend on such beneficiary's behalf, so much of the net income derived from the Separate Trust as the Trustee may deem advisable to provide properly for his or her health, education, maintenance and support, and may incorporate any further income not so disbursed into the principal of the fund. Upon the beneficiary of a Separate Trust attaining the age of twenty-one (21) years, the net income of the Separate Trust shall be paid to the beneficiary in quarter annual or more frequent installments.

(2) Trustee shall also distribute to or for the benefit of the beneficiary such amounts of the principal as the Trustee, in its sole discretion determines is required for the health, support, maintenance and education of the beneficiary.

(3) The Trustee may also invade the corpus of a Separate Trust for the benefit of the beneficiary in order to educate said beneficiary (including technical or trade training; camp, travel or other informal training; college, post-graduate and professional training; if the beneficiary strives therefor in good faith); to provide said beneficiary with a home of his or her own; to enable the beneficiary to embark upon or to pursue a business or professional venture; to meet extraordinary requirements occasioned by illness or other misfortune; and to pay expenses of last illness and burial. In exercising this discretion, Trustee shall consider all other resources available to said beneficiary, including earnings or potential earnings, and if said beneficiary is a married person not working, the earnings or potential earnings of the beneficiary's spouse.

(4) Upon attainment by a beneficiary of a Separate Trust of the beneficiary's twenty-fifth (25th) birthdate, Trustee shall pay over to the beneficiary one-third (1/3) of the corpus of the Trust; upon the beneficiary's thirtieth (30th) birthdate, Trustee shall pay over to the beneficiary one-half (1/2) of the then corpus of the Trust; upon the beneficiary's thirty-fifth (35th) birthdate, Trustee shall pay over to the beneficiary the remaining corpus of the Trust.

(5) If any beneficiary shall have attained any of such respective ages at the time when such Separate Trust is directed to be set apart for that beneficiary, the Trustee shall distribute to such beneficiary such part or parts or all, as the case may be, of such

Separate Trust fund (instead of holding same in Trust) as are directed to be distributed to such beneficiary upon attaining such respective ages.

(6) If the beneficiary of a Separate Trust dies before complete distribution, Trustee shall pay over the corpus, including any accrued but undistributed income of the Trust, as said beneficiary may appoint by said beneficiary's Last Will and Testament. The Power of Appointment granted hereunder shall be a General, rather than a Special, Power of Appointment.

(7) In default of the exercise of such general power of appointment by said beneficiary, or insofar as such appointment shall be void or shall not take effect, then upon the death of a beneficiary of a Separate Trust, Trustee shall pay over the corpus to said beneficiary's then living issue, if any, per stirpes, subject to the provisions of Section 4 hereunder; otherwise to the beneficiary's parents' then living issue, per stirpes; provided, that if any such distributee is the original beneficiary of a Separate Trust hereinabove created and said Trust has not been completely distributed, the amount to be distributed shall be added to said Separate Trust.

Section 4   Whenever the provisions of this Article direct the outright distribution of all of or a share of any trust upon its division or termination and, if outright distribution is directed to a person who has not reached the age of twenty-one (21) years or who is not legally competent, the interest of such person shall vest, but the Trustee may, in its discretion, continue to hold and administer the share of such person in further trust until that person reaches the age of twenty-one (21) years or is restored to legal capacity, as the case may be. During such period, the Trustee shall distribute to or for the benefit of such person so much of the income and the principal from the trust as the Trustee determines, in its discretion, is required for the support, comfort, education and welfare of that person, periodically adding any undistributed income to the principal. When that person reaches the age of twenty-one (21) years, or is restored to legal capacity, the entire share shall be distributed to him or her outright. If that person should die before he or she is entitled to distribution under the provisions of this Section, Trustee shall pay over the corpus, including any accrued but undistributed income of the Trust to said beneficiary's estate.

Section 5   If the all of the beneficiaries of any trust administered under this Article die and none of the persons entitled to receive distribution of the trust estate are then living, the trust shall immediately terminate and the remaining trust estate shall be divided into two (2) separate equal shares. One share shall be distributed to the persons who would be entitled to receive ANDREW D. WESTHEM's property and the other share shall be distributed to the persons who would be entitled to receive the property of EMILY WESTHEM, such persons taking in the proportions provided by the laws of the State of California as if ANDREW D. WESTHEM and EMILY WESTHEM had both died at that time intestate, each surviving the other and domiciled in California.

ARTICLE VII
PROCEDURES FOR RESIGNATION OF TRUSTEES, REMOVAL OF
TRUSTEES AND APPOINTMENT OF SUCCESSOR TRUSTEES

Section 1   Any Trustee shall have the right at any time to resign by mailing written notice to the beneficiaries pursuant to Article IV, or to their legal guardian(s), acting on their behalf. Such resignation shall take effect sixty (60) days after the date of such notice. The resigning Trustee shall deliver to each said beneficiary a statement of all receipts and disbursements of the trust made by it and an inventory of assets then held by it belonging to the trust.

Section 2   Upon the resignation of any Trustee the beneficiaries pursuant to Article IV, upon the vote of a majority of said beneficiaries or of their legal guardian(s) acting in their behalf, shall, upon a majority vote, appoint a successor Trustee, pursuant to the provisions of Section 3 of this Article.

Section 3   The beneficiaries pursuant to Article IV, or their legal guardian(s) acting in their behalf, upon the vote of a majority of said beneficiaries or of their guardian(s) acting in their behalf, shall have the right to remove any Trustee and select a Successor to the Trustee which shall be only a banking association or a corporation regularly involved in the business of trust administration and counseling, under the following terms and conditions:

(a) Any Successor Corporate Trustee shall be an institution or the wholly owned subsidiary or affiliate of an institution having not less than Fifty Million ($50,000,000.00) Dollars in assets and capital of not less than Ten Million ($10,000,000.00) Dollars.

(b) The removal of the Trustee shall be made effective twenty (20) days after a letter in writing has been sent to the Trustee discharging the Trustee and informing the Trustee of the identity of the selected Successor Trustee.

(c) The Trustee, upon the effective date of its discharge, shall deliver to the Successor Trustee and to each such beneficiary of the trust a statement of all receipts and disbursements of each of the trusts together with an inventory of the assets belonging to the trust.

8

(d)   When the Successor Trustee shall deliver its receipt for the assets of each of the trusts to the Trustee so removed, the latter shall be discharged of all its duties and obligations hereunder.

Section 4   If, for any reason, a Successor Trustee is required but is not appointed by the effective date of a Trustee's resignation, the resigning Trustee may select and appoint its successor or, at the expense of the trust, seek the appointment of a successor by a court of competent jurisdiction.

Section 5   Whenever a Trustee ceases to act, the Successor Trustee shall have all of the titles, powers, rights, discretions, obligations and immunities of its predecessor Trustee.

Section 6   Whenever the provisions of this Article authorize the appointment or selection of a Successor Trustee upon the resignation or removal of any then serving Trustee, if a Successor Trustee is provided for pursuant to Article I hereof, then the terms of Article I shall govern notwithstanding any term or provision contained in this Article to the contrary.

ARTICLE VIII
TRUSTEE'S POWERS, RIGHTS AND DUTIES

Section 1   It is Settlor's intention that the Trustee's powers to conserve, protect, manage and invest property of the trust shall be the same as Settlor possesses in the management of Settlor's own affairs, notwithstanding the provisions of any rule of law or statute now in existence or later enacted pertaining to powers which may be properly exercised by fiduciaries.

Section 2   Without limiting the broad scope of the powers intended by this Article, Settlor grants the Trustee the following specific powers:

(a)   IN CONNECTION WITH REAL PROPERTY, the Trustee may, in its discretion, exercise or refrain from exercising the following powers:

(1)   To buy or sell real property upon such terms and conditions as the Trustee may deem advisable.

(2)   Notwithstanding any other provision of this Agreement of Trust or rule of law to the contrary, Trustee shall pay, first from income, and then from principal, ALL costs necessary to maintain any real property held as a part of any Trust hereunder. Such costs shall include, but not be limited to, maintenance and upkeep of every kind and nature, any and all taxes which may be imposed and insurance in an amount sufficient to fully and adequately rebuild any

9

real property held within the Trust which may be damaged due to fire or other like disaster.

(3) To make ordinary or extraordinary repairs or alterations in buildings or other structures, demolish any improvements, or erect new party walls or buildings.

(4) To subdivide and develop land, or dedicate land to public use; make or obtain the vacation of plats and adjust boundaries; adjust differences in valuation on exchange or partition by giving or receiving consideration; or dedicate easements to public use without consideration.

(5) To enter for any purpose into a lease as lessor or lessee with or without option to purchase or renew for a term within or extending beyond the term of the trust.

(6) As to oil, gas, and mineral interests, to drill, test, explore, mine, develop, and otherwise to exploit the interests; in connection therewith to pay from principal or income all delay rentals, lease bonuses, royalties, overriding royalties, taxes, assessments, and other charges; and to surrender or abandon an interest; to enter into farmout pooling, unitization, or dry hole contribution agreements in connection therewith; and to produce, process, sell or exchange the production from the interest in a manner and extent as the Trustee, in its sole discretion, deems advisable.

(7) To execute and deliver a deed of conveyance for cash payment of all sums remaining due or a purchaser's note for the sum remaining due secured by a mortgage or deed of trust on the land.

(8) To deliver a deed in escrow with directions that the proceeds, when paid in accordance with the Escrow Agreement, be paid to the Trustee, as designated in the Escrow Agreement.

(b) To collect, hold and retain assets received from Settlor until, in the judgment of the Trustee, disposition of the assets should be made, and the assets may be retained even though they include an asset in which the Trustee is personally interested and to receive additions to the assets of the trust which are acceptable to the Trustee.

(c) To sell any trust asset upon such terms and conditions as the Trustee may deem advisable; to acquire an undivided interest in a trust asset in which the Trustee, in any trust capacity, holds an undivided interest; to invest and reinvest trust assets; to deposit trust funds in a bank or trust company, including a bank or trust company operated by the Trustee and including any common trust fund of any such depository bank or trust company; to vote a security, in person or by general or limited proxy, including the power to retain in trust and vote a security issued by a bank or financial institution; to pay calls, assessments, and any other sums chargeable or accruing against or on account of securities; to sell or exercise stock subscription or conversion rights; or consent, directly or through a committee or other agent, to the reorganization, consolidation, merger, dissolution, or liquidation of a corporation or other business enterprise.

(d)   To hold real property or a security in the name of a nominee or in other form without disclosure of the trust, so that the title to the real property or security may pass by delivery, but the Trustee is liable for any act of the nominee in connection with the land or security so held.

(e)   To insure the assets of the trust against damage or loss, and the Trustee against liability with respect to third persons.

(f)   To borrow money to be repaid from trust assets or otherwise; and advance money for the protection of the trust, and for expenses, losses, or liabilities sustained in the administration of the trust or because of the holding or ownership of any trust assets, for which advances with any interest the Trustee has a lien on the trust assets as against the beneficiary.

(g)   To pay or contest a claim; to settle a claim by or against the trust or the trust assets by compromise, arbitration, or otherwise; and to release, in whole or in part, a claim belonging to the trust to the extent that the claim is uncollectible in the opinion of the Trustee.

(h)   To buy, sell, trade and deal in, stocks, bonds and securities of every nature, including puts, calls, straddles and other options, covered and uncovered, of every kind or nature, and commodities of every nature, and contracts for the future delivery of commodities of every nature, on margin or otherwise; and, pledge any and all trust assets for the future delivery thereof.

(i)   To employ and pay persons, including attorneys, auditors, investment advisors, or agents, even if they are associated with the Trustee, to advise or assist the Trustee in the performance of its administrative duties; act without independent investigation upon their recommendations; and instead of acting personally, employ an agent to perform any act of administration, whether or not discretionary.

(j)   To prosecute or defend actions, claims, or proceedings for the protection of trust assets and of the Trustee in the performance of the Trustee's duties.

(k)   In performing enforceable contracts by the Settlor of the trust, among other possible choices of action, to effect a fair and

11

reasonable compromise with a debtor or obligor, or extend, renew, or in any manner modify the terms of an obligation owing to the trust. A Trustee who holds a mortgage, pledge, or other lien upon property of another person, may, in lieu of foreclosure, accept the conveyance or transfer of encumbered assets from the owner thereof in satisfaction of the indebtedness secured by lien.

(l) To abandon property when, in the opinion of the Trustee, it is valueless, or is so encumbered or is in condition that it is not of benefit to the trust.

(m) To pay taxes, assessments, compensation of the Trustee, and other expenses incurred in the collection, care, administration, and protection of the trust.

(n) To make distributions, divisions and allocations of property in cash or in kind, or partly in each, and to resolve doubtful questions as to the value of property for such purposes. Whenever the provisions of this Agreement of Trust direct the division of the trust estate into separate equal shares or trusts, it shall not be necessary for the Trustee actually or physically to divide the trust estate into as many parts as there may be trusts, but an undivided part of the entire trust estate (or any lesser portion thereof) may be deemed, and shall be duly evidenced by appropriate book entries, to have been definitely allocated to each such trust.

(o) To determine the identity of all persons having a vested or non-vested beneficial interest in the trust, with or without legal proceedings.

(p) To make determinations as to the allocation of receipts and the apportionment of expenditures between income and principal. The Trustee shall not be required to follow any provision of law regarding such determinations.

(q) To pay any sum distributable to a beneficiary under legal disability, without liability to the Trustee, by paying the sum to the beneficiary, or by paying the sum for the use of the beneficiary or to a legal representative appointed by the court, or if none, to a relative, for the use of the beneficiary.

(r) To purchase any property belonging to the estates of either Settlor or property belonging to any revocable trust established by either Settlor and to borrow from or lend to the Personal Representatives of either Settlor such amounts as the Trustee may deem necessary to protect and conserve the assets of either Settlor's estate and the assets of the trusts under this Agreement upon such terms and conditions, whether secured or unsecured, as the Trustee may deem proper and necessary.

12

(s)   To purchase policies of life insurance insuring the life of either Settlor, or any beneficiary hereunder, either individually or collectively. The Trustee shall not be obligated to pay any charges with respect to any life insurance policies held as assets of this trust. However, upon notice at any time during the continuance of this trust that the premiums due upon such policies are in default, or that premiums to become due will not be paid, by either Settlor or by any other person, the Trustee may apply any cash values attributable to such policy to the purchase of paid-up insurance or of extended insurance, or shall borrow upon such policies for the payment of premiums due thereon. If the Settlor or any other insured becomes totally and permanently disabled within the meaning of such insurance policies containing a waiver of premium clause, the Trustee upon the receipt of such knowledge shall promptly notify the insurance company which has issued such policies and shall take any and all steps necessary to make such waiver of premium provisions effective. The Trustee shall be under no duty or obligation to invest and/or keep invested any cash of nominal amount that was initially deposited and described in the schedule attached hereto. Notwithstanding the foregoing, however, prior to making payment for any insurance premiums, from the income of the trust, the Trustee shall obtain the consent of all of the beneficiaries of the trust in order for the Trustee to make payments of any insurance premium from the income of the trust.

(t)   At either Settlor's death, the Trustee may purchase any property forming a part of the probate estate of said Settlor.

Section 3   Notwithstanding anything to the contrary in this Agreement of Trust, the beneficiaries, pursuant to Article IV of this Agreement of Trust, at any time, shall have the right, to appoint or discharge any individual or firm as Investment Advisor, under the following terms and conditions:

(a)   Upon a unanimous vote, the beneficiaries pursuant to Article IV, may appoint such an Investment Advisor and shall notify the Trustee in writing of the Investment Advisor selected by such beneficiaries.

(b)   The Trustee, in its sole discretion, may accept or decline the directions for the purchase, sale, investment, and reinvestment of the trust assets given to the Trustee by the Investment Advisor in writing.

(c)   The Trustee shall not be liable or responsible in any manner whatsoever to any person interested in any trust under this Declaration of Trust for any losses to the trust estate of any such trust by reason of purchases, sales, investments or reinvestments of any assets of the trust estate by the Trustee pursuant to directions given by such Investment Advisor.

(d)   At any time a majority of the beneficiaries, pursuant to Article IV, may discharge an Investment Advisor. A written notice of the discharge of an Investment Advisor shall be given by said beneficiaries to the Trustee.

(e)   If an Investment Advisor is discharged, and a substitute Investment Advisor is not appointed by the beneficiaries, pursuant to Article IV, within ten (10) days after written notice of the discharge of the Investment Advisor, the Trustee shall thereupon again assume all the duties and responsibilities with respect to the purchase, sale, investments, and reinvestment of the trust assets previously granted to the Trustee under the provisions of Sections 1 and 2 of this Article.

Section 4   Notwithstanding anything herein contained to the contrary, no powers enumerated herein or accorded to the Trustee generally pursuant to law shall be construed to enable either Settlor or the Trustee, or any other person to purchase, exchange, or otherwise deal with or dispose of the principal or income of this trust for less than an adequate or full consideration in money or money's worth, or to enable either Settlor or the Trustee to borrow the income or principal of this trust, directly or indirectly, without adequate interest or security. No person, other than the Trustee, shall have or exercise the power to vote or direct the voting of any stock or other securities of this trust, to control the investment of this trust, either by directing investments or reinvestments or by vetoing proposed investments or reinvestments, or to reacquire or exchange any property of this trust by substituting other property of an equivalent value.

ARTICLE IX
RIGHTS AND DUTIES OF TRUSTEES BETWEEN THEMSELVES

Section 1   No Trustee who may be entitled to a discretionary distribution under any provisions of this instrument shall participate in any determinations relating to such distribution.

Section 2   If more than two Trustees are acting at any time, all matters requiring or permitting the exercise of discretion by the Trustee shall be determined by a majority of the Trustees then acting.

Section 3   A Trustee not permitted to exercise discretion or foreclosed from exercising discretion by a majority vote of the remaining Trustees shall not be liable to any person for any damage resulting from such exercise of discretion.

14

ARTICLE X
INSURANCE BENEFITS

Section 1   At Settlor's death, the Trustee shall make a diligent effort to collect all death benefits payable to the Trustee and the Trustee may take any action necessary to enforce payment of death benefits. However, it need not take any such action until it has been indemnified to its satisfaction against all expenses and liabilities to which it determines it may be subjected.

Section 2   The Trustee is authorized to settle claims arising out of any instrument governing the payment of death benefits and its decisions shall be binding upon all persons having a beneficial interest in the trust estate, whether or not such interest is a vested one.

ARTICLE XI
GENERAL PROVISIONS

Section 1   Notwithstanding any other provisions in this Irrevocable Agreement of Trust, the trust established hereunder shall terminate not later than twenty-one years after the death of the last survivor of the beneficiaries named in Article IV who are living at the date of execution of this Agreement. At that time, the property held in trust shall be discharged of any trust, and shall immediately vest in and be distributed to the beneficiaries of the trust.

Section 2   Unless otherwise specifically provided for in this Agreement of Trust, all matters requiring or permitting the exercise of discretion by the Trustee shall be determined by the Trustee in its sole and absolute discretion, and shall be conclusive on all persons having a vested or non-vested beneficial interest in the trust.

Section 3   The Trustee shall render a statement of properties in the trust and of receipts and disbursements during the period covered at least annually to each of the adult and otherwise legally competent beneficiaries (and to the natural or legal guardian) then receiving or entitled to receive income from any of the trusts hereunder. The Trustee may also at any time, at its sole option, secure approval of an account of their proceedings by a court of competent jurisdiction. The books of account of the Trustee shall at all reasonable times be open to the reasonable inspection of the income beneficiaries and such other person or persons as they may designate for that purpose.

Section 4   The principal and income of the trusts established hereunder shall not be liable for the debts of any beneficiary hereunder, nor shall the same be subject to seizure by any creditor or any beneficiary under any writ or proceeding at law or in

15

equity, and no beneficiary hereunder shall have any power to sell, assign, transfer, encumber or in any other manner anticipate or dispose of his or her interest in the principal or in the income produced thereby.

Section 5   The Trustee may make payments to a minor by making payments to (a) the Guardian of that minor's person or estate, (b) a custodian of property held for the minor's benefit under the Uniform Gifts or Transfers to Minors Act of any state, (c) any suitable person with whom the minor resides, or (d) the minor directly if, in the Trustee's judgment, the minor is of sufficient age and maturity to spend the money properly.

Section 6   If any provision of this Agreement is held by a court of competent jurisdiction to be invalid or unenforceable, the remainder of the Agreement shall continue in full force and effect and shall in no way be impaired or invalidated.

ARTICLE XII
DEFINITIONS

Section 1   When the term "trust" or "trust estate" is used without other words of description, it shall mean any or all of the trusts being administered under this instrument at the time the term is applied.

Section 2   The terms "child" or "children" of Settlor shall mean any child born to or legally adopted by either Settlor before or after the date of this instrument. The terms "child" or "children" with respect to any other person shall mean all natural born children as well as all legally adopted children, whether born to or legally adopted by such other person before or after the date of this instrument.

Section 3   The term "descendant" or "descendants" shall include all lineal descendants by blood or legal adoption of the named ancestor.

Section 4   When the terms "income beneficiary" or "income beneficiaries" are used without other words of description, they shall mean all persons who may be entitled to receive a distribution of income from any trust under this instrument at the time the term is applied.

Section 5   The term "education" shall mean any kind of formal education or training, including undergraduate, postgraduate or professional schooling.

Section 6   The term "person" or "persons" shall mean any natural or legal person, or any association of natural or legal persons.

16

Section 7   The term "right of representation" means that the children of a deceased descendant of any person shall share equally in the share their parent would have taken if living.   Posthumous children are to be considered as living at the death of their parent.

Section 8   The term "Corporate Trustee" shall mean any national banking association, corporation, or other institution, part or all of the business of which involves the regular administration of trust accounts and of counseling in connection with trust business.

Section 9   As the context of any provision may require, nouns and pronouns of any gender and number shall be construed in any other gender and number.

Section 10   The term "future interest" shall have the same meaning and effect given said term in Section 2503(b) of the Internal Revenue Code of 1986, and as amended, and the Regulations pertaining thereto.

ARTICLE XIII
GOVERNING LAW

The validity of this Agreement shall be determined under the laws of California and any questions of construction of this instrument and administration of the trusts under this Agreement shall be determined under the laws of California.

The Settlor has signed this Agreement on the 1st day of May, 1991.

_____   _____
Witness   ANDREW D. WESTHEM, Settlor

_____
Witness

_____   _____
Witness   EMILY WESTHEM, Settlor

_____
Witness

17

STATE OF CALIFORNIA   )
COUNTY OF LOS ANGELES   )

    On this 1st day of May, 1991, before me, the subscriber, personally appeared ANDREW D. WESTHEM and EMILY WESTHEM, to me known, and known to me to be the persons described in and who executed the within instrument, and they duly acknowledged to me that they executed the same.

OFFICIAL NOTARY SEAL
RANDOLPH J LEAVENWORTH
Notary Public — California
LOS ANGELES COUNTY
My Comm Expires JUL 12,1994

Notary Public
My commission expires:

    The foregoing instrument, consisting of nineteen (19) pages, including this page, was subscribed published and declared by ANDREW D. WESTHEM and EMILY WESTHEM to be their Irrevocable Trust, in the presence of us, who in their presence, at their request, and in the presence of each other, have subscribed our names as witnesses.

Address: 1494 A Pico Blvd
Los Angeles California

Address: 33 Linden Drive
Los Angeles California

ACCEPTANCE OF TRUSTEES

Witness

Witness

DAVID WESTHEM, Trustee

OFFICIAL NOTARY SEAL
RANDOLPH J. LEAVENWORTH
Notary Public — California
LOS ANGELES COUNTY
My Comm. Expires JUL 12,1994

STATE OF CALIFORNIA   )
COUNTY OF LOS ANGELES   )

    On this 1st day of May, 1991, before me, the subscriber, personally appeared DAVID WESTHEM, to me known, and known to me to be the person described in and who executed the within instrument, and he duly acknowledged to me that he executed the same.

Notary Public
My commission expires:

18

STEVEN A. SCIARRETTA
PROFESSIONAL ASSOCIATION

ATTORNEY AT LAW

LL.M. IN TAXATION
TAXATION AND BUSINESS PLANNING
ESTATE PLANNING AND ADMINISTRATION

ONE BOCA PLACE
2255 GLADES ROAD, SUITE 405 EAST
BOCA RATON, FLORIDA 33431

TELEPHONE: (407) 241-6600
TOLL FREE: 1-800-545-8454
FAX: (407) 241-6617

RE: Charitable Remainder Trusts

Dear

Pursuant to our recent telephone conversation, I have drafted this letter in an attempt to provide you with more information as regards Charitable Remainder Trusts in general, and as regards your situation in particular.

As you are aware, Charitable Remainder Trusts have recently met with great favor because they allow the Settlor to retain an income from highly appreciated property, while not paying the customary capital gains tax.

In short, you, as the Settlor would contribute highly appreciated property to the Charitable Remainder Trust, retaining onto yourself an income interest for your lifetime, while passing the capital gains tax onto the charitable remainderman, which, as a qualifying charity, will be tax exempt. Additionally, you will receive a charitable deduction, albeit somewhat limited, for the property contributed.

Alas, as with any tax code provision that appears to good to be true, there are a number of limitations and steps which must be followed. Failure to properly follow these steps can cause denial of the charitable deduction, Settlor realization of the capital gains tax and possibly even full inclusion of the value of the trust corpus into your estate.

Obviously, then a Charitable Remainder Trust is not for everyone. First and foremost, if you are not yet ready to depart with control of the asset, a charitable trust is not for you. If, however, you are willing to give up control of the property in exchange for the life income as noted above, then, perhaps a Charitable Remainder Trust is the way to go.

SOURCE: Steven A. Sciarretta, JD, LL.M., of Steven A. Sciarretta, P.A., Boca Raton, Florida.

I

Charitable trusts have many rules and limitations which must be followed. Those of most major importance are listed hereafter:

1. All Charitable Remainder Trusts must be irrevocable.

2. The Settlor, the Settlor's spouse and/or the Settlor's children may act as Trustee of the Charitable Remainder Trust, if the Settlor so chooses. A word of caution here, however. If hard to value assets are transferred to the Charitable Remainder Trust it is advisable for an Independent Trustee for the Limited purpose of Special Evaluation to be nominated. This trustee must be independent, ie. not a family member or person or other entity which would fall under the dominion and control of the Settlor. In this way, decisions regarding valuation and therefore Charitable Contribution Amount would be outside the control of the Settlor.

3. The property contributed must be the Settlor's entire interest in the property. That is, an undivided interest as opposed to all of the property owned by the Settlor. For example, if you owned 100 shares of XYZ Corp., you need not contribute all 100 shares, but you must contribute the entire interest in each share to be contributed. You would not be able to retain an otherwise as yet undeveloped easement in real property that is to be contributed to the trust.

4. The required income amount must be paid to, or for the use of, a named person or persons, at least one of which is not a qualifying charitable organization. Persons include an individual, a trust, estate, partnership, association, company or corporation.

5. Special rules apply if tangible property (artworks, automobiles, etc.) comprise a portion or all of the property to be contributed. Also, you must be extremely careful if certain types of intangible property are contributed to the trust. These unique intangibles would include items such a royalty rights.

6. Due to assignment of income principals, you may be taxed adversely, if you transfer property to a Charitable Remainder Trust that is expressly or impliedly required to sell or exchange the property and reinvest the proceeds in tax-exempt securities. This often creates problems as it therefore becomes very difficult for the income stream retained to be invested in such a way as to pass out tax-free income.

2

STEVEN A. SCIARRETTA, P.A.

7.   A Charitable Remainder Trust can be established to last for the lifetime of one or more individuals, no matter how long or short that may be, or for a fixed period not to exceed twenty (20) years.

8.   No Amount, other than the specified income, may be paid out at any time. Therefore, you must be absolutely certain that you will not be in need of the funds at a later date.

9.   If the property to be contributed is mortgaged or otherwise encumbered, then the bargain sales rules will apply.

10.   Charitable Remainder Trusts are exempt from taxation unless they have unrelated business taxable income. Since debt-financed income qualifies as unrelated business taxable income, the trust must not be funded with mortgaged property nor incur any indebtedness, as noted in Item 9 above. If these rules are violated, the trust will be taxed as a complex trust, the charitable deduction will be lost and the capital gain will be taxed at current income rates.

11.   The minimum annuity amount for a Charitable Remainder Annuity Trust is five (5%) percent of the initial fair market value of the trust assets. By contrast, a Charitable Remainder UniTrust must distribute, at least annually, a fixed percentage of not less than five (5%) percent of the net fair market value of the trust assets. No maximum amount is established for either type of trust. However, the charitable deduction afforded through use of a Charitable Remainder Trust is directly tied to the amount of annual return received. Therefore, in simplest terms, the higher the annual return you receive, the smaller the charitable deduction afforded.

12.   Contributions of appreciated, intangible property to a Charitable Remainder Trust may well cause the imposition of the Alternative Minimum Tax (AMT). The AMT preference amount will be the amount by which your charitable deduction exceeds your basis in the property contributed. Of course, the timing of the recognition of this preference item is of paramount importance. You should speak with your tax accountant in order to determine if your contemplated contribution will give rise to AMT problems.

II

As noted above, Charitable Remainder Trusts come in two (2) varieties: annuity trusts and unitrusts.

3

STEVEN A. SCIARRETTA, P.A.

A Charitable Remainder Annuity Trust (CRAT) is a trust where the annual income payment is based on the fair market value of the initial contribution. The annual amount received by you then, is fixed, regardless of whether the value of the underlying trust corpus increases or decreases.

Conversely, a Charitable Remainder UniTrust (CRUT) is a trust where the annual distribution is based on the current fair market value of the property held thereunder. As a result, a CRUT affords two opportunities not otherwise available through a CRAT.

First, contributions may be made in later years to the CRUT but not to the CRAT since the CRAT's payout is determined at the time of initial funding while the CRUT's payout is redetermined annually.

Second, the CRUT affords the opportunity to further defer income by inserting a provision into the CRUT that requires distributions not to exceed income. In this way, if the income earned by the CRUT does not equal or exceed five (5%) percent, then, the income may be paid in a later period when there is sufficient income to make up the shortfall. Low income productive assets would then be placed into the CRUT to afford you the opportunity to recognize income years later in the future. Many planning opportunities are available here depending on the asset(s) to be contributed. However, as the current maximum income tax rate is only thirty-one (31%) percent, your tax accountant should be consulted in order to determine whether such deferral would be economically productive.

You should also be aware that while the Charitable Remainder Trust is a tax-free entity, the character of any asset passed out to the Recipient, will be retained. This means that if the income of the trust is comprised of interest, dividends, rents, royalties and/or capital gains from the sale of held assets, then, those items will flow over to the Recipient. This is most important when the income earned by the trust has it's basis in capital gain. If the trust were to sell assets contributed to it, any gain incurred will be tax-free to the Trust, however, if the Trust were to pass out these proceeds, the Recipient of the proceeds would be responsible to report the income as arising from the sale of a capital asset. This fact should be kept in the forefront when planning distributions from the Trust.

III

Several methods are used in order to determine the charitable contribution amount for the various charitable trusts. The IRS has proscribed many tables to be used in order to determine the charitable contribution amount. These tables are based upon the amount of income interest retained by the grantor, as well as the applicable federal rate

4

STEVEN A. SCIARRETTA, P.A.

(AFR) in existence for the month in which the contribution is made.   The
AFR in effect for June, 1991 is 9.20%.

As we have discussed previously, it is your desire to transfer your
Virginia farm, which has a current FMV of approximately ($1,000,000.00)
One Million dollars, into the Charitable Trust.   Your basis in this
property is approximately ($150,000.00) One Hundred Fifty Thousand
dollars.   It is your intention therefore to transfer this property to
the Charitable trust, and to then allow the Trustee of the trust to sell
the property therefore having the capital gain occur through the trust,
where it will be tax exempt.

I have therefore made the computations which follow, based upon the
following facts:

   1.   You are sixty-three (63) years of age.

   2.   You will contribute real property having a value of
         $1,000,000.00 to the Charitable Remainder Trust.

   3.   You desire a ten (10%) percent return on your contribution.

Based on the assumptions as noted above, if you were to establish a
CRUT, paying $100,000.00 annually to you for your lifetime, your
charitable contribution amount would be equal to approximately 22.159%
of the value of the property contributed, or approximately $221,590.
The charitable contribution amount, however, will be further limited as
discussed in part IV, below.

IV

Through the use of the tables as noted in III above, the charitable
contribution amount is determined.   This amount, however, is not the
amount of charitable deduction available to you, for the year in which
the gift is made.   Rather, the charitable contribution amount is subject
to the charitable deduction limitations which are imposed by the
Internal Revenue Code on all contributions, whether through trust or
otherwise.

Charitable contribution deductions are limited to three (3) basic
categories: 50% deductions, 30% deductions and 20% deductions.
However, the contributor must be a United States citizen and must
itemize deductions on Schedule A of Form 1040 in order to be able to
avail herself of the deduction.

Contributions in cash or of non-appreciated assets going to a
"public" charity are deductible against up to Fifty percent (50%) of
adjusted gross income.

5

STEVEN A. SCIARRETTA, P.A.

Contributions in cash or of non-appreciated property going to "semi-private" or "private" charities or contributions of appreciated property to a "public" charity are deductible against up to Thirty percent (30%) of adjusted gross income.

Finally, gifts of appreciated property to a "semi-public" or "private" charity are deductible against up to Twenty percent (20%) of adjusted gross income

"Public" charities are, for the most part, those charities you would normally consider to be public. "Private" charities are for the most part private foundations. Obviously, then "semi-private" charities are those which are neither public nor private. Rather than engaging in a detailed discussion as regards which charities are public, semi-private or private, I believe it would be best for us to simply discuss the charities you intend to name in your new Charitable Remainder Trust.

All contributions not used in the year of contribution, may be carried forward for the next five (5) succeeding years.

Finally, one last comment as regards the deductibility of charitable contributions. The disposition of the property upon the death of the measuring life, is of paramount importance. If the charity is to continue to hold the property "for the use of" the charity, then, in no event, will a charitable deduction be allowed in excess of thirty (30%) percent. However, if upon the death of the measuring life or lives, a cash or other non-appreciated contribution is to go directly "to" a public charity, then, the fifty (50%) percent deduction will still hold.

<u>V</u>

Your individual allowable deduction as regards your new Charitable Remainder Trust will vary then based upon the following factors:

1. The federal rate applicable (AFR) at the time of the gift.

2. Your desired time period for receiving income thereunder.

3. The nature and character of the property to be contributed.

4. The amount of your adjusted gross income, and;

5. The category of charity to which you wish to make the final contribution.

6

STEVEN A. SCIARRETTA, P.A.

<u>VI</u>

In conjunction with the Charitable Remainder Trust, you should consider implementing an Irrevocable Life Insurance Trust (ILIT). An ILIT is designed to be a wealth replacement vehicle. That is, it is a vehicle designed to hold life insurance proceeds which will be used to replace the value of the property passing to charity through the Charitable Remainder Trust. ILIT's are special vehicles, because if the Trust is properly drafted and administered, the insurance proceeds coming into the trust will arrive free of all income, estate and generation skipping taxes. In this way, One Million Dollars of life insurance held under an ILIT will produce a true One Million available dollars to your children, whereas One Million Dollars in property held by you at the time of death will provide your children with only approximately Five Hundred Thousand Dollars, as they will be responsible to pay the estate taxes thereon. Please be advised however, that ILIT's do require a small amount of annual administration. If any one or more of your children is business orientated, he or she should have no problems whatsoever in administering this Trust during your lifetime.

You will find Andrew Westhem, of Wealth Transfer Planning, Inc., to be most informative as regards the administration and funding of these Insurance Trusts.

In conclusion then a Charitable Remainder Trust when used in conjunction with an Irrevocable Insurance Trust may well provide you with an increased income during your lifetime and also provide a greater inheritance to your children.

As we discussed, I will need to speak with local counsel and your tax accountant so that we can together, attempt to determine the proper course of action in order to maximize tax savings while still being certain to provide you with the income level you desire.

I look forward to hearing from you in the very near future. Again, thank you for allowing me to assist you with this most important, personal matter.

Sincerely,

STEVEN A. SCIARRETTA

SAS/sms

7

STEVEN A. SCIARRETTA, P.A.

Trustee's Operating Manual

Introduction

1. The following Manual is designed to assist the Trustee of the
   _____Name_____ Family Irrevocable Insurance Trust in implementing its terms.
2. It is important for the Trustee to keep in mind that adherence to the
   deadlines outlined below is critical; failure to meet a deadline could
   result in cancellation of an insurance policy or the loss of tax
   benefits.
3. Any questions in connection with the implementation of the Trust
   terms should be directed to the attorney for the Trust:
   _____**Attorney's Name, Address and Phone**_____.
4. Questions regarding the insurance policies in the Trust should be
   directed to the insurance underwriter, _____**Name, Address**_____
   ____**and Phone**____

Assets

The Trust consists of the following assets:

Payments of Premiums

5. No later than _____**Date**_____ of each year, the Trustee shall
   write a letter to the Trustor(s) requesting they send a check, payable
   to the Trustee, in a minimum amount sufficient to pay the annual
   premium on the ____**Insurance Company, Face Amount, Type of Policy**____ policy. This
   payment must be received by the Trustee within fifteen (15) days of
   the date of the letter. A form of the letter is attached as Exhibit
   "A." The letter should set forth the projected annual premium for
   each year.

6. Upon receipt of the check from ___Insured's Name___, it should be deposited to the Trust bank account.

7. Within fifteen (15) days of receipt, the Trustee, pursuant to Article 6 of the Trust, must give notice to the beneficiaries of the Trust, i.e., ___Beneficiary's(ies') Name(s)___ of their withdrawal rights under the Trust. The letter to the beneficiaries should specify that their withdrawal rights expire thirty (30) days from the date of the letter. A form of the letter is attached to this Manual as Exhibit "B," along with the current addresses of the beneficiary(ies).

8. In the event any of the beneficiary(ies) exercise their withdrawal rights, the Trustee shall pay to the beneficiary the amount the beneficiary is entitled to, pursuant to the Trust terms.

9. The Trustee shall pay the insurance premiums no later than ___Date___ of each year.

10. Prior to November 30th of each year, the Trustee shall review his income position, and with the advice of counsel and the accountant for the Trust, shall distribute any net distributable income in accordance with Article 6.

Tax Returns

11. The Trust will be a calendar year taxpayer and will be required to file tax returns by April 15 of each year. The Trustee must engage the services of an accountant and furnish him with sufficient data to have the returns prepared and filed by the due date.

Trustee Compensation

12. Pursuant to Paragraph _____, the Trustee is entitled to "reasonable" compensation for the Trustee's ordinary and extraordinary services. The Trustee should confer with the Trust's attorney and accountant prior to billing the Trust for compensation.

EXHIBIT "A"
FORM LETTER TO INSUREDS

Dear

The annual premium on the Life Insurance policy owned by the
_____Name_____Family Irrevocable Insurance Trust is due
___Date___of this year. According to the schedule in my pos-
session, the annual premium for this year is $___Amount___.

Please send me a check payable to ___Name of Trustee___ Trustee, in the
minimum amount of $___Amount___. A self-addressed envelope is
enclosed for your convenience.

In order to comply with the Trust terms, this check should be received
no later than ___Date___.

Should you have any questions, please do not hesitate to contact us.

Best Wishes,

___Name of Trustee___, Trustee of the
_____Name_____ Family Irrevocable Insurance Trust

Enclosure

EXHIBIT "B"
FORM LETTER TO BENEFICIARIES
TO COMPLY WITH CRUMMEY POWERS

Date

Name
Address
City/State/ZIP

Re: _____Name_____ Insurance Trust

Dear Beneficiaries:

Please be advised that the Trustee of the _____Name_____ Family
Irrevocable Insurance Trust has received a gift in the sum of
$___Amount___.

Pursuant to Article 6 you have the right to withdraw a proportionate
share of this amount, if you should choose to do so.

In order to exercise your right, you must file with me, in writing, no
later than ___Date___, a written demand for your share of the amount
contributed to the Trust.

In the event you elect not to make demand for distribution, the amount
shall become an asset of the Trust and shall be used for Trust purposes, including, but not limited to, the payment of insurance
premiums on insurance policies held as assets of the Trust.

Should you have any questions, feel free to call the undersigned.

Sincerely,

_____Name of Trustee_____, Trustee of the
_____Name_____ Family Irrevocable Insurance Trust

Glossary of Wealth-Transfer Terms

A-B trust A trust divided into two portions, usually between husband and wife, in which the "B" trust becomes irrevocable at the death of the first spouse, thus passing up to $600,000 tax free directly to the ultimate heirs, who can save $235,000 or more in taxes on estates of $1.2 million or more.

Administrator Person named by the court to represent the estate when there is no will or the will did not name an executor, also called a "personal representative."

Beneficiary The person and/or organization who obtains the benefits of the trust.

Bypass trust A trust set up to bypass the surviving spouse's estate, thereby allowing full use of the $600,000 federal estate-tax exemption for both spouses.

Codicil A written change or amendment to a will.

Community property A form of title for husband and wife that is recognized in 10 states. One of the primary benefits of community property is the income-tax basis step up to fair market value that occurs upon the death of either spouse.

Conservator An individual appointed by the court to administer the affairs of an incapacitated adult.

Credit shelter trust *See* bypass trust.

Double win trusts A charitable remainder trust combined with an irrevocable life insurance trust.

ERTA The Economic Recovery Tax Act of 1981, which contains the largest package of tax reductions in history. ERTA created an unlimited marital tax deduction and a $10,000 (per year per person) gift-tax exemption, and it raised the estate-tax exemption from $225,000 in 1982 to $600,000 in 1987 and beyond.

Estate tax A transfer tax imposed on the value of property and assets left at death; often called an inheritance tax or death tax.

Executor The person or institution named in a will who is responsible for the management of the assets and the ultimate transfer of the property; also commonly referred to as a "personal representative."

Gift tax A tax imposed on transfers of property by gift during the donor's lifetime.

Grantor The person who creates a trust. Also called trustor or settlor or maker. The terms are synonymous.

Guardian One who is legally responsible for the care and well-being of a minor. Appointed by a court, the guardian is under court supervision.

Holographic will A handwritten will. Most states accept holographic wills if they are entirely handwritten by the owner of the estate, then dated and signed.

Intestate Having died without a will.

Irrevocable life-insurance trust An irrevocable trust that is established for the purpose of excluding life-insurance proceeds from the estate of the insured for estate-tax purposes.

Irrevocable trust A trust that the trustor does not have the power to revoke or amend.

Joint tenancy A form of joint ownership in which the death of one joint owner results in the immediate transfer of ownership to the surviving joint owner or owners.

Living (inter vivos) trust A trust, created by a written legal document, which is funded during the lifetime of the trustor. Very often, this will be a revocable living trust that will be used as the ultimate vehicle for the distribution of the trustor's assets when the trustor dies.

Marital deduction A deduction that is available for transfers between spouses, either during their lifetime or at death. Under federal law, there is a complete interspousal exemption from transfer tax for qualifying transfers.

Pour-over will A will used in conjunction with a revocable living trust to "pour over" any assets that are not transferred to the trust prior to death.

Probate Literally, the process of proving that a will is genuine. By custom, this is the legal and bureaucratic gamut through which any estate—with or without a will—must pass.

Qualified terminable interest property ("Q-TIP") trust A terminable interest that will qualify for the marital deduction, if an appropriate election is made by the donor or executor. In order to be eligible for the marital deduction, the trust must provide the surviving spouse with all income from the property during the spouse's life and no person, including the spouse, may have the right to appoint the property to anyone other than the spouse during the spouse's lifetime. This type of vehicle is frequently used to avoid any transfer tax upon the death of the first spouse, but it enables the first decedent to retain control over the ultimate disposition of the property.

Revocable trust A trust plan that gives the grantor the power to alter or revoke the trust terms.

Taxable estate Adjusted gross estate, less marital deduction or charitable expenses.

Tenancy in common A form of joint ownership in which two or more persons own the same property. At the death of a tenant in common, ownership transfers to that person's designated beneficiaries or heirs, not to the other joint owner.

Testamentary trust A trust set up in a will that takes effect only after death.

Testate Having died with a will.

Trust A fiduciary relationship in which one person (the trustor) transfers legal title of property to a fiduciary (the trustee) who manages the property for the benefit of another person (the beneficiary).

Trustee The person or institution who accepts and manages property according to the instructions in the trust agreement.

Unified tax credit An estate- and gift-tax credit of up to $192,800, which permits the transfer of up to $600,000 free of federal estate and gift tax.

Will A legally binding direction regarding the disposition of one's property, which is not operative until death and can be revoked up to the time of death or until there is a loss of mental capacity to make a valid will.

Index

A

A-B trusts, 8–10, 11, 269
Accountants, 48
    and estate planning, 215–16
Administrators, court-appointed, 269
Administrators, of private foundations, 83
Advanced underwriting departments, of
    insurance companies, 85–86, 215
Advisers, financial, 213–21. *See also*
    Accountants; Attorneys; Money
    managers
AIDS. *See* Health-care proxy
Alzheimer's disease. *See* Incapacitation
A.M. Best Company, 65, 161, 205
Annuities
    and income taxes, 103–5
    deferred, 104, 198–200
    fixed, 104
    immediate, 104, 198
    joint-and-survivor, 106, 107
    period-certain, 107
    private, 150–53
    single-life, 105–7
    tax-deferred, 104
    variable, 104
    variable-payout, 107
Annuitizing, 105–8
Annuity remainder trusts, 82
Annuity trusts, 77–78
AP (attending physician's) statement, 217

Appraisal. *See* Value and valuation, present
Appreciation. *See* Capital gains
Arm's-length rules, 122
Art, valuation of, 37
Asset protection, in family limited partner-
    ships, 128–29
Assets, 3, 11–12, 225
    as gifts, 36
    protection of, 16
Attending physician's (AP) statement, 217
Attorney, power of. *See* Power of attorney,
    durable
Attorneys, 18, 68–69
    and estate planning, 213–15
    and offshore trusts, 134
    See also Financial advisers

B

Bahama Islands, as offshore trust site, 132
Bank accounts, 26
Banks
    and estate planning, 216
    as trustees, 46
Basis, of property value. *See* Capital gains
Beneficiaries, 268, 269
    and Crummey power, 69–70
    of a trust, 13, 19, 43, 45
    of CRTs, 77–78, 86
    of Wealth Trust™, 98
Bequests, 19–20

Bonds, tax-exempt
and CRTs, 85
and income taxes, 103
Bonuses, tax aspects of, 115–16
Book value, of a business, 121
Brokerage accounts, and offshore trusts, 132
Brokerage firms, 101
as trustees, 46
Business continuity plans, 119
Businesses, closely held, 113–24, 150
and CRTs, 83–84
and estate taxes, 3–4, 49
and family limited partnerships, 127–28
and private foundations, 138
and Q-TIPs, 58
valuation of, 37
Buy-sell agreements, 119, 122, 150
Bypass trusts, 269

C

"Cannibal life insurance." *See* Universal life insurance
Capital gains, 31–32, 37–39, 76–77, 91–92
and CRTs, 76–77, 81–82
and gifts, 36
and MECs, 199–200
and private annuities, 152
and private foundations, 138
Cash value
in MECs, 195, 196
in policy illustrations, 202–6, 207
in second-to-die insurance, 187–89
of life insurance, in tax-free inheritance trusts, 70–71
of life insurance policies, 163–67
of universal life insurance, 176, 178
Cayman Islands, as offshore trust site, 132
Charging order, and limited partnerships, 131
Charitable deductions, from income taxes, 78–79. *See also* Charitable lead trusts; Charitable remainder trusts; Foundations, private; Public charities
Charitable lead trusts (CLTs), 87–89
Charitable remainder trusts (CRTs), 15, 46, 76–87, 128, 258–64

and private foundations, 138–41, 142
Charities. *See* Public charities. *See also* Charitable lead trusts; Charitable remainder trusts; Foundations, private
CLTs. *See* Charitable lead trusts
Codicils, to wills, 21, 269
Commissions, on life-insurance sales, 167
Community property, 33, 269
Conservators, 27, 269
Contesting, of wills, 28
Continental Illinois Bank, 161
Contributions, charitable. *See* Charitable lead trusts; Charitable remainder trusts; Foundations, private; Public charities
Convertibility, of term insurance, 161
Cook Islands, as offshore trust site, 132, 133
Coopers & Lybrand (accounting firm), 47
Corporate shield, 113–14
Corridor (insurance), 196–97
Cost basis. *See* Capital gains
Creator, of a trust. *See* Maker, of a trust
Creditors
and family limited partnerships, 129
and offshore trusts, 130–32, 133–34
Credit shelter trusts. *See* A-B trusts; Bypass trusts
CRTs. *See* Charitable remainder trusts
Crummey powers, 69–70, 268
Current mortality rate, 176

D, E

Damages, legal. *See* Judgment awards
Debts, 19, 20
Deferred annuities. *See under* Annuities
Demand right. *See* Crummey power
Disability. *See* Incapacitation
Distributions
excess, from retirement plans, 144–49
from annuities. *See* Annuitizing
from CRTs, 84
from family limited partnerships, 127
from MECs, 194
per capita, 19, 94–96
per stirpes, 19, 94–95
Dividends, on life insurance, 170

Divorce, and Wealth Trust™, 98–99
Doctors, and living wills, 23, 24
Double win trusts, 269
Duff & Phelps, Inc., 65, 161
Dynasty trusts, 73–74

Engel, Barry S., 132
Engel & Rudman (legal firm), 132
Equitable Life Assurance Society, 161,
  178–79
ERTA, 269
Escape clauses, 207
Estate freezes, 116–18
Estate taxes, 3, 19, 226, 270
  and CLTs, 88
  and irrevocable life-insurance trusts,
    62–63
  and living trusts, 28
  and tax-free inheritance trust strate-
    gies, 72
Estates, 3
  insurance proceeds as part of, 207
Excise tax, on pension plans, 72–73, 144–
  49
Executors, 20, 270
  and estate planning, 219
  of Q-TIPs, 58
Exemption, gift- and estate-tax. *See* Unified tax credit

F, G, H

Face value, of term insurance policies, 158
Family limited partnerships, 15, 125–35
Fee simple ownership, 30, 33
Fees, legal
  for living trusts, 46–47
  for offshore trusts, 133
  for private foundations, 141
  for tax-free inheritance trusts, 69
Fiduciaries, 100–101
Filing cabinet, to store wills, 18
Financial planners, 85
Fixed annuities. *See under* Annuities
Foreign situs trust. *See* Offshore asset-
  protection trusts
Form 1041, 47
Foundations, private, 16, 68, 83, 136–43

Fraudulent conveyance, to offshore trusts,
  133
Funeral expenses, 19
Future interests, and gift taxes, 69–70

GEICO, 161
General partners, 125–27
Generation-skipping strategy, 15, 90–109
Generation-skipping taxes, 39, 74, 91
Gibraltar (British colony), as offshore trust
  site, 132
Gift taxes, 5–6, 34–40, 226, 270
  and CLTs, 88
  and family limited partnerships, 126–
    27
  and irrevocable trusts, 44–45
  and private annuities, 152
Gifting trusts, 100
Gifts, 5–6, 12–13, 14–15, 34–40
  and family limited partnerships, 126–
    27
  and living trusts, 28
  incomplete, to offshore trusts, 132
  of excess retirement plan distributions,
    148
  to purchase MECs, 195
Government Employees Insurance Com-
  pany. *See* GEICO
Grantor. *See* Maker, of a trust
Grantor trusts, and income taxes, 103
Guaranteed mortality rate, 176
Guaranteed renewable term insurance, 161
Guarantees, on annuities, 104–5
Guardians, 20, 270
Guernsey, island, as offshore trust site, 132

Harvard Medical School Health Letter, 24
Health, and life insurance, 190, 208, 209
Health-care proxy, 23–24
Holographic will, 270
Homestead laws, 33
Hospitals, and living wills, 23, 24

I, J, K

Immediate annuities. *See under* Annuities
Incapacitation, 55
  and business continuity issues, 121
  and trusteeship, 27

Income
    and estate taxes, 49
    and gifts, 36
    from CRTs, 84
    from living trusts, 27, 28, 32
    from Q-TIPs, 58–59
    from tax-free inheritance trusts, 74
    See also Rule of 72
Income taxes
    and CRTs, 78–79
    and gifts, 37–39
    and irrevocable life insurance trusts,
      62–63
    and irrevocable trusts, 44
    and living trusts, 28
    and private foundations, 142
    on life insurance proceeds, 166–66
    on retirement plans, 72
    on trust income, 47
    trustee's knowledge of, 102–3
Incomplete gifts. *See* Gifts, incomplete
Incorporation, 113–14
Inflation, and whole life insurance, 173–74
Insurance. *See* Liability insurance; Life
    insurance. *See also* Permanent insurance;
    Term insurance; and specific kinds
Insurance agents, 186
    commissions, 167
    and estate planning, 216–18
Insurance companies
    and CRTs, 85–86
    and estate planning, 215
    selecting, 65, 160–61, 182, 190, 202–
      10
Insurance proceeds, as part of estate, 207
Interest payments, from trusts. *See* Income:
    from trusts
Interest rates, and whole life insurance,
    173–74
Interest-sensitive life insurance, 174–75,
    178
    vs. universal life insurance, 176–77
Internal rate of return, of life insurance,
    207–8
Interpolated terminal reserve, of life insur-
    ance, 37
Inter vivos trusts. *See* Trusts: living

Intestate death, 17, 270. *See also* Wills
IRAs. *See* Pension plans
Irrevocable life insurance trusts, 45–46, 61–
    67, 228–29, 270. *See also* Tax-free inher-
    itance trusts
Irrevocable trusts, 13–15, 44, 209, 213–21,
    270
    CRTs as, 84–85
    to hold MECs, 196
IRS, and estate freezes, 118

Jersey, island, as offshore trust site, 132
Joint-and-survivor annuities, 106, 107
Joint-and-survivor life insurance policies.
    See Second-to-die insurance
Joint ownership (tenancy), 21, 26, 30, 31,
    270
Judgment awards, 16
    insurance policy's vulnerability to, 129
    and MECs, 196
    and offshore trusts, 130–32, 134
Keogh plan, distributions from, 72. *See
also* Pension plans

L, M, N, O

Land, and Q-TIPs, 58–59. *See also* Real
    estate
Lawsuits. *See* Judgment awards
Lawyers. *See* Attorneys
Liability, 114
    and offshore trusts, 130–32
Liability insurance, and offshore trusts,
    130–32
Life estates, and Q-TIPs, 58
Life insurance, 155–201, 228–29
    and buy-sell agreements, 122–23
    and CRTs, 79–80
    and family limited partnerships, 128–
      29
    vs. MECs, 198
    See also Permanent insurance; Term
      insurance; and specific kinds
Life insurance companies. *See* Insurance
    companies
Life insurance policies, 14–15
    and Q-TIPs, 56–57
    valuation of, 37

Life insurance proceeds
   and income tax, 166–66
   and probate, 26
Life insurance trusts, irrevocable. *See* Irrevocable life insurance trusts. *See also* Tax-free inheritance trusts
Limited partners, 125–27
Limited partnerships, family. *See* Family limited partnerships
Litigation. *See* Judgment awards
Living trusts. *See* Trusts: living
Living wills, 22–24
Loans
    against life-insurance policies, 166–67, 191
    against MECs, 194

Maker, of a trust, 43, 45, 270
Malpractice lawsuits, and offshore trusts, 134
Man, Isle of, as offshore trust site, 132, 134
Marital and nonmarital trusts. *See* A-B trusts
Marital deduction, for estate taxes, 6–10, 270
Marx, Groucho, 27
MECs, 108–9, 193–201
Medical power of attorney. *See* Health-care proxy
Minor children, as beneficiaries, 26, 27, 39, 46, 63
Modified endowment contracts. *See* MECs
Money managers, 101, 216
Moody's Investor Service, 65, 161
Mortality cost, of insurance, 176, 199, 204
Mortality rate, of insurance, 176
Municipal bonds. *See* Bonds, tax-exempt
Mutual funds
    and Wealth Trust™, 101–2
    as gifts, 36
    via variable life insurance, 178–79
Mutual insurance companies, 170

Net investment yield (insurance), 205
Net worth, 11–12. *See also* Value and valuation, present
Nursing homes, 191

Offers, from insurance carriers, 217, 218

Offshore asset-protection trusts, and income taxes, 103, 130–35
Ownership, of assets. *See* Title, to assets

P

Paintings. *See* Art
Partnerships, 125–29
Payable on death system, of bank accounts, 26
Payouts. *See* Annuitizing; Distributions
Penalty tax, on MEC distributions, 194
Pension plans
   and CRTs, 83–84
   and MECs, 200
   and probate, 26
   excise tax on excess distributions from, 72–73, 144–49
   See also Retirement
Per capita distribution, 19, 94–96
Period-certain annuities, 107
Permanent insurance, 122–23, 163–70, 173–83, 186–87
Persistency bonuses, in life insurance, 204, 207
Person, guardian of the, 20
Personal representatives. *See* Executors
Per stirpes distribution, 19, 94–95
POD system. *See* Payable on death system, of bank accounts
Policy illustrations, life insurance, 202–6
Pooled income funds, 86
Portfolio rate, of interest-sensitive life insurance, 175
Pour-over wills, 12, 27, 270
Power of appointment, 54
Power of attorney, durable, 27
   vs. health-care proxy, 23
Power of attorney, medical. *See* Health-care proxy
Preferred risk, in life insurance, 208
Premiums, life insurance, 176, 193–94, 198
   payment of, by life insurance trust, 69
   for permanent insurance, 163, 164, 165–66, 168–69, 170–71
   for term insurance, 158–60
   for variable life insurance, 179
Present interests, and gift taxes, 69–70

Present value. *See* Value and valuation, present
Primogeniture, 43
Principal, in trusts, use of, 74
Private annuities. *See under* Annuities
Private foundations. *See* Foundations, private
Probate, 21, 25–29, 196, 270
Promoters, of CRTs, 85
Property, guardian of the, 20
Prudent-man rule, 100–101
Public charities, 136–43. *See also* Charitable lead trusts; Charitable remainder trusts; Foundations, private

Q, R

Q-TIP (Qualified terminable interest property) trusts, 15, 53–60, 271
Quotes, from insurance carriers, 218

Real estate
   and CRTs, 81–82
   and estate taxes, 3, 49
   and offshore trusts, 132
   as a gift, 36
   title to, 30–31
   valuation of, 37
Remaindermen, 87–88
Replacement cost, of life insurance, 37
Residuary clause, in wills, 20
Retirement
   and business continuity issues, 120–21
   and CRTs, 83–84
   and second-to-die policies, 191
   and tax-free inheritance trust strategies, 72–73
   income needs during, 74–75
   plans. *See* Pension plans
Revocable living trusts, 12, 44, 271
Risk rating, of life insurance, 208
Rule of 72, 40

S

Safe, fireproof, to store wills, 18
Safe-deposit box, to store wills, 18, 23
Salary
   of private foundation administrators, 83
   of private foundation trustees, 137, 139, 142
Savings and loan associations, 160
Sciarretta, Steven A., 128
S corporations, and Q-TIPs, 58
Second-to-die life insurance, 177, 184–92
   and Q-TIPs, 56–57
   and variable life, 181
   escape clauses in, 207
   purchased with excess retirement plan distributions, 148
   with tax-free inheritance trusts, 64–67
Self-dealing, 141–42
Settlor. *See* Maker, of a trust
Seven-pay test, of legal life insurance, 197–98
Shaw, Michael, 47, 48
Shrinking trust principal strategy, 50–51
Single-life annuities. *See under* Annuities
Single-premium life insurance, 71–72, 193–94
SPDA. *See* Annuities: deferred
Split-dollar insurance, 114–15
Sprinkle powers, 74
Standard & Poors Corporation, 65, 161
Standard risk, in life insurance, 208
State inheritance taxes, 227
State taxes, 5
Stepchildren, 53–55
Step up, in basis valuation. *See* Capital gains
Stocks and bonds
   and estate freezes, 117
   and estate taxes, 49
   as gifts, 36, 37–39
   See also Bonds, tax-exempt
Successor executors, and estate planning, 220
Successor trustees
   and estate planning, 220
   of living trusts, 27
   of private foundations, 137
Sunburst trusts, 92–96
Surtax. *See* Excise tax
Survivorship insurance policies. *See* Second-to-die insurance

T

Table 16 (insurance risk), 208

Taxable estate, 271

Tax-deferred annuities. *See under* Annuities

Tax-exempt bonds. *See* Bonds, tax-exempt

Tax-free inheritance trusts, 13–15, 63–75, 187, 191, 231–57, 265–68
  and generation skipping, 92
  and life insurance, 129
  and private foundations, 138–41
  to hold MECs, 200
  with CRTs, 79–80
  See also Irrevocable life-insurance trusts

Tenancy in common, 30, 33, 271

Term insurance, 122–23, 158–62, 186–87
  second-to-die policies, 177

Testamentary trust, 44, 271

Testate death, 271

Title
  to assets, 30–33
  to MECs, 200

Triple submissions, for insurance contracts, 217

Trust departments, in banks, 46, 216

Trustees, 13, 43, 100, 126, 265–68, 271
  and accounting, 48
  and annuities, 104
  and estate planning, 219–20
  and insurance premiums, 69
  and living trusts, 26, 27
  and tax management, 102–3
  of CRTs, 86
  of irrevocable trusts, 45
  of private foundations, 137, 141
  of Q-TIPs, 58
  of sunburst trusts, 93
  of tax-free inheritance trusts, 63
  of Wealth Trust™, 74, 98

Trustor. *See* Maker, of a trust

Trusts, 8, 271
  vs. family limited partnerships, 126
  and gifts, 39
  living (inter vivos), 18, 21, 25–29, 41–109, 270

  and income taxes, 47
  and real-estate title, 32
  See also specific kinds, such as Charitable remainder trusts; Irrevocable trusts; Revocable trusts; Wealth Trust™

Tunnel trusts, 70

U, V, W, X, Y, Z

UGMA. *See* Uniform Gifts to Minors Act

Unified tax credit, 4, 34–36, 69–70, 147, 271

Uniform Gifts to Minors Act (UGMA), 46

Uniform Transfers to Minors Act (UTMA), 46

Unitrusts, 77–78, 84

Universal life insurance, 175–77, 178, 182

Universal variable life insurance, 182

UTMA. *See* Uniform Transfers to Minors Act

Value and valuation, present, 37
  of a business, 121
  of family limited partnerships, 128
  of real estate, 82

Vanishing premium, of life insurance, 165–66, 168–69, 171–72, 194

Variable annuities. *See under* Annuities

Variable life insurance, 177–81, 182–83

Variable-life MECs, 195

Variable-payout annuities. *See under* Annuities

Virgin Islands, British, as offshore trust site, 132

Wealth Trust™, The, 74, 97–98

Whole life insurance, 173–83
  vs. universal life insurance, 176
  See also Interest-sensitive life insurance

Whole life MECs, 195

Wills, 12, 17–24, 27, 271

Wills, pour-over. *See* Pour-over wills

Witnesses, to wills, 20

Wrap accounts, 101

Page

<u>9</u> - Each has 600K   A-B trust / marital trust /
    1st die → Trust → income to spouse.
           to children
    2nd die → 600 K Trust children
          600 K surviving spouse to children

<u>13</u>   - TAX free inheritance trust - irrevocable
    you can't be trustee - ? spouse / Kids
    Put money in to cover inheritance tax-
    Can use life insurance here.

<u>15-16</u>   Summary of ways to divest estate

<u>19</u>   - per stripes ÷ equally to children
      vs per capita ÷ equally among survivors.

<u>Question:</u> If Asset joint then assume
    Loretta has 50% + when 1st dies
    only <u>50</u>% in estate?   <u>See p.147</u>
    How to title property? What about
                    pension plan
<u>22</u>   - Summary of info. in will -   if I die →
                        to LAM +
                      assume part of
26   - Joint property = no probate   her estate to
                        600 K deduction
    but ? wf suit can someone get
      more than 50% of Asset?

    Pension plan - no probate of beneficiary
      <u>not</u> estate.

27 - living trust + pour-over will.

39 - maximizing values of gifts

51 - trust shrinking -
   surviving spouse only takes
      money from his or her
      funds keep 600k in trust &
      let $ build. To children tax free.

54 - Q-tip - trust for xs > 600k to
   control transfer of property. No
      estate tax of all income to spouse.

63 - tax free inheritance trust -

185 - 2nd to die policies